HENRY ANATOLIO BISNAR

January 2, 1935 -

 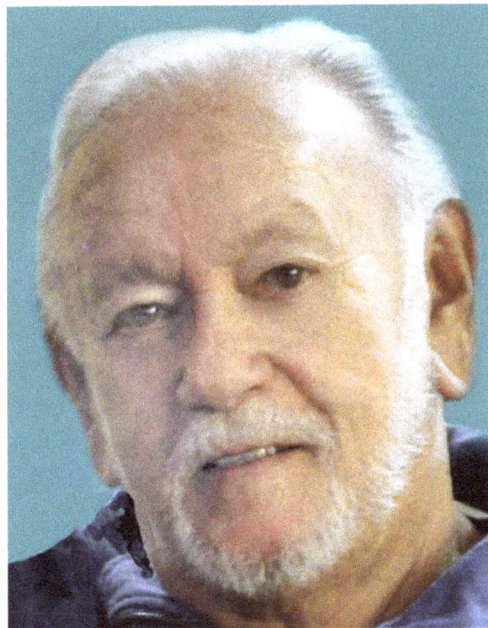

1935   2016

Ramblings as of October 25, 2016

These are the ramblings of Hank Bisnar. They are not necessarily in any kind of order and are not intended to be an autobiography, but more of a life's journal. Many of the dates in my stories are my best guess and may not be exact.

I am the youngest of seven children.

1st - Jimmy who died of smallpox before my birth.

2nd - Thelma who also died before my birth. The story I remember about her was she was playing with matches and set her dress on fire.

3rd - William George – March 18, 1925

4th - Bernaldo Francis – April 8, 1927

5th - Dorothy Effey – June 21, 1931

6th - Constance Thelma - January 14, 1933

7th - Henry Anatolio – January 2, 1935

Left to right: Dot, Bill, Hank, Ethel, Boots and Bernie

At age 82 I am the only surviving child.

I also have three half siblings.

1st - Elizabeth Bisnar Nirza - February 7, 1956

2nd - Evelyn Bisnar – July 14, 1960

3rd - Ferdinand Bisnar - October 21, 1962

I was born in the city of Long Beach California on January 2, 1935. I am of Filipino and Irish descent. My father was full Filipino and my Mother claimed to be full Irish although her maiden name is Brunner. Go figure!

| Flag of America Independence 1776 | Flag of the Philippines Independence 1946 | Flag of Ireland Independence 1916 |

For reasons unknown to me I was born in our home at 120 Golden Ave. 120 Golden Ave. no longer exists. That location and many others were replaced by the Long Beach World Trade Center in the 1980's. During my first year we moved two times. I don't know the address of the first move but it was on Loma Vista Dr. on the west side of Long Beach. The second move was to 820 Dawson Ave. on the east side of Long Beach. That was in 1936 and my family occupied that home until 1988. (52 years)

820 Dawson Ave. Long Beach California

I lived in this house from age 1 thru 22. My Mom bought the house in 1936 for $3,800.00. The ladies that lived next door told us a little history of the house. These ladies (They were really old to me) moved to Long Beach while in their teens from Iowa. They lived on the very west side of town and on Sunday mornings their parents would drive their horse drawn wagon east on 7th to what is now Dawson Ave.

From there they would go north for a quarter of a mile to a farm house to buy eggs and vegetables. The closest farm was about two or three miles away. I'm sure that the house is well over 100 years old and is still a family dwelling.

The neighborhood was middle class residential with vacant lots everywhere which was great for dirt clod fights.

It was a four bedroom house when we moved in, but was later expanded to six bedrooms and a den. Mother was a person that wouldn't take no for an answer. When told she couldn't remove the bookcases between the front room and the dining room because they were part of the bearing wall, she and my brothers removed them themselves. When told she couldn't raise the attic roof up and make another bedroom she kept on until she found a carpenter that would do it the way she wanted it. When told she couldn't move the inside stairs to the outside of the house to make room for another bedroom and enlarge the kitchen, she hired that same carpenter again to do the job. The house was mostly built of redwood and it went through many earthquakes, a few with me in it. It had a storm cellar which we never used, but it was a great place for me and my buddies to play in. Of course it was like all two story houses. If you were upstairs, whatever you wanted was downstairs, and if you were downstairs, whatever you wanted was upstairs. That was my last two story house.

Our yard was big and there were six trees in it. Two Plum trees, two fig trees, one orange, and one lemon. We would climb up and sit in the trees and eat the fruit. Sometimes we would go around the neighborhood and try to sell fruit. I remember walking around the yard and having the fallen figs squish between my toes.

The house pictured at the beginning of this section is one taken at night during the Christmas season. My Step dad Cy made all the decorations and it would take him two weeks to put them all in place and hook up the sound system for the Christmas music.

We were a Navy family and my dad wasn't around much. My Mother pretty much raised us by herself. I know we didn't have much money but I never thought or felt we were poor. As I remember, we dressed like everyone else and I know we never went to bed hungry. We didn't do a lot of family activities or go many places. Mostly it was visiting friends of my Mothers. The only trip we ever took was when I was about 5 or 6. My Mother bought a new Plymouth coup and she drove all six of us and our dog back to New York to visit her family in Brooklyn. I remember our dog got lost and it took a long time before we found him. My uncle lived on a farm, and one of the goats ate the buttons off my new coat. My Mom was not happy.

Christmas and Thanksgiving were always big family gatherings. There were 25 or 30 people for dinner. My Mom was an OK cook, but both my dad and step dad were stewards in the Navy and they cooked to die for.

My memories are from four or five years old. I remember that my mom would drive her car and make me stand next to her right side so she could keep me safe. They didn't know much about safety in those days. I remember I wore short pants a lot which I thought was uncool at the time. I also wore a lot of Navy suits. That was because we were a Navy family. I remember how excited I would get when it was time for the other kids to come home from school. My mom told stories about how I would run to meet my brothers and sisters and warn them if she was "on the war path" and they were in for it. My brothers and sisters were very good to me and always looked out for my well-being.

My earliest memory is a fall I took for which I was hospitalized. Our house was a farm house built back in the late part of the 19th century, and what used to be a barn, was our garage. It was big enough for four cars and had a full loft. The loft had one of those winches for lifting bales of hay, and a trap door for lowering things down to the ground floor. Somehow I fell though the trap door and landed on the dirt floor below. I don't remember exactly what my injury was, but I remember being in a crib-like bed and people coming to see me. I'm sure I was about four or five years old.

As a kid I was very active and loved to climb trees or anything there was to climb. Unfortunately, I took quite a few falls and had many cuts. I stopped counting my stitches at around 100. One time I fell off our front porch and went head first into our car fender. I was big enough to stand up after the fall, but my head was stuck between the bumper and the fender. My brothers had to bend the fender to get my head free. Once I kicked an open tin can that still had the lid attached and it came back and cut my shin. While climbing in one of our plum trees, a friend of mind accidentally hit my hand with a butcher knife. I have stitches on the top of my head from playing football, on my forehead from cancer removal, on my nose and arm from a fall at work, above my right eye from getting my head stuck between a bumper and a fender, below my right eye from getting hit with a stick as a kid, on my hand from a butcher knife and a water glass, on my back from a boil removal, on my left shin from kicking a tin can, on my neck from my Carotid Artery surgery, and on my right knee from my knee replacement in 2009. The last stitches were at age 75. I'm scheduled for my left knee to be replaced, and that will add another 25 or more stitches. I still have time for more stitches. Hopefully, I'm doing something fun when it happens. Only one broken bone. Broke my collarbone playing football.

I lived at 820 Dawson in Long Beach from age 1 until I got married at age 22. I was gone for two years during my Army time. I'll talk about my marriage and the Army later.

820 Dawson, Long Beach Ca.

I remember that there were lots of kids on our block and in the neighborhood. It was a great house to grow up in and I have many fond memories having lived there. Although my brothers and sisters were older, they spent a lot of time with me and often took me places. One vivid memory, is the time it rained really hard and I took my new toy submarine outside and put it in gutter to watch it float down the street. Well, it went so fast I couldn't keep up with it and upon reaching the end of the street, it went down the storm drain. My oldest brother Bill said that all the storm drains dump the water into a place called "The Hamilton Bowl". So all five of us walked what seem to me a very long way. When I got older I realized it was only about a mile or two from our house. When we got there is was as big as five or six football fields and the water was up to my waist. I don't know how long we walked around in the water looking for the submarine but we never found it. When we got home our Mom went "On the War Path" because we were all wet and cold.

Whenever any of us did something not to her liking, she always laid down the law and everybody listened. The rule for eating was that you didn't have to eat anything you didn't want but you had to eat whatever you put on your plate. You always asked for permission to leave the table. She was a non-violent, no nonsense woman. Of course, God help anyone who said anything bad about her kids.

When I was 9 or10 my parents got a divorce. It had very little impact on me because my Dad being in the Navy really wasn't around much and I did not have a close relationship with him. When he retired from Navy in 1952 and came to live in Long Beach we developed a very close friendship.

My Mom married my stepfather Cy Bicaldo. I believe if I could have picked from all the fathers in the world, I could not have picked a better person than Cy.

He gave everything a father could give and treated my Mom with love and care.

Long Beach was a wonderful city to grow up in. You could go anywhere and be safe. As a young boy I covered the entire town on my bicycle and motor scooter and even hitchhiked at times. My favorite places were the Beaches. (Long Beach, Seal Beach, and Huntington Beach), Marine Stadium, Signal Hill, The Pike, Rainbow Pier, The Lagoon, Sand dunes in Seal Beach and some I'll think of later.

My parents bought their first TV when I was about 12 years old. It was Phil Co 12" black and white. They also bought a magnifying bubble that increased the image to about 15" but you had to sit right in front of it or everything was distorted. The stations went off the air at midnight after playing the National Anthem. When there was no programming, all you could see was a test pattern. The stations came back on a 6:00am.

We had only one telephone in our house. The first one was a candlestick type and was kept in the living room. I remember everybody was on a party line. We had four other people on our party line. You had to lift the ear piece and listen to see if anyone else was using the phone.

I was the youngest, and that was by far the best spot in the lineup. By the time I was 14 or 15 my parents were financially set and I was in hog heaven.

We had our share of pets. Two dogs, two rabbits, one snake, white rats, and homing pigeons. They were not there at the same time. My favorite was my dog "Cubby." We were the same age and he lived to be 14 or 15. He would go everywhere I would go. He would follow me to school and be there when I got out. A few times they called me out of class to get him out of the hallway. He did that until I went to high school. Dogs didn't have tags and they pretty much went anywhere they pleased. He liked everybody but the mailman and our rabbits. One of them bit his tail. He wouldn't go near them but if they got out of their cage he would corner them and bark until someone came and put them back in the cage. He would chase cars and try to bite the tires. He hated baths. After you gave him a bath you had to keep him in the house until he was dry because if he got out he would immediately go under the house and roll in the dirt. When I was 15 he just disappeared. I think he may have been hit by a car or just passed away somewhere. I missed him and it was my first experience of losing something I loved. About a year, later my sister Boots brought home a puppy that was some kind of terrier. She named it Tito and it became my dog in a very short time. She was a good dog and actually had puppies on my bed.

St. Matthew's Grammar School   St. Matthew's Church

When I was 5 years old I started school. The year was 1940. They didn't have kindergarten at my school, so I went into the first grade. I think I was the smallest kid in the class.

My Mother wanted them to keep me back so I would be the same age and size as the other kids in my class. It took her until I was in the 3rd grade to prevail. I remember not wanting to be held back because I was afraid the kids would make fun of me. No one ever did, and I soon realized that I could not only compete, but for the most part, be ahead of my classmates. I wasn't a great student, but I did well enough to get passing grades.

Of course what I liked most about school was the sports. I was always one of the better players in all the sports. As seventh grader, I played on the 8th grade teams.

I was a Captain on the Crossing Guard squad. I guess that was my first management job. Things went along pretty good at St. Mathews until the 8th grade. Our football coach quit after only one game. There was no one to replace him, so I was selected by the players to be coach and captain. I guess this was my second management job. The schoolyard was very small, so Mother Superior had the yard painted with strips, and each grade had their own area to play in. Then, she picked eighth graders to be leaders for each class. She picked me as the leader for the eighth grade boys. Third management job. It was cool at first, until I figured out that I never got to participate in the games and had to settle all the arguments. After about 3 or 4 weeks, my friend (who was the seventh grade leader) and I asked Mother Superior if we could rotate as leaders with other kids. Mother Superior said ok, but the next day she announced that if anyone quit as a leader they could not be on the basketball team. So, although I was the best player, I couldn't play. Another rule was that you were not allowed to kick footballs on the schoolyard. Well guess what! One day before school started, I was talking with my buddies when a football bounces right into my hands. Some kids on the other end of the yard were calling for the ball. So not thinking of the "no football kicking rule" I booted it back to them. Unfortunately, it took one bounce and hit Mother Superior in the back of her head. That very afternoon she came to our classroom and expelled me from school for breaking the "no kicking the football" rule.

Needless to say when I got home and told my Mother, she went ballistic. Not so much at me, but at the @#%$ Nun that did such thing to her "perfect son". She immediately went to see Monsignor Lynch. No telling what she said, but he overruled Mother Superior and said I could return to school. One problem! I didn't want to go back to St. Mathews.

I finished out the year at SCMA (Southern California Military Academy), where my older brother Bernie had gone. It was a great school and I really liked it. Of course Bernie had been the all-time "Mr. Cadet" and there was no filling his shoes. In fact, I started off by getting into a fight on my first day. Some guy tried tell me I couldn't save a seat for someone. Although I did get a lot of demerits and had to do extra work on week-ends, I liked the small classes and the great sports program. The following year, they cut the school back to only the sixth grade, so I couldn't return. SCMA wanted me to go to Browns Academy in Encinitas CA. (a prep school fashioned after the US Military Academy) I chose not to go and enrolled in St. Anthony's High School.

St. Anthony High School Long Beach

As a freshmen, my best friends were John Thielen, Danny Vessey, Gene Kelly, Al Tossas, Tom Hibbison, and Roger Lorge, and Charlie Wieland. High School was a good time in my life. St. Anthony's is a Catholic school with two high schools. One for boys and one for girls, on the same campus. All the classes were separated and in different buildings. The boy's school was taught by the Holy Cross Brothers, and the girl's school was taught by the Holy Cross Sisters.

The Brothers were a no nonsense group of teachers. As a freshman, I had heard stories of how tough they could be. On the second or third day, I was in the study hall where they had a double desk that two people could sit in. Me and the guy I was sitting next to were talking, and one of the oldest brothers (Br. Theoplous) told us to be quite. We did for a few minutes and then started to talk again. He came to our desk and gave us a slap across the face. It was so light-handed I thought, if this is all they do there's no problem, and just as I finished that thought, he came with a backhand and knocked both of us out of our seat. He definitely got our attention. I didn't get hit again until my senior year, and it was Brother Theoplous again. I guess he remembered me form that study hall and sat me in the front row of his class. He would stand right next to me as he lectured the class. Thinking he couldn't see me, I tossed a piece of paper in the trash can. Before the paper hit the can he smacked me in the back of my head. I have total respect for all of my teachers and never saw anyone get hit that didn't have it coming.

The great thing about an all boy's class is that you do things that wouldn't happen in a mixed class. Once we had a substitute lay teacher and he wasn't familiar with the class bells. For three weeks we left class when the girl's school bell rang. It was 15 minutes before our class was over, but he didn't know the difference. Sometimes we would get to class early and carried the teacher's desk to the other end of the room and turned all our seats the wrong way. It was a good ten minutes before Brother Philip realized everything was backwards. There are many other stories I'll' think of later.

I liked the sports of course, and all those great looking girls. I didn't really apply myself to school work until my junior year. I kept my grades just good enough to be eligible to play sports. My freshman and sophomore years were

pretty much sports (Football, Basketball and Track). I played 'B' football and "B" basketball for one year. That's like JV is today. As a senior, I finished 5th in the state CIF 1A finals in the low hurdles. Our football field was about 15 miles from the School and we had to ride on the back of a flatbed truck to get to and from practice. My sister Dot who had been a cheerleader in both high school and college, talked me into trying out for varsity cheerleader. I made it, but it was really tough. I played B-football and was a cheerleader at the varsity games. I took some ragging from some of the football guys, but I made my sister happy for at least one year.

At the start my junior year, Brother Frances the principal, called me to his office and asked if I intended to graduate from St. Anthony's. Of course, I said yes. He said the only chance of that happening was if I got away from my current friends and started to study and bring up my grades. Although none of my buddies did anything really bad, only myself, John, Tom, Charlie, and Roger from our group finished High School. I don't know why he singled me out, but I've been forever grateful. After that talk, Brother Frances and I became friends. He would always stop me in the hallways and ask how I doing (he already knew) and would reach out and grab my shirt pocket and church my cigarettes. He also knew I had a car and would send me on errands for school supplies and to mail packages.

One of my favorite stories about high school is about cigarettes. All through high school, my cousin Tommy lived with me and we were the best of friends. One day, I went to the office and asked Brother Frances if I could go to my car and have a smoke. He said NO, that leaving the campus during school hours was a no-no. Then he handed me his keys to the Chemistry Lab and said not tell anyone and make it fast. About three weeks later, my cousin Tom wanted to sneak off campus to the car and have a smoke. I told him Brother Frances would give him the keys to the Chemistry Lab. When Tom asked for the keys, Brother Frances took him by the back of his shirt and tossed him out of his office.

On First Fridays, the entire High School would go to mass before 1st period started. Tom and I would sneak away to a café called Humpy-Dumpty's for hot chocolate and doughnuts. We always got back just as mass was over and in time to be in our first class. That is, every time but one. One time, we got back after our History class started. As we walked into the room we didn't see Brother Francis sitting in the back of the room. Thinking we made it without being caught we started to laugh. That's when Brother Francis told us to go the office.

He sent us home and said we could not return until he spoke with our parents. Tom's Mom got really mad and made him stay in his room for rest of the day. My Mom thought it was funny and told me not to do it again, and let me go to the beach. What a great Mom.

When I was a junior, my dad retired from the Navy and bought a new 1953 Ford Victoria hard top convertible. He didn't know how to drive and the plan was for me to teach him to drive. After only three or four lessons, he gave it up and said that my two sisters and I could have the car as long as someone would drive him wherever he needed to go.

He was a boxing champ on one of his ships, and won a trophy for ballroom dancing but could not handle driving a car.

That worked out great for me because my oldest sister Dot was an Airline hostess and traveled, and my younger sister Boots was in nursing school and had a boyfriend. The car was mine.

I had two steady girl friends in high school. As freshman, I dated several girls. As a sophomore, Sandra Sayers and I went steady for almost a year.

At the end of my junior year I met Val Pegg and we stayed together until I went in to the Army in 1954.

I attended LBCC for one year. I really didn't have my heart into studying and wasn't making much headway. I did try out for the track team but always seemed to come in third in our inter team meets. You had to finish at least second to compete in the regular meets. After one year, I left school and took a job at the American Can Co.

Things I did and Places I went

Roasting Marshmallows 1946

In our neighborhood there were many vacant lots. One of things we liked to do was to build a fire in a vacant lot and roast marshmallows. On one occasion, I was holding my marshmallow with a coat hanger and wanted something to prop it up so I wouldn't have to hold it. I pick up a good size rock to use as a prop not knowing that someone had just taken it out of the fire.

Needless to say I burned my hand pretty good. I immediately ran home to get help from Mom. She took a cube of butter, put it in my hand and wrapped it with a dishtowel. Then my mom took me to an emergency room for treatment. This was in a time when butter was considered a luxury and the doctor's first question was, "where did you get the butter?" Luckily, it was not a serious burn.

Motor Scooter 1948 - 1950

On my 14th birthday, my parents bought me a new Cushman Motor Scooter. It had a buddy seat on the back and would go about 60 mph. I was the only one of my age to have a motor scooter. I did have two friends a year or two older than me that had scooters. I was able to roam the city of Long Beach on my bicycle, but now I could begin many more adventures. Jimmy, Ralph, and I went from Santa Monica to San Diego and almost every town in between. In those days there were no freeways, so we traveled up and down Highway 101. The scooter brought about the end of my paper route. By delivering the papers on the scooter I could do it in one fourth of the time it took on my bicycle. The problem was on the morning route, the paper was to be delivered no later than 6 am. There were too many complaints about noise. It was stop using the scooter, or give up the route. Of course, by now I was way beyond riding my bike. I only took one fall on the scooter. As I was rounding a corner I hit some loose gravel and the scooter slid out from under me. I had a friend on the back but we were not hurt. I got my driver's license when I turned 16, and that was the end of the scooter.

Skin diving 1951-1954

Danny, Charlie, and I began skin diving when we were 16 years old. We started our diving at Whites Point in Palos Verdes, Crescent St. in Laguna, and the Long Beach Breakwater. We didn't have any money for good equipment, so we made our own. We used 1¼" wood dowel 6' long with surgical tubing tied with a loop on the top and a five prong spear head at the bottom. You would put your hand into the loop and stretch it half way the length of the pole and hold it tight. When you released your grip, the pole would surge forward with great speed and force. We speared many fish with our poles. The largest for me was a 4' Sand Shark and an 18" Stingray. Charlie once got a 13lb. Lobster.

About two years later, Charlie and I bought dry Diving Suits and Arbalete Spear Guns. The suits were made of rubber and cover your entire body. They had a hood and boots. The front had a large hole where you would slide your feet into the boots and slip the top over your body and head. You tied the front with surgical tubing. If you did it just right you could stay dry and warm. If you didn't get it tied right, you'd end up wet and cold. We made our own weight belts out of army gun belts and lead molded in tuna cans. The guns were 4' long with a pistol grip and shot a 3½' spear.

When we got a little older, we began going to Catalina Island and Estero Beach in Mexico. Once, we built a 6' dingy to take to Estero Beach. We would swim out about 100 yards and tie the dingy to the kelp, and use it to hold whatever we might spear. It was really a rough place to get into the water. We had to climb down rocks as the waves came in hard. On our last trip there, Charlie's hand got caught between the boat and the rocks and dislocated his finger. His finger was at a right angle to his hand. Danny held him from behind and I pulled it back into its place. I know it hurt like hell, but he never showed it. Those were great times and great memories.

Fishing Boat 1952

I and three of my buddies (Danny, Kelly and Charlie) bought a cabin cruiser. Well, not exactly a cabin cruiser, but an 18ft. fishing boat. It cost us $200.00, and we had to move it from Balboa Island to Long Beach. Danny's uncle gave us an old beat up 1935 Ford Coup which we took to Charlie's dad's machine shop and made a trailer. We used Kelly's 1939 Chevy to hall it out the water (nearly burned the clutch out), and took it to my parent's house. They were none too happy about having it on their driveway. We spent the next two months scraping off about four layers of old paint and working on the engine.

It had a 1934 Durant Star four cylinder engine which blew out the head gasket the first time we started it. Danny's uncle helped us with repairs. After going to all the parts dealers in Long Beach, we ended up in Los Angeles somewhere. The guy that sold us the head gasket said it was probably the last one in existence, and if we ever needed another one we would have to have one made. With a new paint job, new wiring, and the engine running good, we were set to go fishing. Actually, we were in to skin diving, not pole fishing. We took it down to the Alamitos Bay and lunched it for a trial run. Everything was going great for the first few minutes and then a fire broke out inside the cabin. Two guys jumped over the side and Charlie and I put the fire out with the fire extinguisher. The new wiring loom was lying on the engine and got so hot it caught on fire. We had many great days on that boat, skin diving along the coast from the Palos Verdes kelp beds to the east end of the Long Beach Breakwater. We would get lobster, Bass, Corbina, Crabs, Abalone, and other kinds of fish. We did have to be towed in to the dock a few times.

The way we would dock the boat was to put it in into reverse just before the nose would hit dock. The foot pedal that worked the clutch was broke, so we used a pipe wrench to engage the clutch and shift to reverse. One day, as I went to engage the clutch the pipe wrench was missing and I knew we would hit the dock very hard so I jumped on the dock and ran around to the front and tried to stop the boat by pushing it backwards. The force of the boat just pushed me backwards and into the water. The water was covered solid with green moss and totally gross. When I came up from falling in the water I had this really bad smelling moss form head to toe. It's funny now, but it wasn't then.

Where we moored the boat, there was a 40ft. commercial fishing boat on one side, and a 60ft. racing sail boat on the other side. I would work on the sail boat shinning brass and washing down the decks. The owner offered to take me and Danny to Mexico for a race, but our Moms would hear none of it.

After I went into the Army, they lost interest in the boat and got behind on the mooring fees. They finally gave the boat to the Sea Scouts.

Water Skiing 1952-1958

I started water skiing in my junior year of high school. The pictures below were taken at the Marine Stadium in Long Beach CA.

Marine Stadium 1952

The boat belonged to my friend Charlie's dad.

The stadium was originally built for the 1932 Rowing Olympics.

Today, it's used for public water skiing and boat races. We also used another boat that belonged to John Wavle's dad. One time John, Dennis, and I invited our girl friends to go water skiing. Upon getting the boat into the water, John said he wanted to take a run around the stadium to warm up the engine. He was just showing off for the girls. He took off like a bat out of hell and on the first turn he flipped the boat. The flip threw John and the three girls out of the boat and the boat landed upside down in the water. Luckily, a nearby boat got there just in time to tie a rope on to the bow before it sank. No one was hurt but the engine was toast. Needless to say, that was the last time John's dad let use his boat.

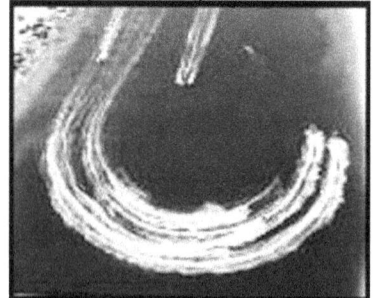

We also skied at Golden Beach on the west end of Long Beach. From the launch area, we would go out to the breakwater. In the mornings and early afternoon, the water was calm and smooth as glass.

Charlie and I decided to make our own water skis. We cut and laminated the wood in Charlie's dad's machine shop. Mine were a little too narrow, but Charlie's were good enough that he tried to sell them in ski shop. That didn't work so he sold them at the stadium. They were the first "Banana Skis" at the stadium and he sold quite a few before he quit making them.

After I got out of the Army, I bought an 18' ski boat. It was an inboard with a converted 1949 Ford car engine. When it was running good it was pretty fast and fun to ski behind. I think I spent more time trying to keep it running then I did skiing. One time we were at Golden Beach and it blew a head gasket. We didn't brother to put in on the trailer to work on it. We just beached it. While me and Charlie started removing the head gasket, Danny and Kelly went to the parts shop. We were ready go in about 1½ hours, but now we had a new problem. We were so focused on the engine repair that we didn't notice that the tide had gone out and the boat was high and dry out of the water. I don't know what the weight was but we couldn't move it by ourselves. We went up and down the beach to get people to help.

I guess we had about twenty people helping us pushing it back in the water. We got it back and had a great day skiing.

I sold the boat a few years after I got married. With two small children, a wife who really didn't like water skiing, and no money for maintenance, it didn't make sense to keep it.

Car Accident 1953

One time I let my girlfriend Sandy drive my parents new Oldsmobile. She didn't have a driver's license. The car needed gas and I asked her to pull into a gas station. She pulled in but went a little too far past the pump. When she backed up, she knocked down the pump cover. The attendant was about our age and was really cool. He said he would tell his boss that it was me because Sandy didn't have a license. Nothing ever came of it but I never went to that station again.

I borrowed my parents new Oldsmobile to go the mountains for the day. We were in Big Bear and it started to snow pretty hard so we headed for home. As we were going down the mountain (without chains), I lost sight of my friends so I pulled over to the side of the road to wait for them. When they caught up to me they tried to pull over and stop but slid into the back of my car. My parents said they were just glad nobody got injured. I knew they were also sick about their new car.

On my way home from Val's house around 5:30 pm, I was going south on Orange Ave. driving about 30 mph. As I entered the intersection of Orange Ave. and 11th St., a woman driving a 1948 Buick ran the stop sign and hit me broadside. She was drunk and had two adults in the front seat, and two small kids in the back. The car was a convertible and the kids were sitting up on top of the back seat. Luckily, when she hit me it threw the kids down to the floor and not out of the car.

She was so out of it she couldn't remember the next day if I had a passenger or not. I was pretty sore for a few days, but the worst of it was I was without my car for two weeks while it was in the repair shop.

Riding the Rails 1948-1952

As young beach bums, we loved body surfing. Board surfing wasn't the thing to do in those days. Body surfing was a great sport. We all had 12" duck feet, (Swim fins) and could swim hard and fast to catch and ride the breakers. If you caught the wave right, you could ride it all the way up to dry sand.

Breakers were good at Cherry Beach, Belmont Beach Pier, Huntington Beach Pier, and Tin Can Beach (Sunset Beach). Huntington Beach was the best, with waves anywhere from 4ft. to 8ft. Once or twice a year they would get up to 10ft or 12ft. The problem was, we didn't have any way to get to Huntington Beach. Somehow, we discovered that there was a freight train that went through town right in our neighborhood. It slowed and came almost to a stop at Anaheim and Redondo. It was slow enough that we could hop on it and ride it all the way to Huntington Beach. We would catch it at 10:00 am on the way down and 4:30 pm on the way back.

We did have two occurrences that didn't go so well. The train passed though the Naval Ammunition Depot in Seal Beach on its way south. We would hide in a box car or a gondola while it passed though. On one occasion we were in a gondola with big 4ft. pipes in it and well hidden. We felt the train come to a stop and heard some activity. What we didn't know was that they had unhooked our gondola and left us in the Depot. After about ten minutes we looked out to see we were in the middle of the Depot about ¼ mile for the gate. We got out and started for the gate and within minutes two Marines with guns told us to halt. After our explanation of how we got in there, they took us to gate and let us go. Luckily, we were not too far from home and we hitchhiked back.

On another occasion, I jumped off on the return trip and I fell and cut my hand on a small, but very sharp rock. It was bleeding pretty good and we couldn't get it to stop. Danny disappeared for a while, and then caught up to us with some gauze and band aids. He had gone in to a Drug Store and swiped the first aid stuff to help me out. We stopped riding the rails when Danny got his driver's license.

Summer Playgrounds 1944-1947

Many of the public Grammar and Jr. High Schools were open to kids during the summer months. They had baseball leagues for ages eight thru thirteen, all kind of games to check out, and field trips to the beach and other places. The school near my house was Burbank. We played softball against Franklin, Jefferson, and Rogers. Nearly every day, we would have a softball game in the morning and then go to the beach. We would be home for eats by lunch time and then back to the beach again. One time, we got a bunch of starfish from Rainbow Pier and put them in a gunny sack under the checkout bungalow. After the second day the smell was so bad you couldn't go near the bungalow. They had to jack up the bungalow to remove the sack.

Home Deliveries

When I was a kid (1940) there were several home deliveries right to your door step.

The **Helms Bakery Man** would blow his whistle to let people know he was there with all his bakery goods.

The **Ice Man** would blow his horn. He would deliver ice blocks of 25 or 50 lbs. Many people didn't have refrigerators and they use ice to keep their food cool. My family had both a refrigerator and an icebox.

The **Milk Man** would leave your milk on the porch, or on the front steps very early in the am. We would get 3qt's every other day.

The local newspapers were delivered in both the AM and PM. I had two paper routes, **The Independent** in the morning, and the **Press Telegram** in the evenings. The Independent is no longer published and Press-Telegram is now a morning paper.

Before I moved to Arizona, I knew my mailman by his first name and we spoke almost every day. The mailman would walk his route and put the mail in your own mailbox. Here in Arizona, they have cluster mailboxes, and you have to drive a few blocks to get your mail.

Cluster Mail Box

Carnation Ice-cream Distributor

Just a few blocks from my house was a Carnation Milk and Ice Cream distributor. If you got there late in the afternoon, when the trucks came back from their deliveries they would give ice cream they couldn't keep. There were many times we all got a half gallon each.

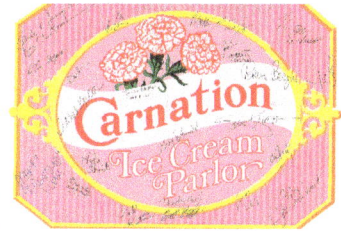

This is the original Ice Cream Distribution building. Sixty Five plus years later it's an Auto Repair Shop. 11th St. and Freeman Ave. Long Beach, Ca.

The Boys Club 1945 - 1950

The Boys Club was near my house. It was converted from an old church to the Boys Club. They didn't have any Girls Clubs in those days. I liked to go there and play pool and board games.

Rainbow Pier 1932-1975

Rainbow Pier was in downtown Long Beach. It started on Pine Ave. and went out over the ocean and back in to Alamitos Av. Maybe a ½ mile. You could drive cars on it, and it had a fishing pier at the center of the bow. We would fish from the pier and climb down on the pilings and get starfish and crabs. The crabs were 4" to 6" and good for eating. The starfish weren't good for anything. On the west end of the pier, there was a "Spit & Argue Club". This was a place where anyone could get up on the podium (soap -box) and talk about or say anything they wanted to. It was mostly old men and they did a lot of hand waving and yelling. It was fun to see how excited they would get.

On the inside of the pier was a lagoon for swimming, paddle boats, and canoes. When I was about five years old, my brother Bill threw me off his shoulders out over my head and told me to swim back to him. That's how I learn to swim.

This is what replaced the Pier in 2009

The Municipal Auditorium 1932-1975

The Municipal Auditorium was the place in Long Beach where all the big events took place. Things like The Circus, The Globe Trotters, Boxing and Wrestling matches, conventions, and special events. It was replaced by the new Long Beach Convention Center and the Performing Arts Theater in

1962. Visit Google: Scotty Moore Municipal Auditorium-Long Beach for a complete history.

The Alamitos Bay

 The Alamitos Bay was another popular beach in Belmont Shore. When I was a kid, there was no marina and the bay just went straight out to the ocean. In wasn't unusual to have Harbor Seals in the bay. In fact, one time, three friends and I found a baby seal behind an old boat wreck when the tide was low. Its mother must have swam off when she saw us coming. We didn't know what to do with it so we carried it to a friend's house on the Naples Canal. We put it in the canal, but it kept barking and following us along the canal. A man with a saltwater pool took it off our hands. There was a big fine for catching a seal.

Naples Canal

The Naples Canal was part of the bay, and it has many bridges over the canals. We liked to dive off the highest one called Chinese Bridge. Each year at Christmas time there's a boat parade though the Naples Canals.

Terminal Island Bridge

Terminal Island is a small island at the west end of Long Beach. When I was a kid, it was a Navy Shipyard as well as a Navy Base. There were two bridges used to cross over the channels. One was a floating pontoon bridge, and the other was a draw bridge. In 1970 the pontoon bridge was replaced by the new Desmond Bridge.

Seal Beach Pier 1950's

Seal Beach and the Pier is just south of Long Beach. We liked to fish on the pier and body surf next to the pier. The pier has been damaged many time from storms. It was closed for a few years but now it's repaired and has a Ruby's Café at the end

of the Pier. They also have charter deep sea fishing boats from there.

The Long Beach Pike 1902 – 1979

The Pike was an Amusement Park. It was a place where you might see anything. Lots of Sailors, Hookers, Conmen. It was like a permanent carnival with bright colored lights, noise and game barkers trying to get people to try their luck. For me, it was the rides, The Fun House, and The Plunge.

My favorite rides were the Cyclone Rollercoaster (named The Jack Rabbit Racer) coaster, and the Spinning Tubs called the Tilt-a-World. The Plunge was an indoor freshwater swimming pool about haft the size of a football field. I swam there a lot and when I got to High School, that's where our swimming team practiced and had the Swim Meets.

Visit Google: The Pike-Wikipedia, The free encyclopedia for a complete history.

Shady Acres 1950 - 1953

Shady Acres was miniature Golf and Arcade. This was a place to go on a first date or just with a group of guys.

Hines Ice Skating Rink 1948-1953

The Hines Ice Skating Rink is in the city of Paramount. At age of seven or eight, my sisters would take me ice skating. We would ride the bus and have to transfer two times to get to Paramount. In High School, it was another place to take a date. It was, and still is, owned by the Zamboni family. I went to High School with Richard Zamboni, the son of the owner. He invented the "Zamboni Ice Machine" that all the NHL rinks use to condition the ice.

Long Beach Roller Rink 1950 – 1953

The Roller Rink was the place I took my very first date. Her name was Louie and she lived right across the alley from me. She was a year younger than me and we knew each other from about age six or seven years old. We only dated three times but were close friends.

Dirt Clod Fights 1944 – 1948

One of our favorite games was dirt clod fights. In the spring, all the vacant lots would have grass as tall as 24". If you grabbed a hand full of grass at the ground level and pulled hard, you'd come up with a big piece of dirt and grass. Now you had a dirt clod with a 24" tail to throw with. We would choose sides and agree to the amount of clods and throwing distance. You were on the honor system to keep track of how many times you got hit. The team with the most hits on the other team was the winner. We would make all kinds of silly bets. One time we were tossing clods across the street at each other. I was next to an apartment building and couldn't see anything to my right. As a joke I picked up a big rock and tossed it into the street. Just as the rock reached the middle of the street a car came from the right and the rock hit in the door.

I didn't wait to see how much damage it did. I just started running and didn't stop for four or five blocks. I went down to the Marine Stadium for the rest of the day. When I got home, nothing was said so all was well. I asked my buddies the next day about the car. No one knew because they ran too.

Signal Hill 1947 - 1950

Signal Hill is a city inside of a city. Signal Hill is within the city limits of Long Beach. Back in the early 1920's oil was discovered. As a kid growing up near there, it was a great place to roam and have what seemed like daring adventures. The hill was cover with wooden oil derricks and pumps. We would climb up and ride the pumps, and climb to the top of the derricks where you could see for miles all the way to the ocean, Palo Verdes and to down town Los Angeles. In the spring, the hillside would be covered with grass as tall as two feet high. We would find some old sheet medal sidings and bend the end like a toboggan. There were places you could slide down the hill for several blocks.

On the east side of the hill was a street named Shell Hill. It was named Shell Hill because at the top was where Shell Oil Co. drilled its first well. Back in the 1930's, they had Model T races up the hill. It was a ¼ of a mile ride on an eight degree slope, and a run for your life on bicycles. Once I was riding on my

friend's handlebars, and as we started down the hill the chain came off and we had no brakes. We swerved off the road into the tall grass and didn't get hurt. Lucky for us it was spring and the grass was really tall and thick. As we got older, Signal Hill was a great place to go with our girlfriends and make out.

The Lagoon 1932-1951

The Lagoon was a great place to swim. It is located next to Recreation Park and was originally built for the 1932 Olympics for Diving Competitions. It had three separate piers. Two piers for just jumping off and swimming.

The diving pier had two 3-meter boards and three different towers. I don't remember what the height of the towers were, but

only qualified divers could dive or jump from it. I did sneak up and jump off each tower one time. In the winter time, we would take our bicycles to the pier for jumping and tie a rope to the bike and the pier railing. Then, we would ride as fast as we could off the end of the pier. The idea was to see who could ride out the farthest from the pier.

Recreation Park 1947 - 2013

Concert Stan

I believe Recreation Park is one of the oldest parks in Long Beach. It has two golf courses, a casting pool, outdoor stage for all kind of performances, several tennis courts (Home court for Billy Jean King), lawn bowling courts, shuffle board, Blair Field (minor league baseball field), and for many years the site for the Iowa State Picnic. When I was growing up, Long Beach had a big population of people from Iowa.

Casting Pool   *Blair Field*

Softball Field   *Billy Jean Tennis Park*

Blair Field is a part of Recreation Park in the city of Long Beach, Ca. In 1923, the City built a baseball stadium with grandstand seating for 1,000. The first official game was between the Los Angeles Dodgers and the Chicago Cubs. Several minor league teams trained there over the years. The Salt Lake Bees, Seattle of the Pacific Coast League, Denver of the Western League, the Philadelphia Athletics. The Los Angeles Rams also used it for their practice filed. For many years it was use for the city softball league. It had four softball diamonds and was the site for the World Series of Softball.

In 1956 the city relocated the softball diamonds to the Hamilton Bowl and a new stadium was built. It was named after Frank T. Blair a sports editor who campaigned for the new stadium for many years before his death in 1953.

The field is used by many levels of baseball. The Long Beach State University, Long Beach City College, High Schools, American Legion, Connie Mack and other youth baseball games.

My two sons played there in High School, Connie Mack, American Legion, and Long Beach City College. As a bat girl my daughter Jacki was hit by a foul ball and lost her hearing in one ear. I can't say how many games I watched over a thirty year span but it has to be in the hundreds.

The Movies 1940 - 1968

When I was younger, I only went to the movies in the summer time. There were four theaters. The Cabart, The Ebell, The Dale, and The Art. The Cabart was only five cents and on Wednesday you could get popcorn, see a news reel, two cartoons, a cowboy serial, and two major films for ten cents. The Art Theater is still there. There was no profanity or violence. When I got older and could drive to more theaters, there was The United Artist, The Town, Pacific Coast, The Crest, and five drive in movies. We would put three or four guys in the trunk and only pay for two at the drive-ins.

Years later, when I was married and had two kids, we would take two cars to the drive-in. I would drive our VW and Brent and Andy would watch from it. Val would drive our other car and she and I would watch from it. I would make two big groceries bags of popcorn and take our own drinks. That was our family entertainment.

The Paramount Drive-in   *The Lakewood*

The Los Altos

The Spruce Goose 1947

Hughes Aircraft built the largest flying boat ever built in 1947. It was built for WWII, but the war ended before it was complete. It could carry 750 troops and one Sherman tank. It was built  of wood (birch) and had eight Pratt & Whitney R-4360 Wasp Major Engines. It had crew of three, could cruise at 250 mph, had a range of 3000 miles, and was 218' long, a wingspan of 320', Height of 79', and a loaded weight of 400,000 lbs. It made one flight on Nov. 2, 1947 in the Long Beach Harbor. I was 12 years old and was there to see it take off. Although it was on display in Long Beach for many years, it now resides in The Evergreen Aviation Museum, McMinnville OR.

The Queen Mary

The Queen Mary came from London England in 1967. On Its last trip it left South Hampton, around the tip of South America and north to Long Beach Harbor. It was greeted by hundreds of boats, helicopters, planes, blimps and thousands of spectators. It took a year to refurbish before it was finally towed to its permanent place on pier J. My line crew at GTE was the crew that constructed the cable system for its communications.

The Pacific Coast Club 1948-1952

The Pacific Coast Club was a private men's club. It looked like an old castle on the outside but it was a five star hotel for the members. It had an Olympic size swimming pool, a gym, and handball courts. The front faced Ocean Blvd., and the back led out to the beach and the ocean. We would sneak in though the back door and go swimming until they caught us and kicked out.

The Villa Rivera Hotel

The Villa Rivera Hotel was built in the 1929 and was the second tallest building in Southern California. It has 16 stories with 132 homeowners, and cost $2M dollars to build. It was built as an "own-your-apartment", but became a hotel after the great depression. In the 1950's it returned to residential apartments. It became recognized as a National Historical Landmark in 1996. I made many deliveries there when I worked for the Wine Mess.

The Long Beach Grand Prix

The Long Beach Grand Prix began in 1975 as an open wheel race on a street circuit with Formula 5000 cars. It's the largest event in Long Beach with attendance that regularly reaches 200,000 people. It has 11 turns and is 168 miles. I attended the race three times. Twice with my dad Cy, and one time my son Brent (his company provides two-way communications) got me in to the drivers pit to take photos.

Cub Scouts / Boy Scouts / Sea Scouts

I don't remember much about the Cub Scouts. I liked the uniform but wouldn't wear short pants. My older brother Bill was the Scout Master when I was in the Scout Troop. I think he made it harder for me to pass all merit badges because he was my brother. I liked the camping trips and made Star Scout, but really wasn't in to the scout meetings. When Bill moved to Huntington Beach I dropped out of scouting. I did join the Sea Scouts for a short time. After the first day trip out on the ocean I never when back.

Drive- In Restaurants 1949 - 1953

Drive-In restaurants were the place to hang out during my High School days. There were two in Long Beach. The "Clock" was the where the kids from East Long Beach hung out, and "Grisenger's" was where the kids from North Long Beach hung out. We did go to both just to see who was there and meet some different girls. There weren't many problems between the kids from either side of town. The best treats were Hot Fudge Sundaes and Deep Dish Pies with ice cream on them.

Kens 1953

Kens was another place to hang out. It was a fast food walk up just like McDonalds, but it was a few years before McDonalds got started.

Big Bear 1952 - 1953

Big Bear was the place to go for skiing and tobogganing. Every year after Christmas, a lot of kids would go to Big Bear for a few days. I didn't ski, but I loved tobogganing. One year, we made two toboggans. We bought some Masonite and used Charlie's dad's machine shop to build the toboggans. They were long enough for four people to sit on and looked great.

The run we liked to use was about five hundred feet long and had a little stream about twenty inches wide to get over at the end. The first run was fast and we went way past the usual finish spot. Only one problem, when we got up and picked up the toboggan, four round holes the same size as our butts fell out of toboggan.

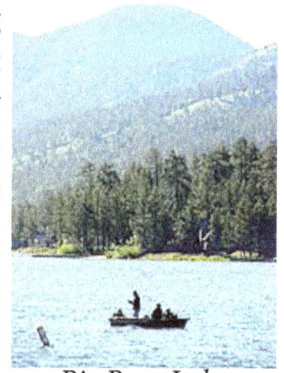

Big Bear Lake

Yosemite National Park 1952

Half Dome

Half Dome

Yosemite Valley is in the California Sierra Mountains. John Muir the naturalist, persuaded many influential people to visit the valley and it was through his diligent campaigning to save the valley it became a National in Park 1890. I have visited Yosemite many times, but my favorite story is the summer of 1952. Four of us went to Yosemite for a week.

There was my cousin Tommy, Tom Hibbison, Don Macken and myself. One day, we were just driving around the mountain roads and Tommy said, "I can see our camp site down there". We were quite a bit higher, but he and Don insisted they wanted to climb down from where we were.

After they got out we headed back to the camp site. About two hours later they showed up with two gallons of red wine. They got lost on their way down and were given a ride back to camp. On the way, the guy who picked them up stopped at store and they asked him to buy some wine. He did. That night we drank all of the wine and of course got very drunk. In the morning when we woke up, we didn't see Tommy anywhere. We had all decided to sleep outside of the tent because it was too hot. Sometime during the night, Tommy went into the tent to sleep and it collapsed on him. It's a wonder he didn't suffocate under it. We had planned to climb up to Half-Dome that day, but we were not feeling to good. The couple camping next us took pity on us and fed us breakfast. About 9:00 or 9:30 we decided to make the climb anyway. The trail is easy and not too steep, but it still takes four hours to get to the top. This was Tommy's first time to be in mountains (he was raised in Brooklyn) and he didn't know how to pace himself. He would run up the trail as far as he could and stop and wait for us. He was a smoker, out of shape, and the altitude was making him sick. He might have killed himself if we hadn't stopped him. The last mile or so is on rock with a rope to hold on to as you climb. The view from the top of Half-Dome is magnificent. You can see the whole Yosemite Valley. Because we left so late, we were really late coming back down the mountain and it got dark before we got back to the car. We were taking things out of our wallets and burning them as torches just to see where we going. When we got to the parking lot it was so dark we couldn't find the car. Don finally found it by walking into it by mistake. That was one very long day. I didn't have another glass of wine until I was in the Army four years later, and that was my last drink of wine.

Top Left:
El Capitan

Top Right:
Yosemite Falls &
Tuolumne Meadows

Left:
Mirror Lake

Sequoia National Park 1953

An National Park in the Southern Sierra Nevada, east of Visalia, California, in the United States. It was established on September 25th, 1890.

In the summer of 1953 I spent some time in Sequoia National Park. Below are pictured myself, Gene Kelly, Don Mackin, and John Thielen at our campfire. Years later, while camping with friends Jan & Dick Sherman, we encountered a black Bear on our hiking trail. Luckily for us, he went off the trail and walked around us and into the forest.

Deer Hunting 1955

After I got out of the Army, I went deer hunting with Danny, Kelly and Don. We had all taken an archery class at Long Bach City College. We went to the Santa Monica Mountains with our bows and arrows. After hiking all day and never seeing one deer, we were back at our camp site sitting on the camp bench having a drink with the bows leaning against the car, when a big five point buck ran right though our camp. Needless to say, we didn't even move for our bows. So much for deer hunting.

Sears & Roebucks 1950

One day Danny, Chuck, John, and I were in Sears & Roebuck just browsing around. We were in the Sports Department and I saw this really neat baseball hat. I tried it on and put it back. Unknown to me Danny had put the hat on and was walking around the store with it. As we walked out of the store (Danny still wearing the hat), a guy grabbed both of us by the collar and said "come with me". I didn't know what was happening so I just took off running. He was able to hold Danny and took him back inside the store. I must have run a mile or more before I stopped. I couldn't decide if I should go back or not. After about ten minutes I headed back to Sears. I met Danny about a block from the store. The guy took him to his office and read him the riot act and let him go. Lesson learned.

Linden Beach 1950 – 1953

Linden Beach is one block west of Alamitos Ave. and South of Ocean Blvd. It was the Beach where all the kids from St Anthony's hung out during the summer. We played Volleyball and did some bodysurfing. One time, I lost my class ring playing volleyball and we searched for a long time but didn't find it. About three weeks later while we were playing volleyball, I reached down and got a hand full of sand and found my ring.

This is where I saw my first "Bikini" swimsuit. We were just lying around when a crowd started to gather just down the beach from us. It turned out that a woman was walking on the beach wearing a Bikini. She was a gorgeous blond and had figure like Marilyn Monroe. The crowd got so large that police showed up and took her away. She didn't speak English and I think she didn't know what all fuss was about. In 1950 no one in Long Beach had ever seen a Bikini up close.

Kick the Can

One of our favorite games was "kick the Can". It was a version of hide & Seek. We would place a can in the middle of the street and someone would kick it as far as possible. The person who was "it" would have to run after it and bring in back to where it was kicked from before he or she could go looking for the other players. If you were found by the "it" person you would race back to see who could kick the can first. If you kick it the "it" person would have to retrieve it and you could hide again. If the "it" person beat you and kicked the can you were caught and had to be the next "it" person.

Touch Football and Fly-out

We played a lot of touch football in the street in front of our house. There was no kicking allowed because the street was lined with 30' palm trees, and if a ball got stuck up in the thorns there was no getting it back. I can't say how many balls of all sorts we lost in those damn palm trees. Fly-out was played with any kind of a ball. It could be a baseball, softball, tennis ball or any kind of ball you wanted to use. The "up" person was determined by the bat game. The bat was tossed up and one person would grab it with one hand. Then, another person would grab it above the first person. Each player grabbed the bat until there was no room to hold the bat. The last one still holding the bat was the winner. The winner would hit grounders at the other players. If you caught it on one bounce it was worth 25 points. On two bounces 15 points. Three or more 5 points. A missed ball deducted 5 points off your score. The first person to reach 100 points got to be the "up" person. If the "up" person hit a fly ball at any time he was out and the person with most points was "up".

Ball-Over - Red Rover

The house I lived in was a two story and had a very high roof line in the front, and a long sloping roof line in the back. One person would be on each side of the house and the idea was to call out "Ball Over - Red Rover" and then throw a tennis ball over the roof so that it would land on the other side and rolled down. The person on that side was supposed to catch the ball before it touched the ground. Whoever got three misses first lost the game.

Step Baseball

This was a game I played by myself for hours at a time. Our house had five concrete steps and concrete walkway leading up to it. The walkway was about 15' long from the steps to the sidewalk and about 6' wide. I would make up baseball situations and throw a tennis ball against the steps. If I was on defense I would have to field the ball and throw it to a certain spot to get an out. If I was on offense, anything that got by me was a hit some kind.

Trick or Treat

Halloween was always a fun time when I was growing up. At age 12 or 13, I was able to cover quite a large area on my trick or treat rounds. As a 14 and 15 year old, it was all tricks and no treats. We would do the dog crap thing. You get a paper bag and fill it with dog crap, then place it on the porch, light the bag on fire and ring the doorbell. Then, run to some place where you could watch. More times than not, someone would come out and stamp out the fire.

We made a dummy out of a manikin. It really looked like a person with hair, arms, legs, shoes, and a hat. We would throw it out into the street when a car was coming, and just before it got to the dummy, we would pull it back with a rope. We would climb up into a tree and drop it down just in front of people as they came walking down the sidewalk. We used that dummy for about four years. When we got our licenses and could drive, we would go down town on a Friday or Statuary night and find a movie theater with a line of people waiting to get in. We would drive up to the curb in front of the theater, open the door and throw the dummy out and drive off. The dummy had a rope tied to it, so it got dragged behind the car. The reaction of the crowd was very funny to us. We would also have one of us sit on a bus bench where there were other people. Then we'd drive up to the bus stop and jump out and pull our buddy into the car. We'd drive about a half a block, stop and toss the dummy out of the car, and drive off dragging the dummy down the street.

CYO (Catholic Youth Organization)

Two good things about the CYO; there was a basketball league I played in, and the dances on Friday nights. My two older sisters taught me how to dance when I was only nine or ten years old, so I was the one of the few young teenagers that would actually dance at the CYO.

Pier Point Landing

Pier Point Landing was a good place for sea food and great for sport fishing. There was a bait shop and you could feed the Harbor Seals.

Grunion Runs

When I was a kid, there were many people who didn't believe there was such a fish as a Grunion. They thought it was like snipe hunting. A Grunion is a little

fish that looks like jack smelt or a top smelt. They are called Leuresthes Tenuis and are members of the Silversides family. They appear mostly from Northern California (Monterey Bay) to Baja California (San Juanico Bay Mex.) They can be caught on nearly all Southern California beaches. It requires a fishing license for anyone over 16 years old and can only be caught with your hands. There is no limit on how many you can catch. The California Department of Fish and Game posts a chart of locations and predicts the nights and times they will run. Google 'Grunion Run' for all the information on Grunion.

I was very young when my older siblings would take me Grunion Hunting. They usually run around midnight and later. We would fill up our buckets and take them home to clean and fry. When I got older, I would go to the beach on my motor scooter with a buddy. We would dig a hole in the sand about 6' long, 3' wide 1' deep. When the wave came in, the hole would fill up with fish. We would take off our pants and tie knots in the legs and fill the pants with Grunion. (digging holes to entrap them is not permitted anymore) I don't know if Long Beach is still a good place for Grunion Hunting.

YMCA (Young Men's Christian Association)

Three good things about the YMCA; you could get a pick-up basketball game almost any time, the swimming pool was fun (I didn't really like swimming in the nude), and I joined a Fencing Club years later in my twenties. A friend of mine was a good enough Fencer to qualify for the Olympic Fencing Team. He didn't go because he got injured. He got me interested in Fencing and I joined the club.

I did pretty well for a beginner, but the instructor didn't like it that my buddy and his friends were teaching me stuff that a beginner wasn't supposed to be doing. I won first place in two tournaments. It started to get expensive with the equipment and the traveling, so I gave it up after a year. My clearest memory is the time I was practicing with a guy who didn't wear the proper mask and I rammed my blade right though his mask and cut his forehead. It just missed his eye.

Airplane Hill

In Long Beach, at the corner of 6th and Winslow, is a street we called Airplane Hill. You would start your car about 50 yards back from the top of the hill and go as fast as you could. By the time you reach the drop off your car would go airborne for about 20 or 30 yards before it came back to the pavement.

Jobs I had

Newspaper Routes 1947 – 1948

When I was twelve, I had two paper routes. A morning route with the Long Beach Independent, and an afternoon route with the Long Beach Press-Telegram. They covered the same area. Junipero Ave. on the East to Cherry Av. on the West. From 7th St. on the South to 10th St. on the north. I delivered about 250 papers on each route. The morning route had to be delivered no later than 6:00 am. All the delivery boys would meet in front of Ralph's Market at 5:00 am. to pick up the papers. They had to be boxed (folded a certain way) so you could toss them a long way. We had L-Brackets on our handle bars which would hold a wooden box with the papers in it. My folks bought me a new bike that had a small wheel on the front with a big basket that sat straight on top of the wheel. It was great for delivering papers. Once a month we had to collect for the papers. They gave us a book with receipt tickets to give to the customers when we collected the money. As I remember, the monthly rate was $1.50 and they paid us .25 per paper. So, 250 X .25 = $62.50 per month X 2 routes was $125.00 a month for me. That was very good money in those days for a kid.

The Wine Mess 1952 - 1953

When I was a junior and senior I had part-time job at a liquor store as a delivery boy. Any order over a dollar they would deliver. I worked after school from 6:00 pm to 9:00 pm, and on Saturdays from 1:00 pm to 6:00 pm. They had an old green panel truck which we used to deliver orders. My job was to deliver orders to the customer's house and collect the money. As a young boy of 17 and 18, I got a good look of what alcohol could do to you.

 Many of the customer's order on one day and wouldn't even remember me on the next day. I met a lot of really strange people and saw some really strange things. One time I made a delivery to an apartment and this young woman answered the door. She was maybe in her mid-twenties. She invited me in while she went for her purse. When she came out of her bedroom, she stood in front of an open flame floor heater. She was wearing a bathrobe and she backed up to the heater and it caught on fire. She immediately took off her robe and started to stamp out the fire. I was in shock because she was totally nude and jumping around trying to put the fire out.

I grabbed a pillow off her sofa and smothered the flame. She just stood there looking at me with tears in her eyes. I excused myself and waited outside until she brought me the money. She thanked me and gave me a nice tip. I never delivered to her again.

One of the regular customers was a Marine and his wife. I must have gone there at least once a week for months. One day I made a delivery and the woman introduced me to her husband who had just returned from overseas duty. He wasn't the guy that been there all the previous times.

More than once when I made deliveries to parties, I was invited to come back to the party after I got off work. I never did.

One evening I was going to a football game after I got off work. About ten minutes before quitting time, an order called in and the guy who was coming on shift hadn't shown up. I had to make the delivery. I was really racing back to the store when an off duty cop pulled me over and gave me a ticket for rolling though a stop sign. I had to go before a judge with my Mom. The judge asked me if I really needed my job to support myself. I knew he would know I didn't and I wouldn't have said that in front of my Mother. I told him I use my earnings to buy gas for my car and to pay for any extra things I wanted. He smiled at me as if that was the right answer and said the only driving I could do was at work for thirty days.

That was the only job I ever got fired from. It was New Year's Day and I stayed home to watch the Rose Blow game. When I went in later, Mrs. Goldstein (the Owner) said I was fired for being late on one of their busiest days of the year. I wasn't happy about being fired but it was the time of the year I would start training for the Track season.

Years later I wondered how an underage kid could have a job delivering liquor.

Edgington Oil Co. 1953

The summer between High School and LBCC, I worked at Edgington Oil Co. This was a small independent oil company in Long Beach. They would hire day labors every day. About fifty guys would show up in the morning and they would hire about twenty five or thirty just for the day. It took eight days before they hired me. The pay was $1.87 per hour which was very good in 1953. This was the most dangerous place I ever worked. It seemed like someone got injured every day. My first job was handling empty 55gal. oil drums. They would be delivered in box cars and we would unload them by hand. It was dangerous because sometimes they would be jammed or wedged together, and we'd have to tie a cable around them and pull them out with a fork lift. When the jam broke loose there no telling where those drums would go. We would load them on to pallets and move them to the stacking yard. This is where they were stored until they were needed for filling. The stacking was the hardest job I ever had in my life. We would stack them five high. At first, I really had a hard time lifting them to the top row, until the smallest guy in group showed me how to toss them.

It was all about leverage. After the first day, I got home and went to bed and didn't get up until it was time to go to work. My next job was on the barrel filling platform. The platform was about haft the size of a football field. It had a big arm in the middle and would rotate 360 degrees. We would place the empty barrels on the platform, and the operator would move the arm around to fill the barrels with oil. After they were filled, one guy would hammer a plug in the fill hole, and then we would use special dollies to load them on to a flatbed truck. If anyone dropped a barrel he would be fired on the spot. I worked in the barrel making factory on the machine that punched holes in the lids of the barrels. I worked on barrel painting crew and got covered with black paint every day. I worked on the Tar platform, stapling the lids of the cardboard containers. They would fill these cardboard containers with hot tar and let them sit overnight to cool before you could staple the top closed. Once, a guy sat on a container that was still hot and burned his butt pretty bad. I worked there until school started at LBCC.

American Can Co. 1954

When I left LBCC, I took a job at the American Can Co. It wasn't much of a job and I worked in the shipping department. I did work in the can factory once or twice testing for leaks. Very boring.

I worked there for three months and then went down to the Draft Board and volunteered for the Army. (Sep. 1954) By volunteering, I moved my name to the top of the draft list. This way I could get my military obligation taken care in only two years' service.

US Army 1954-1956

In 1954, the US had a mandatory draft. The only way you could avoid it was some kind of exemption like college, special employment, or medical waver. After leaving LBCC, I wanted to get my service obligation out of the way. All of the Arm Forces had minimum of three years of enlistment. Two years was the shortest amount of time in service through the draft. I went to the Draft Board and had my name placed on the top of the list.

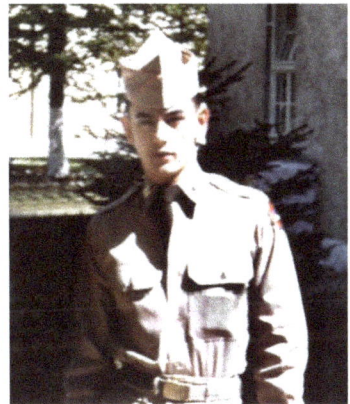

Induction

My plan was to say my goodbyes at home and have my buddy take me to Union Station in Los Angeles where I was ordered to report. The induction into the Army was conducted at the Train Station. I can't remember all the details of it, but I do remember a sergeant saying "All those who agree take one step forward". Funny thing about that, was that there was no other way get out of room without stepping forward.

My family would not hear of me going off alone. My Mom & Dad, my brother Bernie, sisters Dot & Boots, my cousin Tom and two of my nephews all made the trip to Union Station. Some of the other guys had family but not nearly as many as I did. When we started to board the train, my cousin Tom yells out goodbye Uncle Henry. Needless to say that Uncle Henry stuck with me all though basic training. Even my platoon sergeant ragged on me.

Fort Ord, Monterey Ca.

Basic training was hard, but time went by so fast it didn't seem like two months. Our platoon was in a two story barracks. Luckily, I was able to get a downstairs bunk and in the middle of the room. You always want to be in the middle of everything. Never stand on the end of any line, in the front row, or the back row. Whenever they want a detail (workers) for a crappie job, they say 'you guys on the end or in the first row or the back row'. The worst part was all the crawling we did. Our Field Sergeant had a bad foot and couldn't run so he wouldn't double time us. Worse than double time was crawling. He would march us out to the boondocks and send us about fifty yards out and make us crawl back to the road. I had scabs on my keens the entire time in basic training. We did all the things you see in the movies. Crawling under barbwire while they fired machine guns over our heads, lots of pushups, bayonet training, gas mask training, KP, and more marching. I was given an expert shooter medal.

Everyone had to pull KP. (kitchen police) There were three basic jobs in KP. 1. Pots, pans and tray washer. This was the worst job. Can you image all the pots, pans and trays for 300 troops?

 2. Server, mess hall cleanup, and cooks helper. Serving and helping the cook was easy but the mess hall cleaning was hard. All the tables, chairs, and floor had to be scrubbed down three times a day. 3. Garbage man. This guy stood outside in the back of the mess hall and cleaned the grease pit and made sure the troops put their garbage in the right can. The grease pit was a pit about 12" X 12" and 20" deep. All of the grease from the kitchen would end up in that pit. The garbage guy would have to scoop it out and put in a special barrel. It took about 30 minutes, once a shift. After all the troops were gone, he would wash down with a hose. It was actually the best KP job. The first

one to sign in would have his pick of jobs. I always got there before the cooks (4:30 am) so I could have my pick of jobs.

After basic training I was sent to Clerk Typist School. For eight weeks we typed forms and did clerical work in the company command office. While in CTS, I found out that one of my high school buddies had a brother who worked in the office for troop assignment. He told me to see him two weeks before I was to get out of CTS and he would get me assigned to where I wanted to be stationed. I was thinking Hawaii. One problem, he was on leave when I went to see him. I got assigned to a Headquarters Company in Stuttgart Germany.

The trip to Germany was one I'll never forget. It started in a small Monterey airport. They loaded us on to a C41 aircraft. It held about 100 guys. It was night time and when they started up the engines, a big ball of fire came out of the engine on my side. You could see some kind of fluid pouring out of the engine. Just as I said to the guy next me, "We're not going anywhere in this airplane", it started taxiing to the runway. It spit out fire all the way to Oklahoma City where we stopped to eat and changed airplanes.

Fort Dix, New Jersey

We flew to New Jersey and stayed at Fort Dix for three days before boarding a merchant troop ship and headed for Germany. It took nine days to cross the Atlantic to Bremerhaven, Germany.

The weather was so bad for several days we couldn't go topside. We were packed like a can of sardines with our bunks stacked three high. I never saw the guy above me get out of his bunk one time he was so seasick.

I didn't get sick, but I took all pills they gave me. When the waves hit the bow of the ship it sounded like someone was hitting us with a wrecking ball. There were no assigned bunks, so they couldn't really keep track of anyone. I was sent to galley duty on the second day. I think the galley must be the most dangerous place on the ship. Things were flying everywhere as the ship rolled back and forth. The next time they called on the PA "Bisnar, Brown, and Clyborne report to the galley", we didn't go. We just took our chances they couldn't' find us in the mass of bodies. It worked.

Bremerhaven, Germany

Bremerhaven is in the northeast corner of Germany and one of Germany's important seaports. It was founded in 1827 and has a long history of trade. During WWII, the city was bombed but the port was spared to provide a usable harbor for supplying the Allies after the war.

Stuttgart, Germany

From Bremerhaven I took a ten or twelve hour ride to Stuttgart. Stuttgart is in the southern part of Germany and its 6th largest city. It had a population of about 600k and was founded in the 10th century.

I was stationed at Kelly barracks near a small town of Mohrengen, just 10 miles southeast of Stuttgart. It was a German Army base built in 1938, and during WWII named Hellemen Kaserne. Shortly after WWII it was renamed in honor of Staff Sergeant Jonah E. Kelly, West Virginia, 311th Infantry, and 78th Infantry Division. Kelly was awarded the Medal of Honor for his actions at Kesternich (The Battle of The Hurtgon Forest) in January 1945.

Kelly Barrack, Mohrengen Germany

In 1995, Kelly Barracks became the home of Headquarters VII Corps and

the Corps Headquarters unit until it was deactivated in 1992. There were only 14 buildings and about 200 troops. The officer to enlisted men ratio was so great that we didn't salute anyone under Captain. I was assigned to the Headquarters Company VII Corps. Upon my arrival, the First Sergeant told me that he didn't need any clerks and to take a day to decide if wanted to be a lineman or a cook. He assigned me to the cook's room temporarily. Finding out that the cooks worked one day and had two days off,

I chose to be a cook. Also the cooks were exempt from guard duty, room inspections, reveille, and Saturday parades. The way the shifts worked was you reported to the Mess Hall at 12:00pm and worked until it close around 6:00pm. The next day you reported at 4:00am and worked until 12:30 pm. Then you were off work for the remainder of that day, all of the next day and the morning of the next. With some creative trading of work shifts you could get several days off for traveling without using your leave time.

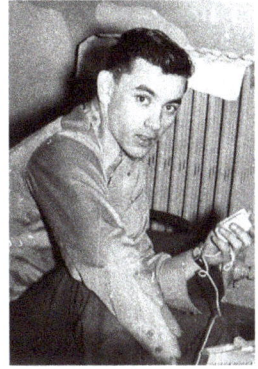

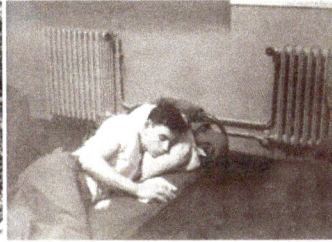

Bivouac

On my third day, we went out on a forty day bivouac. These bivouacs were always unannounced and you were supposed to have your duffel bag ready for field duty at all times. There was always some guy who ended up out there with nothing but fatigues and his rifle. We drove for a few hours to a wooded forest and set up our camp site. I slept in a large squad tent with the cooks.

It was February, snowing and very cold. Of course being from California and a tenderfoot, I didn't know how to live in the snow. Every time I pulled up the zipper to the top of my sleeping bag it would come unzipped. I spent the whole night trying to keep warm. When I got up in the morning my boots and fatigues were frozen. After two

or three days of seeing me struggle, they took pity on me and gave me a few life saving tips.

The sleeping bags were designed for quick release by pulling the zipper all the way to the top. Never pull the zipper to the top unless you want out. You need to put your boots and fatigues in your sleeping bag, and put everything you're not going to need the next day between you and the ground. I actually did pretty well after I got the hang of it.

Life in the field was hard, interesting, and at times fun.

We took two of our civilians with us for KP duty. They were young men and very funny. One day they took the garbage and trash down to the pit for burning. They must have poured a whole five gallon can of gas on it because the explosion, when they lit it, sounded like a bomb. We also had heaters that fit in big trash cans. You would put the heater in the can and fill the can with water. The hot water was used for cleaning the kitchen utensils and the troop's mess kits. They had a small gas tank on the top which dripped in to a fire box at the bottom of the heater and heated the water. More than once, the KP's managed to blow up a trash can.

The German's hunt deer by building a corral and tree platform to sit in while they wait for a deer to feed in the corral. One day, we saw a mother and a fawn, and we tried to catch the fawn. Needless to say, it kicked the crap out of us and ran off.

As a communications company, we strung a lot of wire in the trees. After a few days, a local guy from the nearest town or village would come out and count the number of holes left in the trees left by our linemen. There was a charge for each hole.

The officers had a large squad tent with a wooden floor for their meals. One day, we ran out of fresh eggs and were served powdered eggs. The colonel was so mad he threatened to demote the mess sergeant down to a private if it ever happened again. The very next day, a truck load of fresh eggs was delivered to our camp.

The cooks had to get up early to prepare breakfast for the troops and officers. One day, we couldn't get the generator started for the lights. As we were kneeling over the generator, our Major came up and asked if we needed any help. He was standing there in shorts and boots. He was one tough guy. He knelt down in the snow and in a minute or two he had it running. He said we owed him some extra bacon. As if he couldn't get all the bacon he wanted.

Every day they would have sick call. Anyone that was sick could go in the company ambulance (army 4X4) to the nearest post to see the doctor. They were never close, and it was always a full day's trip. We cooks took turns going to the post for showers and a trip to the PX.

Being in the field for forty days or longer was not fun, but what made it even harder was we would move our camp as many as three or four times. It felt like all we did was load the trucks and unload the tucks.

I really didn't know anything about cooking. The Mess Sergeant was a good guy and just used me as a cook's helper. He did ask me to make chocolate cake one time. He said all I had to do was follow the recipe and it would turn out ok. Well, they turned out to be the best dam Brownies they ever had in that mess hall.

I was only a cook for a few months. The Mess Hall Clerk was sent home for discharge and I took his job. My duties were to order the rations, type the menus, supervise twelve civilian workers, and manage their payroll. I still had all the privileges that the cooks had. Cooks had many privileges that others didn't. They could get clean bed linen whenever they wanted it, have their rifles serviced and cleaned by the arms tech, laundry done with no waiting, get in to the movies free, no inspections, no reveille, no parades, and could

trade work days. Of course these privileges also applied to the Mess Hall Clerk.

One of my buddies was on the Company Bowling Team. I would go and watch him quite often. When one of their team members went home they asked me to take his place. I informed them my highest bowling score was about 140. They said that would be ok and that I would be an alternant to fill in when someone didn't show up. The first time I bowled my best score was 132 and that established a handicap of 21 pins for me. The very next time I bowled my lowest score was 162 and with my handicap I was able to win a trophy for highest score with handicap. Of course it was a fluke but I took the trophy anyway. The other teams called me a ringer. I never bowled that good again.

I shared a room with five guys and it was big enough for maybe eight or ten. I taught them all how to play chess and we would have chess tournaments which would last for a week or two. We all put in $5.00 and winner took all.

For the first few months, I would go to Stuttgart every chance I got. It was a short train ride and cost very little money. The trains were always right on time and right to the minute. It was a big town and had lots of hangouts for GI's. There were many times that five or six guys would go in on a cab back to the post. The cabs were Volkswagen Beetles and could barely make it up the long hill out of town.

Many of us would take gifts and clothing to the Kinderheim (Children's Home) in Waiblingen, Germany. The orphanage was adopted by the VII Corps. In Oct. 1955.

Pfc Eisner, Cpl Wallace, Cpl Minron, and Sgt Jackson are shown paying a visit to the Kinderheim (Children's Home) at Weiblingen, Germany. The orphanage is adopted by the 34th Sig Bn, Corps. 20 May 55.

Photographer: Cpl. Rick Hansen
Hq. Co. 34th Sig Bn, Corps

The Mess Hall was a very interesting place to work. There was always something going on that was just a little crazy.

One of the male civilians' KP's was gay. In those days, gays in the Army were treated pretty badly. Being a civilian he got ragged on even harder. One day he reported me to our major claiming I harassed him with my remarks. I don't remember saying anything to him because he was a nice guy and a good worker. The major called me to his office and asked what I had said to him. After telling him I didn't remember saying anything he laughed and told me not to do it again.

The Major was the same one that fixed the generator for us. He was what they call a Mustang Officer. That's an officer that raises up through the ranks. He was given a battle field commission during the Korean War. He would go to the Motor Pool to inspect the vehicles and drop down in full dress uniform on the palms of hands and look under the trucks, and then push himself up without bending his knees. One time he was inspecting the Mess Hall and found a toilet he said was not cleaned properly.

He asked me to bring him the KP that cleaned the head. (Restroom) When the guy got there, the Major rolled up his sleeves and got on his knees and showed the guy how he wanted him to clean the toilets.

It was discovered that food kept missing from the mess hall. Butter, canned goods, fruit, condiments, and other items. I suspected the same KP that accused me of making gay remarks. He rode a motor bike to work which had saddlebags. The saddle bags were always bulging when drove off at the end of the shift. The Major asked me to phone him the next time I saw him leave with full saddlebags. It happened only a few days later and when I called the Major he came to the mess hall in his personal car.

We followed him for a mile or so then pulled him over. The Major found several items from the mess hall kitchen in his saddlebags. He held him there until the MP's and German police came. They released him, but the Major fired him on the spot. The next day, the company that provided civilian workers got his job back. Turns out that the only one that can legally fire civilians is the employment company that sent him to work for us. He didn't last long because the Major made sure he was harassed by everyone in the mess hall.

I wanted to buy a new camera and the one I wanted was $120.00 in the PX. A lot of money for me in those days. The pots & pans KP was a Russian guy who spoke pretty good English. He told me he could buy the same camera in town for about $80.00. I couldn't pass that deal up. I gave him the money and never saw him again. He gave up a well-paying job for $80.00. Live and learn.

Cigarettes were $1.20 a carton and you needed a coupon to buy them. Everyone was issued two coupons per month. I didn't smoke and was able to sell my coupons near the end of the month for $5.00 each. I tried to save as money as I could for traveling.

VII Corps

Private

E-4 Specialist

Rifle

Bayonet

Grenade

Machine Gun

Good Conduct Medal

Travel While in the Army

I saved my money and my leave time so I could travel as much as possible. I got thirty days furlough a year, and by trading work shifts I was able to travel. I traveled by car to many German towns, villages, forests, and cities. I traveled by train to other countries. Traveling by train was always an experience. They sold tickets by class. 1st class got you a seat in a private compartment. 2nd class got you a seat in a regular passenger car. 3rd class got you on the train and maybe a seat in the passenger car. We would buy the cheapest ticket (3rd class), and then go to the private compartments and stay there until the conductor asked for our ticket. We would act like we didn't understand him and sometimes he would let us stay there.

Together, the five guys in our room bought a 1934 Mercedes. I don't know how many guys owned it before us, but it was on the base long before me. It was pretty banged up but ran good, and we covered a lot of country side in it.

One time, we were out in the country and were approaching a small village. A Honey Wagon (horse drawn wagon with manure) was coming towards us and it took up more than half of the road. Just as we started to go around it, another car came out from behind the wagon and tried to pass on the same side. We got pinned between

the car and the honey wagon. The other driver and the guy on the honey wagon could not speak English. Speedy Minion, our driver, was a Jewish boy from New Jersey, but could speak pretty good Spanish. The local policemen could also speak Spanish. They exchanged information while the rest of us walked to the village and had a couple beers.

The Black Forrest Germany

The Black Forrest is a beautiful forest in the heart of Germany. We took many trips to the country side to spend time away from the Post and enjoy the people.

Amsterdam

I went to Holland with my buddy John. We stayed in a pension (family-owned guesthouse) with a really nice family. The owner was also a tour guide and we spent two days sightseeing in his car. He took us in his car to visit his brother who lived in a Windmill.

We went to the flower auction where they bought huge barges from the flower fields and auctioned them to be shipped all over the world. We drove all over the city of Amsterdam and canals.

Amsterdam has a very large Cantonese (Chinese) community and we went there for dinner. Of course we couldn't speak their language or read the menu. The menu had pictures, so we just pointed to what we thought looked good. They had to bring a second table to put all the food on. We had no idea what we were eating but we didn't leave much. One night, we walked to Canal Street. This is the red light district where the prostitutes did business. They would sit in their windows and invite you in for a good time. At that time in Amsterdam, the cars used only their parking lights at night. I came very close to being hit by a speeding car.

They also have sidewalk urinals for men. This was my best friend John Hindelmier.

Lichtenstein

Lichtenstein is between Austria and Switzerland, and is the sixth smallest country in the world. (pop. About 35k) Vaduz is the capital. It was neutral during WWII and is the world biggest producer

of dentures. They have a Prince as the head of State. There isn't much to see there except the Royal Castle.

Italy

Florence

I took a train from Germany to Florence and spent two days sightseeing. Lots of history and beautiful buildings.

Rome

It would take a couple of weeks to see Rome. I was there for only three days, but covered a lot of ground. Here a list of what I remember after sixty years. St. Peter's Basilica, The Sistine Chapel, St. Peter's Square (I'm actually in the third picture from the left), St. Peter's Fountain, The Pope's Balcony, Vatican Museum, The Pantheon, The Roman Forum, The Spanish Steps, Tivoli Fountain, Four Rivers Fountain, Piazza del Popolo, and the Coliseum.

Venice

Venice is in northern Italy with a population of 270,000. The city stretches across 117 small islands in the marshy Venetian Lagoon along the Adriatic Sea. I spent three days there in 1956. As I walked out of the train station, a women approached me and spoke in Italian. When I said I didn't speak Italian she switched to English and said, "do you know where the Post Office is"? I couldn't tell you were an American". Turns out she was born in Venice but was raised in the US. She guided me to the pension where I stayed.

Short timers

Most guys had a short timer's calendar. It was a sheet of paper we taped in our lockers with the total number of days of our enlistment. The idea was to cross off the days as they went by. You were not considered a short timer until you got under three months. There was a Short Timers Club and the guy with the shortest time got to wear this really cool fatigue hat. It was a crusty old hat that someone donated to the club. The story was the hat was from the Korean War. Short Timers signed the hat with their name and date they went home. The night before the Short Timer went home we would have a party and a passing of the hat ceremony. With beer only 5c a glass, needless to say a good time was had by all.

Departure and Mustering Out

I only got to wear the Short Timers Hat for a few days because the guy ahead of me left just four days before me. We had another tradition we called "Thanks for the Memories". The idea was to do something that everyone would remember about you. Wallis hated to get up for those 4:30am duty calls, so he bought a brand new alarm clock, and on the day he left, he took his trenching tool and mashed it to pieces. Speedy always complained about living on the third floor and having to carry everything up three flights of stairs, on the day he left, he threw all his linen and duffel bag out of the third story window.

My parting shot was the very best. About two months before I left, the First Sergeant assigned our new Mess Sergeant to our room. He was there because the other sergeants didn't want him in their quarters. He was some weird guy from the south that was messy and didn't shower all that much. We tried several times to get him assigned to another room but failed. Being the mess hall clerk, I had contact with him daily and it wasn't a pleasant experience. So, on the day I left I made sure he was in the mess hall, and just before I left I nailed his foot and wall locker shut with some 2" nails.

Azores

I was lucky to be able to fly home rather than go by ship. We made stops in the Azores and New Jersey before going on to California. They call the discharging process mustering out. Each day they would call out a list of the guys to be discharged that day. If you weren't

on that list they would have some kind of detail for you to do. As soon as the last name was called, everyone would scatter trying not to be put on a detail. I and about ten other guys would run around the first building and line up like we were marching somewhere, and I would lead them to the PX or the movies. It took about a week for me to get discharged.

I realize how fortunate I was having served my military duty without going in to combat. When I got home, I had seen more of Europe than the US.

Born Brother Warehouse 1956

After I got out of the Army I didn't do anything for about a month. A friend of mine told me they were hiring where he worked, which was a big warehouse (Born Brothers) in La Brea. It was owned by Thrifty Drugs Store. My job was to load the trailers with goods to be delivered to Drug Stores. It was kind of a no-brainer job, but it paid $2.25 an hour and I worked overtime almost every day. I worked there for about three months until I took a job with the telephone company.

General Telephone Co. 1956-1993

I only took the job at the telephone company as a temporary means of income while I was going to Barber College. My intensions were to get my Barbers License and own a Barber Shop with my brother Bernie. When I applied at the Phone Company I was told they weren't hiring at the time, but when the Personnel guy saw it was my birthday he said, "I'm going to give you a birthday present," and he hired me as a Cable Splicer's Helper. So I worked at the Phone Company during the day and went to Barber College at night.

What is a **Cable Splicer's helper**? This was an apprentice type job for becoming a Cable Splicer and paid $1.25 per hour. When I left Born Brothers, I was making $2.25 an hour and all the overtime I wanted. I lost a $1.00 per hour and all that overtime but it was worth it in the end. Basically, you were the splicer's right hand man and assisted him by maintaining the tools and truck in good order, and were expected to know what he needed before he asks for it. Kind of like a nurse in an operating room. I was a Helper for two years, and worked with a Splicer named Buck Bond. He was a no nonsense guy and not easy to please. He was by far the best person to learn the trade from. There were times I really had to control myself from punching him in the mouth. Of course he was a lot bigger than me, so that wouldn't have been a good idea anyway.

What is a **Cable Splicer**? We've all seen telephone cable hanging from one pole to another and it looks like it is one long piece of cable. Well, cables only come in certain lengths depending on the type and the size. All Cables have to be spliced together at some point. The Cable Splicer is the person that makes the splices that connect the cables. A splicer's pay was $2.40 per hour to start, and took six years to reach top pay of $6.50 per hour. Cables have as little as 2 wires in them, and as many as 7,200 wires. Some cables are color coded and some are not, and each wire has to be identified before splicing them together. Different types of cable can transmit different kinds of signals. It's all way too complicated to explain in these ramblings so I won't go any further with it. There was a certain amount of danger as a Cable Splicer or a Lineman. We work anywhere from 20' to 60' in the air and in underground cable vaults. Once, I experienced a minor explosion in a cable vault and once while working on a cable it broke, and I fell about 20' on to a parked car. My arm went through the rear window and I cut my arm and nose.

I was back to work the next day. My helper fell in a bed of ivory and broke two vertebrates and was off work for three weeks. I also worked as a contract splicer on the weekends for a local cable company. I was a Cable Splicer for six years.

After six years with the company I was promoted to Splicing Foreman. At the time, I was 28 years old and the youngest person ever promoted to foreman. The average length of time for Splicing Foreman was 15 years.

What does a **Splicing Foreman** do? The obvious answer is that he supervises Cable Splicer's. By the time a guy becomes a Journeyman Splicer he really doesn't need someone to look over his shoulder. The Foreman's job is 80% administrative and 20% people skills. It's kind of like a 2nd Lieutenant. I had a crew of 15 splicer's that worked throughout the City of Long Beach.

After two years as a foreman I was promoted to Construction Pre-Fielder.

What is a **Construction Pre-Fielder**? As a pre-fielder I would review all the work orders from Engineering to make sure the jobs could actually be done in the field. There was never a job that didn't need at least some changes in order to match the field conditions. After approving a work order, I would assign it to a Foreman. I also

worked with the other departments to coordinate our work order schedule with theirs. Kind of like a 1st. Lieutenant.

Management Cross Training as a Line Foreman.

What does a **Line Foreman** do? Again, we've all seen cables hanging from pole to pole. The Line Crews are the ones that put up the poles and the cables. They also place all the underground cables prior to the splicers doing the splicing. The Line Foreman's job requires more on site supervision due to the heavy trucks and equipment. Most Linemen are tough guys that work hard and play hard. You have to have a strong personality to command their respect and friendship. I was Line Foreman for 18 months.

Management Cross Training as a Construction Analyst.

What does a **Construction Analyst** do? A Construction Analysis is a suit and tie job and 95% behind a desk. He works for the Top Administrator for Construction and Engineering. He prepares and tracks the construction budget for trucks and equipment. He's a problem solver for construction and the go between the Administrator and the Field Superintends. Kind of like a Captain. I was an Analyst for two years.

Management Cross Training as a Conduit Inspector.

What does a *Conduit Inspector* do? The telephone company contracts out the construction of conduit system and cable vaults. A conduit inspector is the go between, between the contractor, engineering, and the city. He's responsible for inspecting and approving all work the contractor does for the company. I was an inspector for two years.

Management Cross Training as a Communication Salesmen

What is a **Communication Salesmen**? As a communication salesmen, I sold key systems and switchboard systems to local businesses in the southern end of Los Angeles County and the west end of Orange County. Although I did pretty well, I didn't like sales and I transferred out

ASAP. My Sales Supervisor wanted me to stay, but my bag was construction and engineering and the pay was better than sales.

Underground Construction Foreman

What does an **Underground Construction Foreman** do? In 1970, the company decided to start construction of underground conduits systems and cable vaults using company employees rather than contract companies. Having experience as an inspector for underground contract work, I was chosen to be the first foreman for the newly formed UG crews. It started with me and two inexperienced linemen. We began with very small and limited jobs. (under $10,000) Two years later, our UG group consisted of three foremen and 30 linemen and we were building full scale conduit systems and cable vaults. ($200,000 and up).

Underground Construction Pre-fielder

What does an **Underground Pre-fielder** do? As a pre-fielder I made sure all the work orders from engineering were workable in the field and all the equipment and materials were on hand before the crews started a new project. I averaged about 150 miles a day looking at job locations and contacting customers that might be impacted by our work force.

Underground Engineering Supervisor

What does an **Underground Engineering Supervisor** do? When our UG Engineering Supervisor died unexpectedly (a good friend) I was picked to replace him. I supervised two clerks, four draftsmen, and ten GU Engineers. We were responsible for engineering work orders for the GU conduit systems and cable vaults for the southern area.

Facilities Manager

What does a **Facilities Manager** do? When I first hired on as a cable splicer's helper, the top man in the Construction Department was called Superintendent. The thought that I would ever be the Superintendent never entered my mind. After eleven different jobs and 27 years, I was promoted to Superintendent, but with a change of title to Facilities Manager. As Facilities Manager, I was the department head over Construction and Maintenance for the Southern Area. (Long Beach, Seal Beach, Surfside, Lakewood, Bellflower, Los Alamitos, and Cerritos. The Department consisted of 1 Manager, 2 Prefielders, 16 Supervisors, 95 Lineman, 200 Cable Splicer's, 2 administrative clerks and an average of 40 contract employees.

I did spend some time training management employees on the Rancho Calamigos dude ranch in the Santa Monica Mountains. The Construction & Engineering Director decided he wanted all management employees to go through a special training course. He chose a staff person to put together a team to develop a Management Training Course. The staff person was a young lady that I had promoted to supervisor a few years earlier and she convinced the Director I would be the best one to head up the team. I declined the assignment, but to no avail. We visited three highly regarded training faculties. The National Forest Ranger Academy in Harpers Ferry West Virginia, The Xerox Training Center also in Leesburg Virginia and the General Telephone Executive Facility in Hartford Connecticut. We developed a curriculum unlike any other the company offered. It was one week on the Rancho Calamigos Dude Ranch. There were sixteen students in each class who came from all parts of the company and for the most part, didn't know each other. In every class, the idea of team work was heavily stressed, so by the end of the week they were like old buddies. I spent a total of twenty weeks as the on site Manager.

General Telephone is now named Verizon

I can say without any doubt that my 37 year career was all I could have asked for and more. I did have a couple of bosses that I didn't have much respect for, but I outlasted them. I made many good friends have many fond memories.

Barber 1956 - 1967

After I got out of the Army I didn't really know what I wanted to do. My brother Bernie wanted me to get a Barbers License and go into business with him. I thought it was a good idea, but I wasn't one hundred percent sure I wanted to be a Barber. I worked days at the telephone company and went to Barber College at night. Barbering seemed to come easy for me and I was on the first chair within one month. The first chair was supposed to be the best student and you gave the instructors their haircuts. It required 1200 hours to be able to test for a license. It took just under twelve months to reach 1200 hours. The test was given in Los Angeles and was in two phases. Thirty minutes for a written exam of about 100 questions, and sixty minutes to give your model a shave, haircut, shampoo, and a facial. I didn't have a model to take with me, so I just picked a guy that was standing on the sidewalk. He was a fairly easy guy to work on and I finished in about forty five minutes but I didn't like his hair cut, so I cut it again and still made it in time. Of the six guys from my Barber College, only four of us passed the test. Those that failed had to go back for 300 more hours.

I knew long before I got my license I didn't want to be a full time Barber. I stayed at the Phone Company and worked part time for ten years. It was a great part time job because I was paid under the table and could work as much or as little as I wanted. I kept my Master Barber License current until I move to Arizona in 2005.

Travel

I have been given the gift of travel, starting as a teenager. My travels have taken me through every state in the US, all of the Canadian Provinces, and 24 countries. I regret I didn't keep all the itineraries of my travels.

Countries

United States, Canada, Mexico, Costa Rica, Ecuador, Peru, the Netherlands, Germany, Liechtenstein, Switzerland, Italy, South Africa, Zimbabwe, Botswana, Zambia, Malawi, Tanzania, Kenya, Egypt, Portugal, Aruba, Columbia, Panama, and Jamaica.

Itineraries

New England
Massachusetts / Vermont / New Hampshire / Maine /
October 3 - 14 1986

Friday Oct. 3 LAX TWA flight #846 depart LAX 8:15 / Arrive **Boston** 4:27

Pick up Van (Chrysler mini-van) at Alamo Car Rentals. $259.99 per wk. & $49.95 per day with unlimited mileage.

I also tentatively reserved a Chevy Cavalier just in case we are too crowded $158.00 per wk & $45.99 per day.

Howard Johnson Southeast Expressway (617-288-3030). Route 3 at Andrew Square (exit 16)

Boston, Mass 4.5 mi. from airport / 1 mi. from downtown. Free parking - Reserved with no deposit until 6pm. $65.00 double / $74.00 twins per room.

Saturday Oct. 4 **Boston MA. to Quechee. VT.** *135 miles.* **Quechee Gorge Motor Inn.**

(802-295-7600) Box Q, Quechee, VT. 05059 1 mile east on 4. $57.00 per room inc. tax / 4 double rooms reserved.

Sunday / Monday Oct. 5 & 6 **Quechee Vt. to Stowe Vt.** *76 miles.* **Edson Hill Manor**

(802-253-7371)Stowe, Vt. 05672. Manor #4 Schreckengost / Manor #5 Healy & Fasciano /

Manor #7 Nelson / Manor #8 Bisnar / Manor #9 Piña & Penaloza. $83+tax+15% surcharge each inc. breakfast & dinner.

Tuesday Oct. 7 **Stowe, Vt. to Jackson, N.H.** 169 miles via Franconia

Christmas Farm Inn (603-383-4313) P.O. Box 176, Jackson, N. H. ¼mi on SR 16B

Cottage #5 - two bedrooms, living room with fireplace. $412.00 ($51.50 ea.) includes breakfast & dinner. Will sleep all eight of us, although a little crowded. Need to send deposit of $51.50 each before June 15th.

Wednesday & Thursday Oct. 8 &9 **Jackson, N.H. to Bar Harbor ME.** 297 miles

Atlantic Oaks by The Sea (207-288-5801) Includes continental breakfast. H-2&3 Piña, Healy, Fasciano & Penaloza. $92.00 + tax per room. H-1 Bisnar & Nelson $62.00 + tax per room. H-4 Schreckengost $62.00 + tax per room.

Friday Oct. 10 **Bar Harbor Me. to Old Orchard Beach, Me.** 179 miles

Sea Cliff House & Motel (207-934-4874) 2 Sea Cliff Ave., Old Orchard Beach, Me. $30.45 per room / Reserved 1 double & 3 twins.

Saturday Oct. 11 **Old Orchard Beach Me. to Danvers, Ma.**

Salem Quality Inn King's Grant (619-774-6800) On SR 128 at Trask, Davers, Ma. 01923

$73.00 per room. Reserved 1 double 7 3 twins newly remodeled. No deposit if arrive before 6 pm.

Sunday & Monday Oct. 12 & 13 **Danvers, Ma. to Chatham, Ma.**

Queen Anne Inn (617-945-0394) 70 Queen Anne Road, Chatham, Ma. 02633

South Shore of Cape Cod / Victorian Hotel. Includes continental breakfast. Prices are per room. Double $86.00 Schreckengost. Twins $96.00 Nelson & Bisnar. Triple Room Piña, Healy, Fasciano & Penaloza. $144.00. Made reservations for dinner for eight in gourmet restaurant for Monday night. Dinners run from $25.00 to $28.00. It is supposed to be "dining experience" and I thought we might want to celebrate. We can always cancel if we want.

Tuesday Oct. 14 **Boston to Los Angles**

American Air Lines flight #103 depart 5:40 pm / arrive 8:50 pm

Please call Richard Mendoza at **Rick's Travel & Cruises** (213-540-5151) and give him a credit card number or send check for airfare in order to preserve flight reservations. Fare is only $300.00 round trip, but tickets must be purchased before May 13, 1986

Would someone like to arrange for an airport service to take us to and from Lax? We could either all leave from the Schreck's house, or maybe a service will pick us up individually in the same van.

1991 F-Stops National PK. and Monument Tour
Utah and Arizona

Day 1 Long Beach to *St. George*

Depart Long Beach	8:00 am
Arrive *Calico Ghost Town* / tour and lunch	11.00 am
Depart Calico	1:30 pm
Arrive St. George	7:00 pm
Stay at the *Budget 8 Motel* 2p /2b $31.00	

Day 2 St George to *Zion* and *Mt. Carmel*

Breakfast	7:30 am
Depart St. George	9:00 am
Arrive *Zion*	10:00 am
Lunch / tour	
Depart Zion	6:00 pm
Arrive *Mt. Carmel*	7:00 pm
Stay at the *Golden Hills Motel* 2p/2B $31.00	

Day 3 Mt. Carmel to *Bryce Canyon*

Breakfast	7:30 am

Depart Mt. Carmel		9:00 am
Arrive Bryce Canyon	lunch and tour	10:15 am
Depart Bryce Canyon		7:00 pm
Stay at the **Bryce Canyon Pines**	2P / 2B	$50.00

Day 4 Bryce Canyon to *Moab*

Breakfast		7:00 am
Depart Bryce Canyon		9:00 am
Scenic drive with view stops and lunch		
Arrive Moab		7:30 pm
Stay at the Apache hotel	2P /2B	$39.00

Day 5 *Arches National Park*

Breakfast		7:30 am
Depart motel		9:00 am
Arrive Arches National Park tour and lunch		9:15 am
Depart Arches National Park		7:30 pm
Stay at the *Apache Motel*	2P / 2B	$39.00

Day 6 Moab to *Chinle*

Breakfast		7:30 am
Depart Moab		9:00 am
Arrive Natural Bridges Nation Monument		11:15 am
lunch and tour		
Depart Natural Bridges		3:00 pm
Arrive Chinle		7:00 pm
Stay at the *Thunderbird Motel*	2P/2B	$62.00

Day 7 *Canyon De Chelly*

    Breakfast   7:30 am

    Canyon De Chelly tour and lunch   9:00 am

    Return to the Thunderbird Motel   7:30 pm

    Stay at the ***Thunderbird Motel***   2P / 2B $62.00

Day 8 Chinle to Long Beach

    Breakfast   7:30 am

    Depart Chinle   9:00 am

    LONG DRIVE HOME

1992 F-Stops Death Valley
Mar. 27, 28 and 29

DEATH VALLEY - TENTATIVE TOUR PLANS

FRIDAY - Leave about 8 AM in order to arrive at Scotty's Castle at around 2 PM. Plan for about 6 hours travel. If you will need gas, it will be cheaper to gas up in Trona as the gas in Death Valley is very expensive.

* Take the **Mosaic Canyon drive** - The road leads up a broad alluvial fan to the canyon's mouth, from which there is a sweeping view of the northern valley. A short walk into the canyon reveals patterned walls of polished, multi-colored rock.

* Then we can take a swim in the pool before dinner.

SATURDAY Travel east, then south on HWY 190 - to see the following sites:

* **Sand Dunes** - The changing contours, deep shadows and ripple patterns make an interesting contrast to the sharply edged mountain ranges silhouetted to the east and west. Morning visitors who look carefully will find many footprints and other traces left by nocturnal animal activities.

* **Stovepipe well** - A rusted, old hand-operated pump marks the location of a waterhole that was important to all pre-automotive travelers in the valley. Old stovepipes were pounded in to the sand to form walls for the well.

* **Salt Creek** - Pick up a self-guided tour of this area where a large freshwater lake covered the area 2000 years ago. The creek is home to a survivor from that era: the inch-long pupfish, which have successfully adapted to the heat, high salinity and intermittent lack of water in their present environment. In the spring, schools of the fish, along with birds and other desert inhabitants, can be seen from the boardwalk trail.

* **Harmony Borax Works Ruins** - A short footpath with interpretive signs leads past the ruins of the refinery and some outlying buildings. The structures were used to process borax from 1882 to 1889. The minerals were then shipped by mule teams 165 miles over rugged desert to Mojave. A trail leads three miles northwest from the ruins across the salt flats to mounds of borax resembling haystacks. A one-way dirt road north of the works cuts through Mustard Canyon, a series of low clay hills colored by salt and oxidizing iron.

DEATH VALLEY PAGE 2

Meet for Lunch and the Ranger Station Visitor Center - see the movie - gas up if
necessary - pick up the self-guiding auto tour for the south highway to Badwater.
Check the book and stop at the following sites:

* **Fault Scarp** - A small gravel bank to the left of the road
* **Mesquite grove** - it grows at the toe of the furnace Creek fan and is one
  of the largest found in Death Valley.
* **Mushroom Rock** - A sculptured boulder of basalt lava.
* **Devils Golf Course** - which is 95% pure table salt
* **Badwater** - The lowest point you can drive to in the Western hemisphere.
  279.8 ft below sea level.
* **Desert Varnish** - A view of the various alluvial fans on both sides of the
  valley.
* **Artists Drive** - with beautiful views

Plan to meet around 4:00 PM at the parking lot at **Artists Palette** for the best picture
opportunities.

Drive back to Stovepipe Wells and meet for dinner and another swim.

SUNDAY   Plan to head home via Emigrant Canyon Road to see the following:

* **Emigrant Canyon** - Harrisburg Flats, in the upper part of the canyon, is
  the remains of the ancient surface which existed before massive block
  faulting and folding lifted the mountains and lowered the basin that is
  now Death Valley.

* **Skidoo Ghost Town** - This was one of the few mining towns in the area
  that actually showed a profit. Only a few scattered ruins remain at the
  site of a once thriving community of 700 people who worked the gold
  mines in the surrounding hills between 1906 and 1917. The residents
  put of a number of buildings, helped run a telegraph line across Death
  Valley to Rhyolite, and piped in water 23 miles from a spring in the
  Panamint Mountains. The town acquired its name because this mileage
  was the same as the number in a popular saying of the era: "Twenty-
  Three Skidoo."

* **Charcoal Kilns** - Although they date back only to 1877, these immense
  structures look like remnants of an ancient civilization. The 10 beehive-
  shaped kilns are each 30 feet in diameter and 30 feet tall. They were
  built to produce charcoal from the surrounding pinon pine forest for the
  Monoc Mine smelter, 25 miles to the west across the Panamint Valley.
  From the kilns a trail leads 4.2 miles to Wildrose Peak. The first 1 1/2
  miles are mostly uphill, but then the trial follows a saddle to the peak and
  some outstanding views of Death Valley.

DEATH VALLEY PAGE 3

* **Ballarat Ghost Town** - Crumbling adobe walls and remnants of old
  cabins are the only remains   of a town optimistically names
  after a famous gold center in Australia. Ballarat flourished between 1890
  and the years preceding World War I as a lively supply town for
  prospectors working claims in the Panamint Valley region.

ALTERNATE PLAN - If some have the time, you may go north to Scotty's Castle on
  Sunday and take the Emigrant Canyon return trip on Monday. You will see:

* **Scotty's Castle** - Construction of this extravagant vision in the Spanish-
  Moorish style began in 1924. The property, formally named Death Valley
  Ranch, was intended as the winter vacation residence of Albert Johnson,
  a Chicago insurance millionaire. Its popular name comes from Walter
  Scott, a cowboy, prospector, publicity hound, prevaricator, storyteller
  and friend of Johnson. Scotty, whose enthusiastic flamboyance was
  financed by Johnson, managed to convince many that the "castle" was
  his personal domain.
  The house and outbuildings cost at least $2.5 million; work was never
  completed. The interior is filled with interesting, well-crafted furnishings
  and innovative features. The rooms are open to the public only during
  guided tours, which are given daily from 9 AM to 5 PM. Admission:
  adults $4, children 6-12 $2, children under 6 free. Visitors can take self-
  guided tours of the surrounding grounds and adjacent structures; the
  ticket booth sells an informative guide booklet.

* **Ubehebe Crater** - A violent volcanic explosion left this crater nearly one-
  half mile wide and 500 feet deep. Oxidizing ores give orange tints to the
  dark volcanic ash of the crater's eastern walls. A trail leads from
  Ubehebe one-half mile south to Little Hebe, a smaller crater whose age -
  perhaps 1000 years - makes it a relative infant on the geological time
  scale.

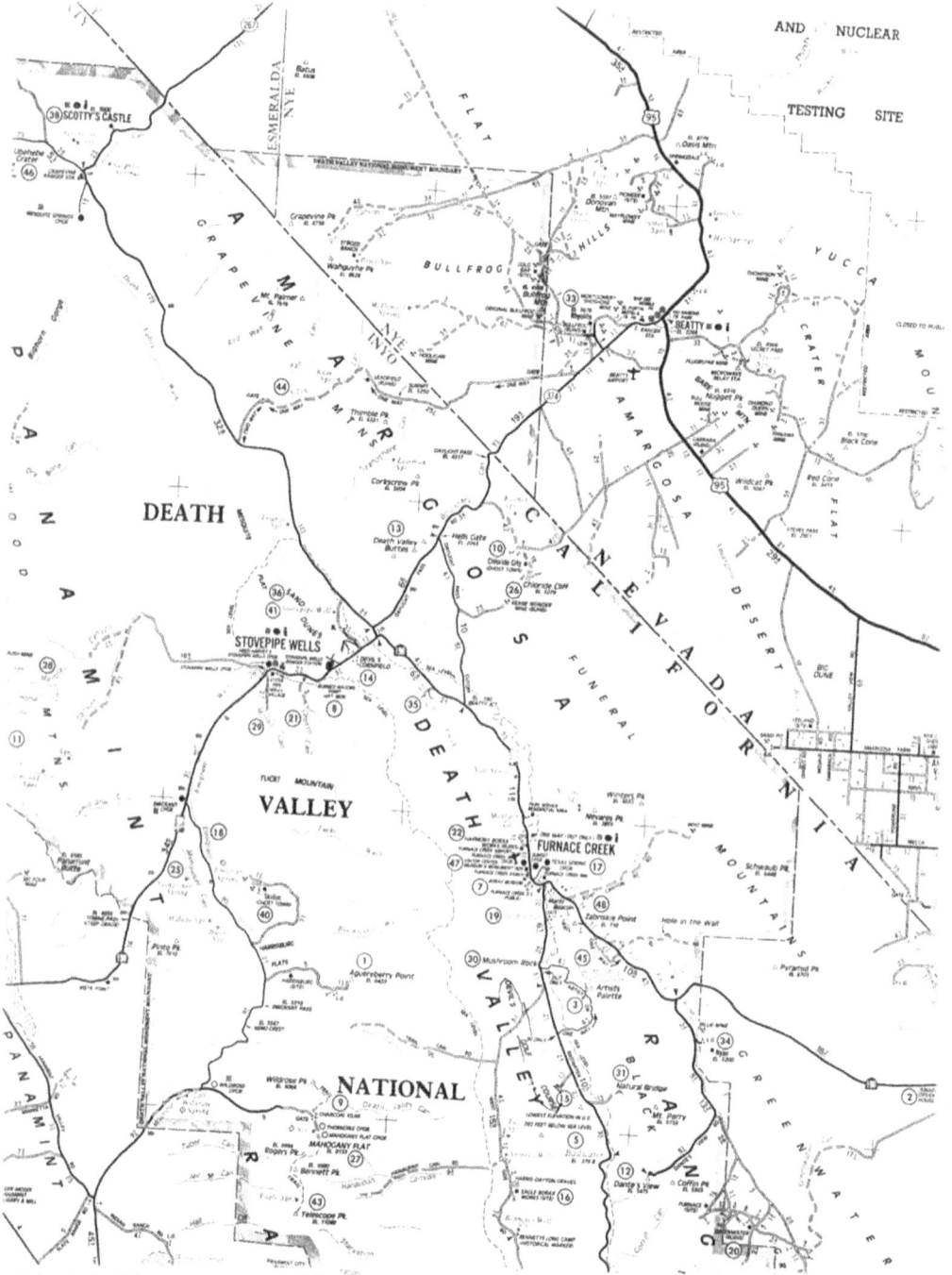

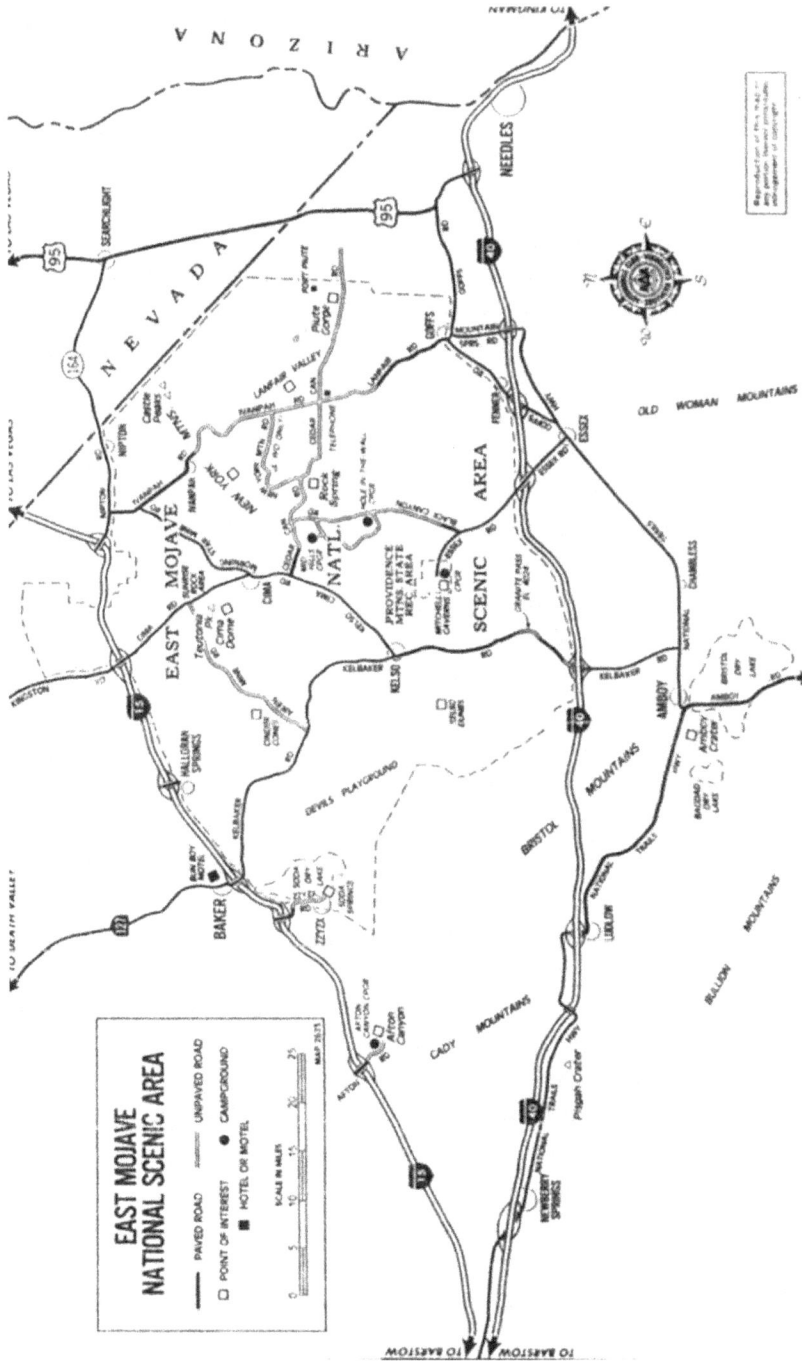

EAST MOJAVE
NATIONAL SCENIC AREA

Mojave National Scenic Area
May 2, 1993

Saturday

9:00-9:30   Meet in **Barstow** at the BLM Desert Information Center, 831 Barstow Road. (619)256-8617.

Follow signs off the I15 directing you there. This drive is approximately two hours from Long Beach.

10:00   Arranged Group Tour of the **Calico Early Man Archeological Site** off I15.

Yvonne is our group leader. This is Dr. Leaky's only North American site. Human remains dated to 200,000 years ago.

11:00   Drive to Baker with photo stop at Soda Dry Lake overlook.

12:00   Check into **Bun boy Motel** at junction of I15 and SR127. AAA rated.

1P=#30.00; 2P/ 1 bed= $39.00; 2P/2 bed=$43.00; extra person in room = $10.00.

No discounts, but Dana will book us together if you mention "f-Stops". She will hold space for May 1 until Saturday, April 10. Reserve with credit card.

Lunch at Bun Boy coffee shop, home of the **World's Tallest Thermometer.**

Gas up and go! Take Kelbaker Road to Kelso Dunes via Photo stops at **Cinder Cones and Kelso Depot.**

3:00   To sunset. Photograph **Kelso Dunes**, a two hour round trip from parking lot. Return to **Baker** for cocktail hour at Pam's room. Dinner at Mad Greek Restaurant.

Optional Campground Arrangements:

After the Kelso Dunes, you may wish to go to either one of the BLM's two campgrounds nearby. **Hole in the wall and Mid Hills** each have 20 sites, charge a fee and have no firewood. You can also park anywhere within 25 feet of an existing road in the Mojave Scenic Area.

There are many commercial campgrounds. for more information call Pam

Sunday

8:00 Breakfast at coffee shop.

9:00 Drive out the I15 to Cima Road and turn right to **Cima Dome**, a batholiths (50 cents to whoever can define this word !) with a thick forest of **Joshua trees**. Then on to **Cedar Canyon Road, black canyon Road** plus its loop road thrown in, probably to **Essex Road** with photo stops along the way.

11:30 **Providence Mountains State Recreation Area.** This place is supposed to have the most spectacular views of all mountains, mesas, valleys and dunes. 100 miles of open view.

12;00 Picnic Lunch. Be sure to plan ahead for this.

1:30 Group tour of **Mitchell Caverns**: $4.00 for a two hour tour of 1½ miles. Make reservation at 1-800-444-park.

Return to Long Bach via I40

Note: Book, maps, pamphlets are available for alternate plans if you have seen these sites or prefer other alternatives such as four wheel driving down the Mojave Trail or seeking out petro glyphs. This place has endless photographic opportunities.

Call Pam at (714)897-3442 for any information you might want.

Baja California Whale Watching
February 13, 1993

Long Beach to Valle de San Quintin. Depart at 8:00 am.

Stop in *San Ysidro* for Mexican Insurance and fuel, cross the border and head south.

Stop in *Ensenada* for lunch and head south to the immigration point. Bring your Visa papers. Head south to *San Quintin.*

Stay at the *Cielito Linda Motel*/ Restaurant. Time permitting, tour of the old water front. (Olde Mill, Olde Pier and the Olde English cemetery)

Day 2, Sunday, February 14, 1993

San Quintin to Guerrero Negro. Depart after breakfast, head south

Stop on the for Photo opps.

Stop in *Catavina* for lunch and fuel.

Stop on the road for Photo opps.

Arrive at *Guerrero Negro*, stay at the *Malarrimo Motel*/ RV Park and Restaurant. ($28.00) Time permitting, tour of The town and/or Olde Lighthouse (El Faro).

Day 3, Monday, February 15, 1993

Whale Watching Trip and/or Ecology Tour, and/or Salt Mine Tour. ($30.00)

Day 4 Tuesday, February 16, 1993

Day trip to picturesque **San Igancio.** Old Mission, Town Square and possible trip to the old Cave Paintings.

Day 5, Wednesday, February 17, 1993

Guerrero Negro to San Quintin. Depart after breakfast, head north.

Stop for Photo opps on the road

Arrive in San Quintin, stay at either the **Cielito Lindo Motel** or at the **Old Mill Motel.** Tour the city and waterfront.

Day 5, Thursday, February 18, 1993

San Quintin to Long Beach. Depart after breakfast. Head north for the border.

Stop for photo opps.

Stop in either **Ensenada or Tijuana** for lunch and shopping.

stop at the border for the traditional wait in the line then head for home.

Things to Bring

Warm clothing, gloves, hat sun glasses

Wet weather gear

Lots of film

Plastic bags for the weather

A sunny smile

At one camera

Flashlight with batteries

Water bottle

Special Note

Days 3 and 4 may be reversed depending on the weather so try to be flexible. Remember we will be in the Land of Manana so nothing is set in concrete.

National Parks
Grand Teton, Yellowstone, and Glacier
September 14 / 29, 1996

Saturday	6:30 a.m. Leave Long Beach
Day 1	Breakfast in Victorville, CA
09/14/96	Lunch in Las Vegas, NV.
Provo, UT.	Arrive at *Provo, UT* approx. 7:00 p.m.
	Motel 6 on I15 @ exit 266 1600 S. University Ave.
	3 rms / 1 night $37.99 + tax 10% AARP Discount.
	Cancel before 6 pm 1-800-466-8356
	Conf Nos. R1584511-0171, R1584528-0171 & R1584535-0171
Sunday	7:00 am breakfast & leave at 8:00 am
Day 2	Arrive at *Jackson Hole, WY.* Approx 3:00 pm
09/15/96	Visitors Center / orientation / slide show
Jackson, WY.	Purchase food for picnic lunches
	Super 8 Motel (307-733-6833)
	1 night 09/15/96 750 South Highway 89, Jackson, WY.
	4 rooms guaranteed on credit card / $63.00 + tax
	Conf. No. JWYO321AMB

Monday	Drive into Grand Teton Rockefeller Parkway
Day 3	Triangle X Ranch, & Moran Junction
09/16/96	Visitor Center / Photograph Teton Range; river overlook
Grand Teton, WY.	Picnic lunch: Wherever we like

Colter Bay Village Cabins (1-800-628-9988)

4 nights Jackson Lake P. O. Box 240 Moran, WY. 83013

Rustic Log Cabins w/1 db & 1 twin bed $64.66 inc. tax/ 4 rooms reserved confirmation Nos. 614892 through 614895 Mail check

$258.64 by 04/04/96

Colter Bay Visitors Center / sunset Photographs around the Lake

Tuesday	**Oxbow Bend** - Photos, hiking, etc. around the area
Day 4	Picnic lunch: Wherever
09/17/96	**Snake River** Dinner float Trip. Pre-paid

8 adults - $42.66 each Reconfirm 24 hours before /cancel up to 24 hours before (check in with **Colter Bay village.**

Meet at 3:45 pm in lobby. Bus to the start site, dinner first. No whitewater. Can be very cold. Steak/ Trout Dinner

Wednesday	Travel back South on Teton Park Road
Day 5	**Hidden Falls; Jenny Lake; Signal Mountain**
09/18/96	Photos / hike / Picnic / photos / etc.
	Picnic lunch: Wherever

Thursday	Open for shopping, horseback riding, another float trip, etc.
Day 6	
09/19/96	

Friday	7:00 am breakfast & 8:00 am leave.
Day 7	Check out of **Colter Bay Village Cabins**
09/20/96	Drive to **Yellowstone Nat. Park** 70 mi. Elevation 7,733' **Old Faithful; Canyon Visitor's Center**
	Picnic lunch: wherever
	Yellowstone Lake Frontier Cabins (307-344-7311)
	North side of Yellowstone Lake
	3 nights 09/20/96 / 09/22/96
	TW Recreational Services P. O. box 165
	Yellowstone National Park, WY 82190 (Cabins $66.78, inc. tax deposit made on my credit card. Confirmation No. X2JZH
	Evening photograph of wildlife at Fishing Bridge.
Saturday	Sunrise photographs around lake
Day 8	**Canyon Country** is the **Grand Canyon of Yellowstone River** with nature's grandest gorges; Largest free-flowing river in U. S.. Walk around south rim trail (1-2hrs). Waterfall at head of river twice as big as Niagara Falls.
	Picnic lunch
Sunday	7:00 am breakfast
Day 9	Travel around in Yellowstone to take photographs
09/22/96	**Beartooh Highway** Trip **("Most Beautiful Highway in America," Charles Karault)** 3½ hour trip (northeast entrance to Yellowstone)
	Picnic lunch
Monday	7:00 am breakfast & 8:00 am leave
Day 10	Check out of Cabins and go towards **West Yellowstone** through 09/23/96 the **Geyser Basin Area.**
	Picnic lunch: Wherever we are at noon

Exit the park to West Yellowstone

Grizzly Park. Approx. ½ day

Call ahead for schedule (406-646-7001 / 1-800-257-2570)

Kelly Inn (1-800-259-4672)

104 S. Canyon Street

West Yellowstone, Montana

4 rooms guaranteed on credit card $63.00 + Tax

1 night 09/23/96

Tuesday	8:00 am leave *West Yellowstone*
Day 11	Lunch: wherever
09/24/96	5:00 pm arrive *West Glacier National Park*
	Mountain Pine Motel Highway (406-226-4403)
	Highway 49 / ½ mi. north Jct. Hwy 2 @ Hwy 4
	3 rooms / 3nights $45.00 per night. Credit card guaranteed
	(2 miles from Two Medicine Lake. Entrance and 30 mi. from *St. Mary Lake* entrance.
Wednesday	*Glacier National Park*
Day 12	Going to the *Sun Road*
09/25/96	Tour *St. Mary Lake and Logan Pass*, if passable
	Mountain Pine Motel / 1 room (Chuck & Dianne) 2 nights
Thursday	*Glacier National Park*
Day 13	*Two Medicine Lake* & Whatever we decide
09/26/96	
Friday	Head for Home. Leave by noon or 8:00 am
Day 14	(Option by 8:00 am we can go to *National Bison Preserve*)
09/27/96	Arrive Idaho Falls, Idaho

Motel 6 / I-15 at exit 118. 1448 W. Broadway

2 dbl. rooms & 1 sgl. room / 1 night $39.77 & $31.99

Conf. Nos. R1584545-0056, R1584560-0056 & R1584566-0056

Cancel before 6 pm 1-800-466-8356

Saturday	8:00 am leave *Idaho Falls, Idaho*
Day 15	(464 miles 8½ hrs.)
09/28/96	4:30 pm arrive *Cedar City, Utah*
Cedar City UT.	Reservations not needed this time of year
	Roadway Inn $43.00 + tax Exit I-15, 57281 S. Main St.
	(801-586-9916)
Sunday	8:00 am leave *Cedar City, Utah*
Day 16	(457 miles 8½ hrs.)
09/29/96	4:30 pm arrive *Long Beach*

2001 Hank & Sylvia's RV Trip
Sept. 4 to Nov. 19

Start: September 4.2001

Countries: USA and Canada

States: California, Nevada, Utah, Wyoming, Nebraska, South Dakota, North Dakota, Minnesota, Wisconsin, Michigan, New York, Vermont, Maine, Massachusetts, Connecticut, New Jersey, Delaware, Maryland, Pennsylvania, Ohio, Indiana, Illinois, Iowa, Kansas, Oklahoma, New Mexico and Arizona.

Provinces: Ontario, Quebec, New Brunswick, Nova Scotia, and Prince Edward Island.

Weather: Good. 75% sunny 25% overcast. It rained 11 times in 76 days.

Images: Hank about 3000 and Sylvia about 400. All are digital.

Miles: 14,198

Fuel: 1,525 gal @ $2,300.68 Avg. price pg gal $1.46 Avg. Miles pg gal. 11.35

Most Interesting Places:

Utah- Dinosaur Nat. Mon.

South Dakota- Mt Rushmore Nat Pk. and Bad Lands Nat Mon.

Minnesota -Itasca St. Pk..

Ontario -Niagara Falls

New York- Coopers Town, Old Forge and Hyde Pk.

Quebec- Quebec

Nova Scotia- Peggy Cove, Cape Breton, and Louisbourg

Prince Edward Island- Fundy Nat. Pk.

Massachusetts- Acadia Nat. Pk. Gloucester, and Stockbridge.

Pennsylvania- Lancaster, Hershey, Intercourse, Bird-in Hand, and Gettysburg.

Missouri- St. Louis.

Most Friendly People: Prince Edward Island CA.

Most Beautiful Place: Cape Breton CA

End: November 19, 2001

THE FALL OF 2001

MAP	HIGHTWAY	FROM	TO	MILES
CA.	15	Long Beach	St. George UT	410
UT.	15/9	St. George	Virgin	20
UT.	9	Virgin	Mt Carmel	45
UT.	89	Mt. Carmel	Sevier	112
UT.	70	Sevier	Salina	37
UT.	256	Salina	Gunnison	14
UT.	89	Gunnison	Fairview	49
UT.	31	Fairview	Huntington	30
UT.	10	Huntington	Hwy 191	30
UT.	191	Hwy 191 No.	Duchesne	45
UT.	40/191	Duchesne	Vernal	58
UT.	40	Vernal	Jensen	13
UT.	149	Jensen	Dinosaur Nat'l Mon.	6

MAP	HIGHTWAY	FROM	TO	MILES
UT .	6/40/191	Dinosaur Nat'l Mon.	Hwy 44	55
UT.	44	Hwy 44 w.	Manila	34
WY.	530	Manila UT	Green River	48
WY..	80	Green River	Walcott	144
WY.	130	Walcott	Larmie	100
WY.	80	Larmie	Cheyenne	43
WY.	25	Cheyenne	Chugwater	37
WY.	25	Chugwater	Weatland	26
WY.	25	Weatland	Jct. 25/26	12
WY.	26	Jct.. 25/26	Guernsey	15
Wy.	26	Gueennsey	Fort Laramie	13
WY.	26	Fort Laramie	Lingle	11
WY.	26/85	Lingle	Torrington	10
WY.	85/26	Torrington	Mitchell	13
NEB.	26	Mitchell	Scottsbluff	9
NEB.	26/92	Scottsbluff	Bridgeport	39
NEB.	385	Bridgeport	Alliance	34
NEB.	385	Alliance	Chadron	60
NEB.	385	Chadron	Jct. 385/79	20
S. DAK.	18/385	Jct. 385/79	Hot Springs	5
S. DAK.	385	Hot Springs	Wind Cave NP Visitor Center	8
S. DAK.	385	Wind Cave NP V/C	Pringle	10
S. DAK.	385/89	Pringle	Sanator	6
S. DAK.	385/89	Sanator	Custer	6

MAP HIGHTWAY	FROM	TO	MILES
S. DAK. 16	Custer	Jewel Cave NM	12
S. DAK. 16	Jewel Cave NM	Custer	12
S. DAK. 16/385	Custer	Carzy Horse MEM	6
S. DAK. 16/385	Carzy Horse MEM	Hill City	9
S. DAK. 385	Hill City	Deadwood	41
S. DAK. 385	Deadwood	Lead	4
S. DAK. 14	Lead	Spearfish	27
S. DAK. 90	Spearfish	Sturgis	21
S. DAK. 90	Sturgis	Piedmont	14
S. DAK. 90	Piedmont	Rapid City	12
S. DAK. 16	Rapid City	Rockerville	11
S. DAK. 16	Rockerville	Jct. 16/16A	5
S. DAK. 16A	Jact. 16/16A	Keystone	3
S. DAK. 244	Keystone	Jct. 244/16/385/87	14
S. DAK. 87	Jct. 244/16/385/87	Jct. 87/16A	20
S. DAK. 87/16A	Jct. 87/16A	Jct. 87/385	16
S. DAK. 385	Jct. 87/385	Pringle	7
S. DAK. 385/89	Pringle	Custer	12
S. DAK. 16A	Custer	Keystone	22
S. DAK. 16A	Keystone	Jct. 16A/16	3
S. DAK. 16	Jct. 16A/16	Rapid City	18
S. DAK. 44	Rapid City	Farming Dale	20
S. DAK. 44	Farming Dale	Scenic	23
S. DAK. 44	Scenic	Cedar Pass	35

MAP HIGHTWAY	FROM	TO	MILES
S. DAK. 240	Cedar Pass	Wall	25
S. DAK. 90	Wall	Murdo	79
S. DAK. 90	Murdo	Chamberlain	68
S. DAK. 90	Chamberlain	Plankinton	42
S. DAK. 90	Plankinton	Mitchell	20
S. DAK. 90	Mitachell	Canistota	41
S. DAK. 90	Canistota	Sioux Falls	40
S. DAK. 29	Sioux Falls	Dell Rapids	19
S .DAK. 29	Dell Rapids	Brookings	34
S. DAK. 29	Brookings	Watertown	47
S. DAK. 29	Watertown	Wahpeton	98
S. DAK. 29	Wahpeton	Fargo N. DAK	42
N. DAK. 10E	Fargo	Detroit Lakes	43
MINN. 34	Detroit Lakes	Park Rapids	40
MINN. 34	Park Rapids	Walker	29
MINN. 200	Walker	Remer	35
MINN. 200	Remer	Hill City	17
MINN. 200	Hill City	Jct. 200/2	27
MINN. 2	Jct. 200/2	Protor	45
MINN. 35	Proctor	Duluth	2
MINN. 61	Duluth	Two Harbors	30
MINN. 61	Two Harbors	Tettegouche St. Pk.	32
MINN. 61	Tettegouche St. Pk.	Duluth	62
MINN. 535	Duluth	Superior WIS.	4

MAP	HIGHTWAY	FROM	TO	MILES
WIS.	535	Superior	South Ridge	6
WIS.	13	South Ridge	Port wing	37
WIS.	13	Port Wing	Cornucopia	14
WIS.	13	Cornucopia	Red Cliff	18
WIS.	13	Red Cliff	Bayfield	3
WIS.	13	Bayfield	Salmo	4
WIS.	13	Salmo	Washburn	8
WIS.	13/63	Washburn	Asland	11
WIS.	13	Asland	Marengo	12
WIS.	13	Marengo	Mellen	12
WIS.	77	Mellen	Upson	13
WIS.	77	Upson	Hurley	13
WIS.	2 E.	Hurley	Wakefield	14
MICH.	28/141/41	Wakefield	Tula	6
MICH.	28	Tula	Merriweather	10
MICH.	28	Merriweather	Burgland	4
MICH.	28	Burgland	Topaz	8
MICH	28	Topaz	Matchwood	3
MICH.	28	Matachwood	Ewen	5
MICH.	28	Ewen	Bruce Corssing	4
MICH.	45/26	Bruce Corssing	Mass City	19
MICH.	26	Mass City	Winona	10
MICH..	26	Winona	Hancock Houghton	38
MICH.	26	Hancock Houghton	Calumet	11

MAP HIGHTWAY	FROM	TO	MILES
MICH. 41/26	Calumet	Cooper Harbor	20
MICH. 41/26	Cooper Harbor	Hancock Houghton	43
MICH. 41	Hancock Houghton	Baraga	28
MICH. 41	Brraga	Jct. 141/41/28	12
MICH. 41/28	Jct. 141/41/28	Michigamme	18
MICH. 41/28	Michigamme	Champion	10
MICH. 41/28	Champion	Negaunee	15
MICH. 41/28	Negaunee	Marquette	11
MICH. 41/28	Marquette	Harvy	4
MICH. 28	Harvy	Au Train	26
MICH. 28	Au Train	Munising	11
MICH. 28	Munising	Shingleton	10
MICH. 28	Shingleton	Seney	25
MICH. 28	Seney	McMillan	13
MICH. 28	McMillan	Raco	49
MICH. 28	Raco	Jct 28/75	15
MICH. 75	Jct 28/75 N.	Sault Ste. Marie	9
ONT. CA. 17	Sault Ste. Marie	Garden River Indian Reserve	20
ONT. CA 17	Garden River I. R.	Echo Bay	5
ONT. CA 17	Echo Bay	Portlok.	20
ONT. CA 17	Portlock	Bruce Mines	19
ONT. CA 17	Bruce Mines	Thessalon	20
ONT. CA 17	Thessalon	Sowerly	10
ONT. CA 17	Sowerly	Iron Bridge	17

MAP HIGHTWAY	FROM	TO	MILES
ONT. CA 17	Iron Bridge	Blind River	26
ONT. CA 17	Blind River	Algoma Mills	15
ONT. CA 17	Algoma	Pronto East	5
ONT. CA 17	Pronto East	Spragge	5
ONT. CA 17	Spragge	Serpent River	6
ONT. CA 17	Serpent River	Cutter	3
ONT.CA 17	Cutter	Spanish	10
ONT. CA 17	Spanish	Walford	10
ONT. CA 17	Walford	Massey	16
ONT. CA 17	Massey	Webbwood	6
ONT. CA 17	Webbwood	Espanola	20
ONT. CA 17	Espanola	Nairn Centre	16
ONT. CA 17	Nairn Centre	Sudbury	31
ONT. CA 17	Sudbury	Waknapitae	35
ONT. CA 17	Waknapetae	Callum	10
ONT. CA 17	Callum	Hagar	22
ONT. CA 17	Hagar	Warren	8
ONT. CA 17	Warren	Sturgeon Falls	31
ONT. CA 17	Shurgeon Falls	Meadowside	15
ONT. CA 17	Meadowside	North Bay	23
ONT. CA 11	North Bay	Callander	5
ONT. CA 11	Callander	Astorville	15
ONT. CA 11	Astorville	Pawassan	17
ONT. CA 11	Powassan	Trout Creek	12

MAP HIGHTWAY	FROM	TO	MILES
ONT. CA 11	Tourt Creek	South River	17
ONT. CA 11	South River	Sundridge	10
ONT. CA 11	Sundridge	Burks Falls	19
ONT. CA 11	Burks Falls	Katrine	10
ONT. CA 11	Katrine	Novar	16
ONT. CA 11	Novar	Melissa	7
ONT. CA 11	Melissa	Huntsville	6
ONT. CA 60	Huntsville	Hillside	18
ONT. CA 60	Hillside	Dwight	6
ONT. CA 60	Dwright	Oxtongue	15
ONT. CA 60	Oxtongue	Algonquin Prov. Pk.	32
ONT. CA 60	Algonquin Prov. Pk.	Whitney	45
ONT. CA 127	Whitney	Lake St. Peter Prov. PK	25
ONT. CA 127	Lake St. Peter Prov. Pk.	Maynooth	12
ONT. CA 127	Maynooth	Birds Creek	20
ONT.CA 127	Birds Creek	Bancroft	4
ONT. CA 62	Bancroft	Madoc	71
ONT. CA 62	Madoc	Ivanhoe	15
ONT. CA 62	Ivanhoe	West Huntington	6
ONT. CA 62	Weat Huntington	Belleville	18
ONT. CA 2	Belleville	Bayside	15
ONT. CA 2	Bayside	Trenton	5
ONT. CA 2	Trenton	Brighton	14
ONT. CA 2	Brighton	Colborne	14

MAP	HIGHTWAY	FROM	TO	MILES
ONT. CA 2		Colborne	Wicklow	7
ONT. CA 2		Wicklow	Grafton	5
ONT. CA 2		Grafton	Brookside	7
ONT. CA 2		Brookside	Colourg	3
ONT. CA 2		Colourg	Port Hope	10
ONT.CA 401		Port Hope	Oshawa	45
ONT. CA 401		Oshawa	Pi;ckering	31
ONT. CA 401/404/DEW		Pickering	Mississauga	47
ONT. CA DEW		Mississauga	Oakville	29
ONT. CA 403		Oakville	Burlington	23
ONT. CA 405		Burlington	Hamilton	12
ONT. CA 405		Hamilton	St. Catharines	44
ONT. CA 405		St. Catharines	Niagara Falls	18
NY. 405		Niagara Falls	Youngstown	21
NY. 18		Youngstown	Wilson	12
NY. 18		Wilson	Olcott	7
NY. 18		Olcott	Somerset	10
NY. 18		Somerset	County Line	4
NY. 18		County Line	Point Breeze	15
NY. 390		Point Breeze	Maniton Beach	32
NY. 490		Maniton Beach	Rochester	20
NY. 490		Rocherter	Webster	8
NY. Sec. Dr.		Webster	Lakeside	9
NY. Sec. Dr.		Lakeside	Pultneyville	9

MAP	HIGHTWAY	FROM	TO	MILES
NY.	Sec. Dr.	Pultneyville	Sodus Point	10
NY.	Sec Dr.	Sodus Point	Alton	4
NY.	14	Alton	South Sodus	4
NY.	14	South Sodus	Lyons	7
NY.	14	Lyons	Alloway	9
NY.	14	Alloway	Geneva	5
NY.	5	Geneva	Waterloo	8
NY.	411	Waterloo	Seneca Falls	4
NY.	414/20/5	Seneca Falls	Auburn	14
NY.	20	Auburn	Skaneateles	7
NY.	20	Skaneateles	S. Onondaga	12
NY.	20	S. Onondaga	Cardiff	6
NY.	20	Cardiff	La Fayette	2
NY.	20	La Fayette	Pompey	7
ONT. CA	11	Melissa	Huntsville	6
ONT. CA	60	Huntsville	Hillside	18
ONT. CA	60	Hillside	Dwight	6
ONT. CA	60	Dwright	Oxtongue	15
ONT. CA	60	Oxtongue	Algonquin Prov. Pk.	32
ONT. CA	60	Algonquin Prov. Pk.	Whitney	45
ONT. CA	127	Whitney	Lake St. Peter Prov. PK	25
ONT. CA	127	Lake St. Peter Prov. Pk.	Maynooth	12
ONT. CA	127	Maynooth	Birds Creek	20
ONT.CA	127	Birds Creek	Bancroft	4

MAP	HIGHTWAY	FROM	TO	MILES
ONT. CA 62		Bancroft	Madoc	71
ONT. CA 62		Madoc	Ivanhoe	15
ONT. CA 62		Ivanhoe	West Huntington	6
ONT. CA 62		Weat Huntington	Belleville	18
ONT. CA 2		Belleville	Bayside	15
ONT. CA 2		Bayside	Trenton	5
ONT. CA 2		Trenton	Brighton	14
ONT. CA 2		Brighton	Colborne	14
ONT. CA 2		Colborne	Wicklow	7
ONT. CA 2		Wicklow	Grafton	5
ONT. CA 2		Grafton	Brookside	7
ONT. CA 2		Brookside	Colourg	3
ONT. CA 2		Colourg	Port Hope	10
ONT.CA 401		Port Hope	Oshawa	45
ONT. CA 401		Oshawa	Pi;ckering	31
ONT. CA 401/404/DEW		Pickering	Mississauga	47
ONT. CA DEW		Mississauga	Oakville	29
ONT. CA 403		Oakville	Burlington	23
ONT. CA 405		Burlington	Hamilton	12
ONT. CA 405		Hamilton	St. Catharines	44
ONT. CA 405		St. Catharines	Niagara Falls	18
NY. 405		Niagara Falls	Youngstown	21
NY. 18		Youngstown	Wilson	12
NY. 18		Wilson	Olcott	7

MAP	HIGHTWAY	FROM	TO	MILES
NY.	18	Olcott	Somerset	10
NY.	18	Somerset	County Line	4
NY.	18	County Line	Point Breeze	15
NY.	390	Point Breeze	Maniton Beach	32
NY.	490	Maniton Beach	Rochester	20
NY.	490	Rocherter	Webster	8
NY.	Sec. Dr.	Webster	Lakeside	9
NY.	Sec. Dr.	Lakeside	Pultneyville	9
NY.	Sec. Dr.	Pultneyville	Sodus Point	10
NY.	Sec Dr.	Sodus Point	Alton	4
NY.	14	Alton	South Sodus	4
NY.	14	South Sodus	Lyons	7
NY.	14	Lyons	Alloway	9
NY.	14	Alloway	Geneva	5
NY.		Geneva	Waterloo	8
NY.	411	Waterloo	Seneca Falls	4
NY.	414/20/5	Seneca Falls	Auburn	14
NY.	20	Auburn	Skaneateles	7
NY.	20	Skaneateles	S. Onondaga	12
NY.	20	S. Onondaga	Cardiff	6
NY.	20	Cardiff	La Fayette	2
NY.	20	La Fayette	Pompey	7

2001 Hank and Sylvia RV Trip
Sept. 4   to   Nov. 19

UT / WY / Neb / S.D. / MI / WI / ON-CAN / NY / VT / N. H. / QUE. CAN / NS. CAN / NB-CAN / PEI-CAN / ME / R.I. / MA / N.J. / MD / PA / W.VA OH / IN / IL / MO / IA / OK / CA

Sep. 4	Long Beach CA. to *Odenville UT*. (*Zion Nat. PK.*) 447 mi. *Mukuntuweap RV PK.*	
Sep. 6	*Jensen, UT.* to *Rawlins, WY.* *Western Hills Campground*	273 mi.
Sep. 7	Rawlins, WY to *Gering Neb.* New RoDetroit Lakebidoux RV PK.	330 mi.
Sep. 8	*Gering, Neb.* to *Keystone S.D.* *Battle Creek Campground*	235 m.
Sep. 9	Keystone, S.D. to *Iron Mt / Custer St. Pk. / Game Lodge Needles Hwy / Crazy Horse* *Battle creek Campground*	
Sep. 10	Keystone, S.D. to *Deadwood S. D.* *Fish 'n fry Campground*	162 mi.
Sep. 11	Deadwood, S.D. to *Wall, S.D.* *Sleepy Hollow Campground*	232 mi.

Sep. 12	Wall, S.D. to *Sioux Falls, S.D.*	319 mi.
	Tony and Lou's house	
Sep. 13	Sioux Fall, S.D. to *Chester S.D.* (Tony's car)	
	Tony and Lou house	
Sep. 14	Sioux Falls	
	Tony and Lou's house	
Sep. 15	Sioux Falls, S.D. to *Detroit Lakes MN.*	307 mi.
	Country Campground, Detroit Lake	
Sep.16	Detroit Lake, MN. to *International Falls, MN.*	*257 mi.*
	International Voyagers RV PK.	
Sep. 17	International Falls, MN. to *Silver Bay MN.*	242 mi.
	Tettegouche St. PK.	
Sep. 18	Silver Bay MN. to *Mellen, WI.*	204 mi.
	Copper Falls St. PK (split rock lighthouse)	
Sep. 19	Mellen, WI. to *Champion, MI.*	306 mi.
	Michigamme Shores Campground MI.	
Sep. 20	Champion, MI. to *Thessalon, ON. CAN.*	351 mi.
	Pine Crest Trailer PK.	
Sep. 21	Thessalon, ON. CAN. to *Tobermory, ON. CAN*	186 mi.
	Happy Hearts Pk.	
Sep. 22	Tobermory, ON. CAN. to *Negara Falls, on. CAN.*	244 mi.
	Niagara Falls Glenview RV PK.	
Sep.23	Negara Falls, ON. CAN. sightseeing	
Sep. 24	Negara Falls, ON. CAN. to *Morrisville, NY.*	243 mi.
	Bucks Woods Campground	
Sep.25	Morrisville, NY. to *St. Johnsville, NY.*	118 mi.
	Crystal Cove Campground	

Sep.26	St. Johnsville, NY. *to Old Forge, NY* *Old forge Campground*	122 mi.
Sep.27	Old forge, NY. to *Gaysville, VT.* *White River Valley Campground*	174 mi.
Sep. 28	Gaysville, VT. to *Rutland, VT.* *White River Valley Campground*	*0 mi.*
Sep. 29	Gaysville, VT. sightseein *White River Valley campground*	
Sep. 30	Gaysville, VT. to *Lebanon, N.H.*	
Oct. 1	Gaysville VT. to *Woodstock, VT*	
Oct. 2	Gaysville, VT. to *Robert Compton Pottery*	
Oct. 3	Gaysville, VT, sightseeing	
Oct. 4	Gaysville, VT. to *Pittsfield VT.*	
Oct. 5	Gaysville, VT. to *Deby, VT.*	178 mi.
Oct. 6	Derby, VT. to *St. Romuald, CAN.*	187 mi.
Oct. 7	St. Romuald, CAN. to *Ferry dock* *Motel ET Campground Etchemin*	9mi.
Oct. 8	St. Romuald, CAN. to *Anse-A-Valleau, QU.CAN.* *Motel Camping Du Ancètres*	407 mi.
Oct. 9	Anse-A-Valleau, QU.CAN. *to St. Omer, QU.CAN.* *Aux Flots Bleus*	228 mi.
Oct. 10	St. Omer, QU. to *Shippagan, NB. CAN.* Camping Janine Du Havre	167 mi.
Oct. 11	Shippagan, NB. CAN. to *Amherst, NS. CAN.* *Gateway Parkland Capming*	347 mi.
Oct.12	Amherst, NS. CAN. to *Dartmouth, NS. CAN.* *Shubie Campground*	144 mi.

Oct. 13	Dartmouth, NS. CAN. to *Digby, NS. CAN.*	135 mi.
	Admieal Digny Inn	
Oct. 14	Digby, NS. CAN. *to Dartmouth ,NS. CAN.*	249 mi.
	Shubie Campground	
Oct. 15	Dartmouth, NS. CAN. to *Hammond Plains, NS. CAN.* 30 mi.	
	Woodhaven Park	
Oct. 16	Hammond Plains, NS. CAN. to *Halifax, Peggy's Cove, Lunenburg*	154 mi.
	Woodhaven Park	
Oct. 17	Hammond Plains, NS. CAN. to *N.E. Margaree, NS. CAN.*	
	The lakes Resort	236 mi
Oct. 18	N.E. Morgarce, NS. CAN. to *Cape Breton NS. CAN.*187 mi.	
	The Lakes Resort	
Oct. 19	N.E. Margarce, NS. CAN. to *Louisboug, NS. CAN.* 100 mi.	
	Louisburg Motor home RVPK.	
Oct. 20	Louisburg, NS. CAN. to *Montague PEI CAN.*	259 mi.
	Montague Recreation Park	
Oct. 21	Montage, PEI CAN. to *New Glasgow, PEI CAN.*	135 mi.
	New Glasgow Highlands	
Oct. 22	New Glasgow, PEI CAN. to *Summerside, PEI CAN.* 204 mi.	
	Green Acres Motel and Campground	
Oct. 23	Summerside, PRI CAN. to *Fundy National Park, NB* 186 mi.	
	Fundy National Park	
Oct. 24	Fundy National Park, NB. to *Pocologan, NB CAN.* 184 mi.	
	Fundy National Park	
Oct. 25	Pocloagn, NB CAN. to *Acadia National PK. ME.* 191 mi.	
	Acadia National Park Campground	

Oct. 26	Acadia National Park ME. to **Rockport ME.** **Camden Rockport Campground**	150 mi.
Oct. 27	Rockport, ME. to **Gloucester, MA.** **Cape Ann Camp Site**	189 mi.
Oct. 28	Gloucester, MA to **Harmony, RI.** **Holiday Acres Family Campground**	140 mi.
Oct. 29	Harmony, RI. to **Stockbridge, MA.** **Patricia House**	187 mi.
Oct. 30	**Stockbridge, MA. to Great Bearington, MA.** **Patricia house**	
Oct. 31	Stockbridge, MA. to **Hyde Park-Culinary Institute of America. Patricia house**	
Nov. 1	Stockbridge, MA. to **Carmel, NY.** **Fahnestock MON. St. Pk.**	214 mi.
Nov.2	Carmel, NY. to **Jefferson Township, NJ.** **Mahlon Dickerson Reservation**	*174 mi.*
Nov. 3	Jefferson Township, NJ. to **Abingdon, MD.** **Bar Harbor RV PK.**	243 mi.
Nov. 4	Abingdon, MD. to **Lancaster, PA.** **Old Mill Stream Campground**	72 mi.
Nov. 5	Lancaster, PA. to **Hershey, Lititz, Ephrata, Intercourse** **Old Mill Stream Campground**	
Nov. 6	Lancaster, PA to **Intercourse, Bird-in-Hand, Paradise, Strasbury. Old Mil stream Campground**	
Nov.7	Lancaster, PA. to **Philadelphia PA.**	
Nov. 8	Lancaster, PA. to **Gettysburg, PA.** **Gettysburg Campground**	63 mi.

Nov.9	Gettysburg, PA. to **Triadelphia, W.VA.** **Dallas Pike Campground**	220 mi.
Nov. 10	Triadilphia, W.VA. to **East Portsmouth, OH.** **Wolford's Landing Campground**	235 mi.
Nov. 11	East Portsmouth, OH. to **Bloomington, ID.** **Paynetown St. Recreation. Area**	304 mi.
Nov. 12	Bloomington, ID. to **Cahokia, IL.** **Cahokia RV PK.**	277 mi.
Nov. 13	Cahokia, IL. to **St. House, MO.** **St. Louis RV PK**	203 mi.
Nov. 14	St Louis, MO. to **Moravia, IA.** **Honey Creek St. PK**	310 mi.
Nov. 15	Moravia, IA. to **Mission, KS** **Mary Jane and Allen house**	*221 mi.*
Nov. 16	Mission , KS. to **Woodward, OK.**	427 mi.
Nov. 17	Woodward, OK. to **Bernalillo, OK.** **Bernalillo KOA RV PK**	487 mi.
Nov. 18	Bernalille, NM. to **Tucson, AZ** **Prince of Tucson RV PK**	467 mi.
Nov. 19	Tucson, AZ. to **Long Beach, CA** **Home**	494 mi.

2005 Hank & Sylvia RV TRIP
3/1/05 to 8/26/05

3-01-05 t   ***Newport Beach CA to Fort Mohave AZ***   328 mi.

3-02-05 w   Avi Resort RV Campground (800) 284-2946

3-03-05 th   10000 AHA Macav Parkway Laughlin NV 89028

3-04-05 f   Visit Andy's family / purchase lot for new house

3-05-05 s

3-06-05 s

3-07-05 m

3-08-05 t   Riverside Adventure Trails RV PK (928) 486-4064

3-09-05 w   4750 Hwy 95 Bullhead City AZ

3-10-05 th

3-11-05 f

3-12-05 s   ***Fort Mohave AZ to Benson AZ***   354 mi.

3-13-05 s   Butterfield RV Resort (520) 586-4400   TL 214

3-14-05 m   251 S. Ocotillo AV Benson AZ 85602

3-15-05 t   Visit Jacki & Lindsay / Two Spring Training games / Tucson
Fea Mkt.

3-16-05 w

3-17-05 th   ***Benson AZ to Las Cruces NM***   220 mi.

	Hacienda RV Resort (888) 686-9090	TL 1122
	Stern St.	
3-18-05 f	***Las Cruces NM to Fort Stockton TX***	284 mi.
	Fort Stockton KOA (432) 395-2494	TL 1489
3-19-05 s	***Fort Stockton TX to Kerrville TX***	254 mi.
3-20-05 s	Guadalupe River RV PK (803) 362-5676	TL 1514
3-21-05 m	2605 Junction Hwy 27 Kerrville TX 78028	
3-22-05 t	Visit Lydia & Joe / Wild Flowers in Dewitt County	
3-23-05 w		
3-24-05 th		
3-25-05 f		
3-26-05 s		
3-27-05 s		
3-28-05 m	***Kerrville TX to Lakehills TX***	48 mi.
3-29-05 t	Lake Medina RV PK (888) 722-2640	TL 1518
3-30-05 w	1218 Leibold's Pt. Lakehills TX 78063	
3-31-05 th	Visit Hortense, Rene & Maryln, and Fluggie / Rodeo & Reba	
4-01-05 f		
4-02-05 s		
4-03-05 s		
4-04-05 m		
4-05-05 t		
4-06-05 w		
4-07-05 th		
4-08-05 f		

4-09-05 s

4-10-05 s

4-11-05 m   *Lakehills TX to South Pardre Island TX*   293 mi.

4-12-05 t   Travelodge Motel

4-13-05 w   Fishing / Brid Watching / Shelling

4-14-05 th

4-15-05 f

4-16-05 s

4-17-05 s

4-18-05 m   **South Padre Island TS to Lakehills TX**   293 mi.

4-19-05 t   Lake Medina RV Resort TL 1518 4-20-05 w Visit family

4-21-05 th

4-22-05 f

4-23-05 s

4-24-05 s

4-25-05 m

4-26-05 t

4-27-05 w   **Lakehills TX to Baytown TX**   250 mi.

4-28-05 th   KOA East Baytown   (800) 562-3418   TL 1514

4-29-05 f   11810 I-10 E Baytown TX 77520

4-30-05 s   Keytown / Johnson Space Ctr. / Houston

5-01-05 s   Astros vs. Clubs

5-02-05 m   **Baytown TX to Nacogdoches TX**   136 mi.

5-03-05 t   Twin Oaks RV Park (936) 560-5207   TL 1529

5-04-05 w   16098 N. US Hwy 59 Garrison TX 75946

5-05-05 th Unv.	De La Baum's house / Dr. Tom Middlebrook / Stephen S. Austin	
5-06-05 f	*Nacogdoches TX to Arlington TX*	196 mi.
5-07-05 s	All Seasons RV Park (817) 277-6600	TL 1457
	2715 S. Cooper Arlington TX 76015	
5-08-05 s	Rangers vs. Indians with Sonya	
5-09-05 m		
5-10-05 t	*Arlington TX to Oklahoma City OK*	225 mi.
5-11-05 w	Rockwell RV PK (405) 787-5992 TL 1245	
	720 S. Rockwell OK City, OK 73128	
	Bricktown / Stockyard City / State Capitol	
5-12-05 th	*Oklahoma City OK to Topeka KS*	317 mi.
5-13-05 f	Capital City RV PK (785) 862-5267	TL 793
	1949 SW 49th ST. Topeka KS	
	State Capitol	
5-14-05 s	*Topeka KS to Kansas City KS*	137mi.
5-15-05 s	Mary Jane & Alan	
5-16-05 m	6126 W. 76th Terrace	
5-17-05 t	Prairie Village KS 66208	
5-18-05 w		
5-19-05 th	Kansas City Royals	
5-20-05 f	T-Bones baseball / Rachel Dance /	
5-21-05 s		
5-22-05 s	*Kansas City KS to Iola KS*	85 mi.
	RV Park of Iola (620) 365-2200	TL 790

5-23-05 m	*Iola KS to Chanute KS*	9 mi.
	Chanute KS to Branson MO	195 mi.
	Drop off RV	
5-24-05 t	Branson MO	
5-25-05 w	The Cabins at Green Mountain (800) 815-6102	
5-26-05 th	3864 Green Mountain Dr.	
5-27-05 f	Branson, MO. 65616	
5-28-05 s	Eureka Springs AK / Showboatn' / Sliver Dollar City / Sohji	
5-29-05 s	*Branson Mo. to Chanute KS*	195 mi.
5-30-05 m	Super 8 Motel	
	Toured the Nu Wa factory / Pick up RV	
5-31-05 t	*Chanute KS to Kansas City KS*	94 mi.
6-01-05 w	Mary Jane & Alan	
6-02-05 th	**Kansas City KS to Halstead KS**	170 mi.
	Spring Lake RV PK (316) 835-3443	TL 790
	1307 S. Spring Lake Rd. Halstead KS 67056	
6-03-05 f	*Halstead KS to Garden City KS*	233 mi.
	RJ's RV PK ( )	
6-04-05 s	*Garden City KS to Colorado City CO*	238 mi.
6-05-50 s	Colorado City KOA (888) 676-3370	TL 477
	Royal Gorge / Canon City / Skyline Dr. / Cripple Creek / Garden of the God's	
6-06-05 m	*Colorado City CO to Montrose CO*	247 mi.
6-07-05 t	Montrose RV Resort (888) 249-9554 TL 515	
6-08-05 w	Black Canyon Nat Pk / Manarch Pass / Blue Mesa Lake Gunnison Rv. Boat ride	

6-09-05 th	*Montrose CO to Salina UT*	277 mi.
	Butch Cassidy Campground (800) 551-6842 TL 1579	
6-10-05 f	*Salina UT to Eureka NV*	294 mi.
	Silver Sky Lodge RV PK (775) 237-5034 TL 1061	
6-11-05 s	**Eureka NV to Cromberg CA**	293 mi.
6-12-05 s	Pine Oaks RV Pk (530) 863-2079	
6-13-05 m	Visit John & Bev	
6-14-05 t		
6-15-05 w	*Cromberg CA to Arcata CA*	291 mi.
6-16-05 th	Mad River Rapids RV PK (800) 822-7776 TL 333	
6-17-05 f	Visit Rick & Olga	
6-18-05 s		
6-19-05 s		
6-20-05 m		
6-21-05 t	*Arcata CA to Ukiah CA*	159 mi.
6-22-05 w	Redwood Empire Fair RV PK (707) 462-3884 $18	
6-23-05 th	1055 North State St. Ukiah CA 95482	
	Visit Judy & Gunther	
6-24-05 f	*Ukiah CA to Paso Robles CA*	369 mi.
6-25-05 s	Wine County RV PK (805) 238-4560 TL 408	
6-26-05 s	Res. # 2800 (Ken) WK $225 Cancel fee $10	
6-27-05 m	From jct of Hwy 101 & Hwy 46E, E 2.2 mi. on Hwy 46E	
6-28-05 t	to Airport Rd., N 0.2 mi. ®	
6-29-05 w	Visit Russell's family and Ursula & boys	
6-30-05 th		

7-01-05 f

7-02-05 s

7-03-05 s

7-04-05 m

7-05-05 t   ***Paso Rbles CA to Santa Paula CA (Ojai)***   160 mi.

7-06-05w   Mountain View RV PK (805) 933-1942 $25 deposit TL 446

7-07-05 th   From jct on Hwy 126 & Peck Rd. exit, N 0.3 mi. on Peck Rd.

7-08-05 f   to Harvard, E 0.2 mi. ® 714 W. Harvard BL. Santa Paula 93060

7-09-05 s   Jacki'a B-day Visit Marisa's family

7-10-05 s

7-11-05 m

7-12-05 t   ***Santa Paula CA to Fort Mohave AZ***   281 mi

7-13-05w   Riverside Adventure Trails RV PK (928) 486-4064

7-14-05 th 4750 Hwy 95 Bullhead City AZ 86426

      Leave RV in Fort Mohave

7-15-05 f ***Fort Mohave AZ to Long Beach CA***   280 mi.

7-16-05 s Rey's House

7-17-05 s Visit Rey's family

7-18-05 m   Dr. Sung 3:pm / Dr. Kim 10:30

7-19-05 t

7-20-05 w

7-21-05 th

7-22-05 f ***Long Beach CA to Laguna Niguel CA***   50 mi.

7-23-05 s Brent's House

7-24-05 s Alex's B-day Visit Brent's family

7-25-05 m

7-26-05 t   Dr. Wang 11:AM Hank / Dr. Kim 10:30 Sylvia

7-27-05 w

7-28-05 th

7-29-05 f *Laguna Niguel CA to Yuma AZ*   238 mi

7-30-05 s *Yuma AZ to Tucson AZ*   237 mi.

7-31-05 s Visit Jacki & Lindsay

8-01-05 m

8-02-05 t

8-03-05 w *Tucson AZ to Fort Mohave AZ*   378mi.

8-04-05 th

8-05-05 f *Fort Mohave AZ to Long Beach CA*

8-06-05 s Jammie's Wedding St. Pan 10:AM

8-07-05 s

8-08-05 m *Long Beach CA to Fort Mohave AZ*

 Riverside Adventure Tarils (928) 486-4019

 4750 Hwy 95 Hwy 95 Bullhead City AZ

8-22-05 m   *Fort Mohave AZ to Long Beach or Laguna Niguel CA*

8-23-05 t   Dr. Arima 8:AM Hank & Sylvia

8-24-05 w   Dr. Sassaki 9:AM Hank Dr. Theis 12:30 Sylvia

8-25-05 th

8-26-05 f   *Long Beach or Laguna Niguel to Fort Mohave AZ*

            Build a house

2005 Peru and Ecuador
Oct. 14 to Nov. 1

Oct. 14 '05	Fly to **Peru**
Oct. 15 '05	Arrive **Lima**
Oct. 16 '05	Explore Lima
Oct. 17 '05	Fly to **Cuzco**. **Inca Quricancha**: **Temple of the Sun**
Oct. 18 '05	**Inca Ruins** at **Sacsayhuamaa** and **Tambo Machay**: **Curandero Healing Ceremony**
Oct. 19 '05	By train into the **Urbamba Gorge** **Machu Picchu**: **Lost City of the Incas**
Oct. 20 '05	Optional day hiking from Machu Picchu: **Inca Bridge**, **Huayna Picchu**, **Gate of the Sun**. Return by train to Cuzco
Oct. 21 '05	Explore **Pisac**, Home hosted lunch Free afternoon in Cuzco
Oct. 22 '05	At leisure in Lima
Oct. 23 '05	Fly to **Quito Ecuador**
Oct. 24 / 29 '05	Fly to the **Gal**ápagos Islands
Oct. 30 '05	Disembark at **San Cristobal Island** Fly to **Quito**
Oct. 31 '05	Quito: Visit **Mindo**
Nov. 1 '05	Return to the U.S.

2007 Hank and Sylvia's RV Trip
Ojai, Paso Robles, Madera and Klamath
Aug. 17 to Sept 6

Aug. 17	Ft. Mohave to *Santa Paula*	314 mi.
	Far West Resort 805-933-3200	$25.00 per night
Aug. 18	*Ojai*	
Aug. 19	Ojai	
Aug. 20	Ojai to *Paso Robles*	178 mi.
	Wine Counrty RV PK. 805=238-4560	$39.00 per night
Aug. 21	Paso Robles	
Aug. 22	Paso robles	
Aug. 23	Paso Robles	
Aug. 24	Paso Robles to *Madera*	115 mi.
	Country Living RV PK. 559-674-5343	$23.00 per night
Aug. 25	Madera	
Aug. 26	Madera	
Aug. 27	Madera to *Red Bluff*	294 mi.
	Red Bluff RV PK. 530-529-2929	$32.00 per night
Aug. 28	Red Bluff to *Klamath*	214 mi.
	Camper Corral RV PK. 800-701-7275	$30.00 per night

Aug. 29	Klamath		
Aug. 30	Klamath		
Aug. 31	Klamath		
Sep. 01	Klamath		
Sep. 02	Klamath		
Sep. 03	Klamath to Red Bluff		214 mi.
	Red Bluff RV PK.	530-529-2929	$32.00 per night
Sep. 04	Red Bluff to *Patterson*		215 mi.
	Kit Fox RV PK.	209-892-2638	$32.00 per night
Sep. 05	Patterson to *Bakersfield*		217 mi.
	A Country RV PK.	661-363--6412	$27.00 per night
Sep. 06	Bakersfield to Ft. Mohave		289 mi.

All of the above is subject to change due to our mood and / or attitude.

Hank's cell 562-400-0419

Sylvia's cell 562-400-1320

ETHEL MARGARET BRUNNER
March 18, 1911 - July 26, 1985
74 years

My Mother, Ethel Margaret Brunner

Born in Brooklyn New York

If only I would have asked questions. I know very little about my Mother's childhood or of her immediate family. Her mother's name was Julia Brunner by marriage and McCormick by birth. I believe she was the fourth generation from Ireland on both her mother's and father's side. She did tell me she only finished 8th grade and left home at a very early age. I think she may have been around 14 or 15. If I calculate correctly, she was 14 or 15 when she had my oldest brother, and 25 when she had me. I remember a story of her Grandfather being either an owner or a trainer of Thoroughbred Horses, and he lost everything he had in the 1929 depression.

This is my Great Grandfather Jack McCormick

I vaguely remember my Great Grandmother when we went to visit her when I was 5 or 6. We were there for her 85th birthday.

In 1934, mom was living in the state of Delaware and moved to Long Beach, California. She had a sister named Viola. Viola was about 4 or 5 years younger than Ethel. She came to live with us in 1948. She married someone from Red Buff, CA. and I only saw her again one or two times after she got married. She and Ethel were not real close sisters.

She was a stay at home Mom with one exception; during WWII she went to work as a forklift driver in the Long Beach Shipyard. With the money she saved, she was able to pay off her first and only home. 820 Dawson Av. Long Beach. Sometime after she married my step dad Cy, they bought the first

801 Alamitos Ave

of their two rental properties. It was near down town Long Beach on Alamitos Ave. It had a four bedroom house, a duplex, and four apartments all on one lot. I lived in one of the apartments for a few months after I got married. A few years later, they bought two duplexes just north of the house. They never owned a credit card and paid for everything with cash. Cy was retired by then and did all the maintenance himself. I did quite a lot of work with him. That's where I learned about water heaters, electrical, plumbing, painting, wall paper, and moving furniture.

My Mom was always crocheting doilies, tablecloths, and bedspreads. She like to play cribbage and solitary. I don't remembering having beaten her in a cribbage game. She only finished 8th grade, but she was very good with numbers. She was a smoker, but never drank any kind of alcohol. She did quit smoking for a few years after she a double mastectomy.

My Mom and Dad took in Foster Children. The first one was only 5 weeks old. She had been abused and neglected by her parents who were both drug addicts. They raised her until she was 3 years old, and then had to give her back to her parents who were both rehabilitated. It was so hard to give her up they never took another baby again. Her name was Lora and her mother was so thankful to my parents that she made sure Lora stayed in contact. She visited them quite often and sent letters and cards long after she moved away. The last time I saw her was at one of our family reunions. She was in her early twenties with a child of her own. My guess is that she is in her mid-thirties by now.

Ethel 1947

They did however, take many teenagers. There was a time they had 5 teenage girls. They even took them to Florida on vacation. Can you imagine my Dad driving his station wagon with my Mom, Grandmother and 5 teenagers to Florida and back? He was a saint.

She also raised my brother's two boys for a short time. With her own children, and all of her foster children, she must have had twenty plus kids in her lifetime.

She had this funny habit I never could figure out. Most of my parent's friends were Pilipino and whenever she was in a conversation with them, she took on the same accent they had. She couldn't speak a word of Pilipino but her accent was exactly like theirs. She never swore. When she got excided she would say "Jesus, Mary and Joseph".

Ethel 1957

The one thing I hated was when she would take me shopping. We would go down to Pine Avenue and start walking on one side of Pine from 8th St. to Ocean Bl., and cross over and walk back to 8th St. She wouldn't buy anything until she had checked every store.

Mom was an OK cook but nothing compared to both my Dad and Step-dad. I know we ate a lot of hamburger. Seems like she had 10 or 15 different ways to use hamburger. She would make big pots of Chile and freeze it in cardboard milk cartons. My favorite was one I think she just made up herself. She would cook the hamburger in a pan until it was nice and brown, and then make roux like brown gravy and mix in green peas. We would eat it over white rice.

117

I remember my mother as being a little plump when I was young, but lost weight as she got older. She had a rather short fuse but was not violent in any way. When she said "no", that was the end of any discussion. Her entire life was lived for her children and every decision she made was with her children in mind.

Ethel 1980

She seemed always to be in good health until 1971 when she had a bout with breast cancer. She was 60 years old when she had a double mastectomy, but recovered with no recurrences. The last two years of her life she suffered from Alzheimer's. Of course, Alzheimer's is no laughing matter, but sometimes you have keep your sense of humor. My office was very close to her house and I would often stop by and bring her flowers. She'd say, thank you and 10 minutes later she would ask my Dad "who bought me the flowers." He'd answer "Hank did". She'd say, "who's Hank? He's your son and sitting right next to you.

My Dad was an absolute saint. Mom would say "let's go for a ride". It could be at any time of the day or night. He would get her dressed, in to the car, and by time they got to the end of their street she'd be asleep. When they got back to house she would say, "I thought we were going for a ride". She was always the money handler. When she started to get sick, Cy would give her a bunch of cash so she thought she was in control of the funds. One time she accused one of

my dad's friends (Ed) of stealing $500.00. She said that she had it under her mattress and he came into the bedroom and stole the money. A few days later, my dad found the money under the mattress but on the other side of the bed.

Mom is buried in All souls Cemetery in Long Beach, Ca.

Between Curb numbers 115 & 125 16 rows back

Anatolio G. Bisnar
July 14, 1899 - December 4, 1967
68yrs.

My Father was Anatolio Bisnar. He was born on July 14, 1899. In the Province of Leyte and the town of Inopacan in the Philippine Islands. He told me he was born in a mountain barrio and was the youngest of 15 children, but I have no evidence of that being correct. His parents were Ciriaco Bisnar and Dorotea Galo Bisnar. His brother was Jose, and his sisters were Tekla and Artemia. I am told he also has half brothers and sisters.

He came to the United States after jointing the US Navy on Feb. 19, 1919. He became a Naturalized US citizen on August 28, 1942 In the District Court of the Territory of Honolulu, Hawaii. He later added the middle initial of 'G' because he said everyone in the Navy had to have a middle initial.

He said he was the youngest of 15 children and left home at age of 15 to join the Filipino Army. His home was somewhere in the mountains of Leyte Island. He told me that when he got only a short way from home he couldn't speak the local dialect. By the time I knew him he could speak Filipino (more than one dialect), Spanish, and English. He served in the Army for three years. He always told the story of how he joined the US Navy. After his discharge from the Army, he and his buddies celebrated their discharge and got drunk. When they came to, they were all in the US Navy and heading for San Francisco. Funny story, but I'm not sure if it's true.

Being in the Navy, he was not home very much. The family did not travel to wherever he was stationed, and he was at sea much of the time. As a result, I didn't know him very well until he retired in 1949.

He served in the Navy for 30 years. He spent the entire WWII at sea. He was authorized to wear one **Silver Star**, four **Bronze Stars**, one **American Defense**, and five **Good Conduct** service ribbons. He also was inducted into **The Silent Mysteries of the Far East** for crossing the 180th Meridian in 1944, and **The Shellback** for having cross the Equator on the USS Makassar Strait on Oct. 14, 1944.

Ships he sailed on

02-23-19		Rec. Ship Cavite P.I.
04-16-19		Rec. Ship San Francisco CA.
05-24-19		Rec. Ship New York NY.
06-30-19	03-16-20	USS Imperator
09-27-19		USS Imperator
03-16-20	01-24-23	USS Pennsylvania
05-01-20		Rec. Ship
07-30-21		USS Pennsylvania
12-31-21		USS Pennsylvania
03-31-22		USS Pennsylvania
06-30-22		USS Pennsylvania
09-30-22		USS Pennsylvania
12-31-22		USS Pennsylvania
12-17-27		USS Camden
06-31-31		USS Reine Mercedes
08-26-31		USS Arkansas
09-13-31		USS Reine Mercedes
09-25-31		USS Reina Mercedes
01-24-23	12-13-35	USS Pennsylvania
12-14-35	03-30-36	USS West Virginia
12-30-35		USS West Virginia
02-08-36		USS Maryland
03-30-36	06-08-36	USS California
06-08-36	07-07-36	USS Tennessee

07-07-36	10-02-36	USS New Mexico
10-02-36	07-12-38	USS California
07-12-38	10-13-38	USS Maryland
10-13-38	12-13-39	USS California
05-10-39	09-14-40	USS New Mexico (Cambator)
12-14-39	05-10-39	USS California (Cambator)
05-10-40		USS New Mexico
09-14-40	01-20-41	USS California (Cambator)

The Flagship USS California was berthed in Pearl Harbor on Battleship Row Dec. 7, 1941 when it was struck by two torpedoes and one bomb from Japanese aircraft. There was considerable damage to the forward and aft of the ship and she sunk in her berth on Dec. 10, 1941. Nearly a hundred officers and men were killed in action during the Pearl Harbor attack. The ship was raised in March 1942 repaired and modernized and returned to duty in January 1944. Anatolio Bisnar was aboard the USS California when the Japanese attack took place.

01-20-41	01-27-41	USS Maryland (Cambator)
01-27-41	05-07-41	USS New Mexico (Cambator)
05-07-41	04-27-42	USS California (Cambator)
04-27-42	4-30-42	Rec. Sta. Pearl Harbor
04-30-42	09-12-42	USS Medusa (Serfor)
09-13-42	08-01-49	unknown
03-18-49		Shore duty
03-24-49		USS Thompson
05-23-49		USS Sierra

USS California

USS New York

Photo # NH 67583 USS Pennsylvania underway, 31 May 1934

USS Pennsylvania

USS West Virginia

USS California

USS San Francisco

USS New Mexico

USS Tennessee

USS Marylyn

USS Sierra

USS Arkansas

USS Thompson

USS Medusa

Just as he was ready retired after 30 years, he was in an auto accident and spent months in the Navy Hospital in White Sands New Mexico.

After he retired, he took residence in Long Beach. That's when we really got to know each other and spent a lot a time together. He never learned to drive a car. He was a Ships Boxing Champ for his weight class and won a trophy for Ballroom Dancing, but could not handle a car. He would come to our house and visit quite often. He liked Logger XXX Beer and cigars. He would walk to the local liquor store and buy one quart of beer and one cigar.

When I was a junior in high school he bought a new Ford Victoria Hard Top convertible. I gave him three or four driving lessons before he gave the car to me and my two sisters.

"The car is yours, I'll call you when I need a ride" Well guess what? My oldest sister Dot was an airline hostess and traveled. My younger sister Boots was in nurse's training and lived on campus and had a boyfriend. The car was mine.

In 1954, he returned to the Philippines for a visit. He was 55 years old and had not been there for many years. At the same time, I joined the Army and was stationed in Germany. Neither of us were good at letter writing, so we lost contact. My sister Dot did keep in touch and she would give me information about him. On Dec.4, 1954 he married Maximina B. Borja a young 16 year old girl. She was under the legal age to get married but lied and said she was 18. The marriage took place in her home town of Dulag, and was witnessed by Simeon Kempis and Rosario Bolasco. The persons that gave consent was Constantina Bisnar, his sister, and Pelagia Gulanza, her mother. They lived at 179 Sto. Rosario St. Inopacan. I met my Step Mother and their children in 1993. My step Mothers name is Maxie, and their children are Elizabeth, Evelyn, and Ferdinand. The story of how we met is quite interesting and I'll write about it later on in these Ramblings.

He died at age 67 on December 4, 1966 on the island of Leyte in the town of Inopacan. He was killed in an altercation. The story goes that he was attending a wedding reception and a fight broke out. He tried to intervene and was stabbed. He is buried in a Roman Catholic Cemetery, Inopacan, Leyte, Philippines.

Anatolio's Children:

George William Bisnar, Bernaldo Francis Bisnar, Dorothea Effey Bisnar, Constance Thelma Bisnar, Henry Anatolio Bisnar, Elizabeth Bisnar, Evelyn Bisnar and Ferdinand Bisnar

On the "Report of the Death of an American Citizen" it states he had a daughter name Mrs. Dennis Taber in Windsor Calif., a brother name Jose Bisnar in Dulag, Leyte, and a sister named Artemia Bisnar Antisoda in Talibon, Bohol, Philippines. . I have no knowledge of these relatives.

Anatolio, Maxie & Ferdi

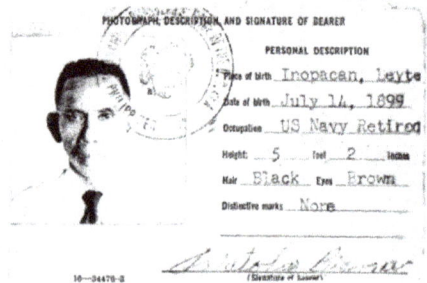

Personal Description Nov. 1965

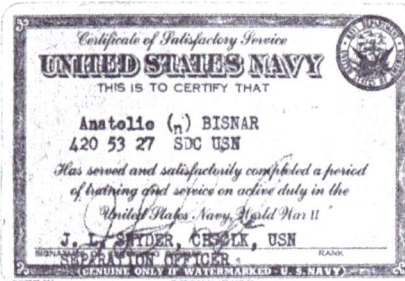

Certificate of Satisfactory Service

ID Card Armed Forces of the United States

Period of Active Duty Feb. 19, 1919 to Aug. 1, 1949

Card No. 193441 Sep. 29, 1964

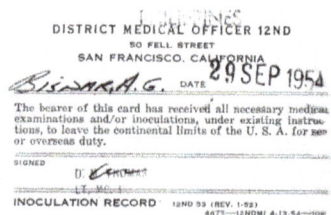

District Medical Officer Sep. 29, 1954

BISNAR, Anatolio, CCK, USN,
Authorized to wear: American Area,
Asiatic-Pacific (1 silver star, 4
bronze stars), American Defense (1
star), Good Conduct (5 stars) service ribbons.

LT. E. THAYER, JR., USNR

Silver Star

Silver Star

Bronze Star

Bronze Star

Bronze Star

Bronze Star

Bronze Star

American Defense

Asiatic Pacific Campaign

Good Conduct

Good Conduct

Navy Service Strips 30 years

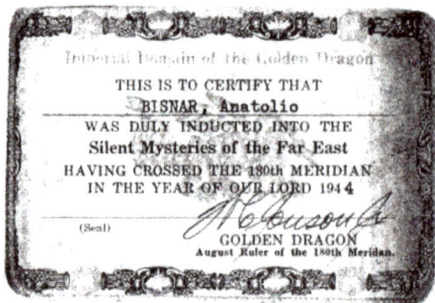

Service Ribbons

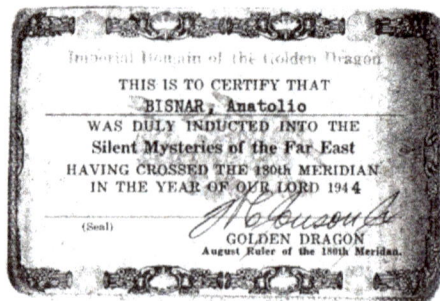

Imperial Dolphin 1944

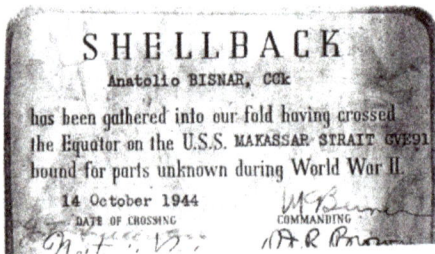

Shellback Oct. 14, 1944

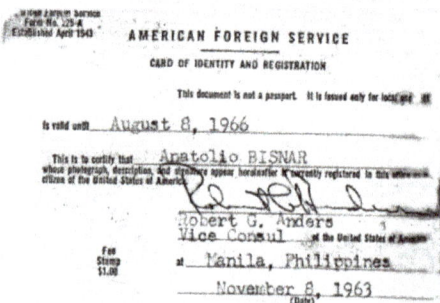

American Foreign Service
Nov. 8, 1963

XC-Folder

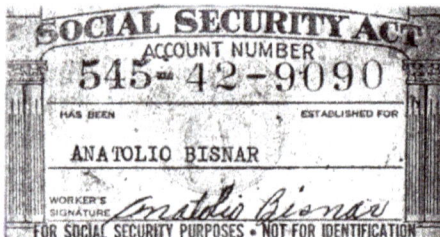

Social Security Card

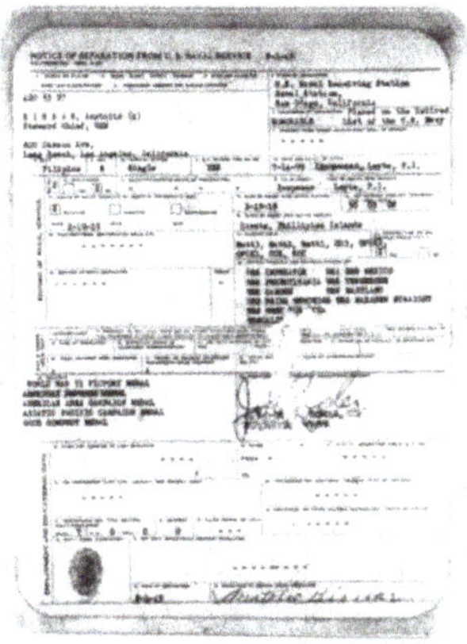

Notice of Separation from Naval Service Aug. 1 1949

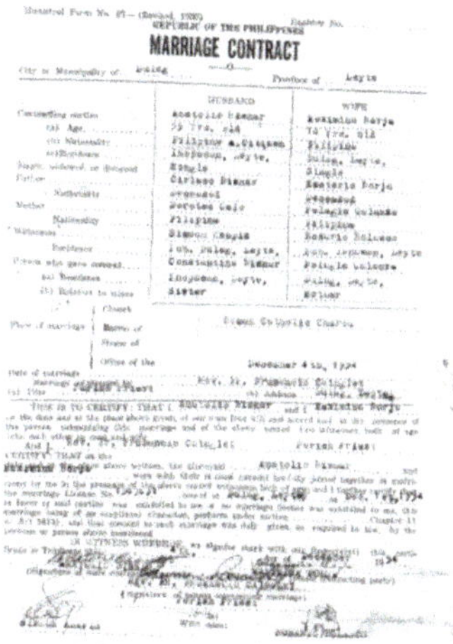

REPUBLIC OF THE PHILIPPINES

MARRIAGE CONTRACT

Marriage Contract
Dec. 4, 1954

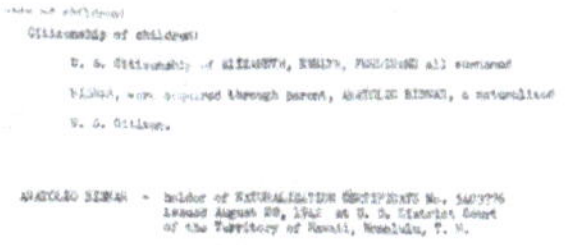

Citizenship or Children
Jan. 19, 1967

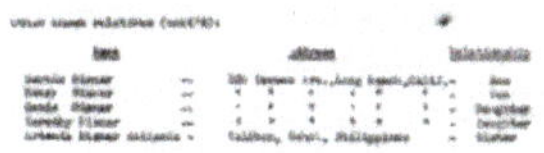

Known Relatives

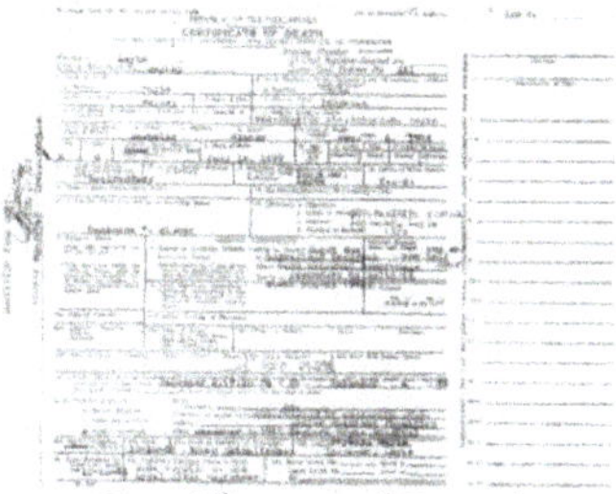

Certificate of Death
Dec. 4, 1967

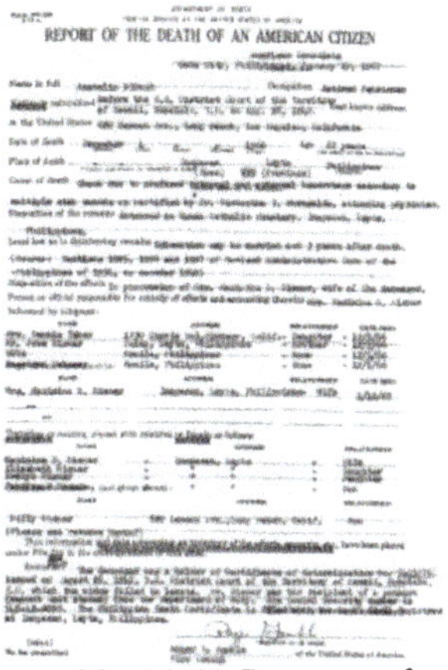

REPORT OF THE DEATH OF AN AMERICAN CITIZEN

Jan. 19, 1968 Report of Death of an American Citizen on Dec. 4, 1967

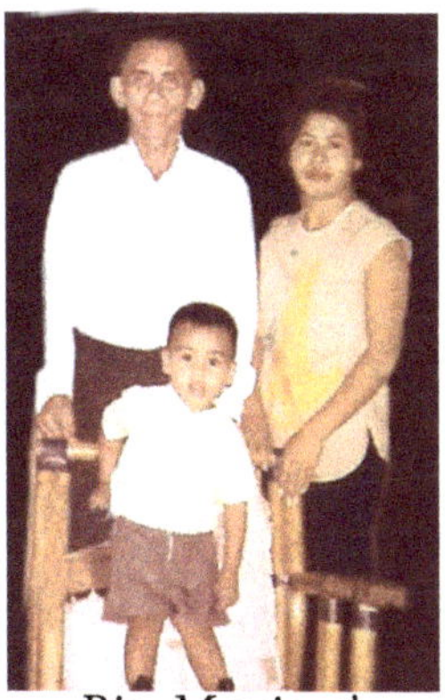

Bis, Maxie, & Ferdie

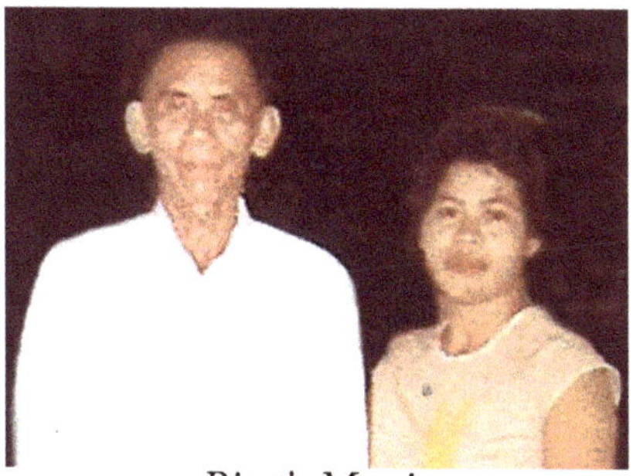

Bis & Maxie

Dad is buried in the Philippines.

Ariston Bicaldo
February 22, 1911 - September 17, 2000
89 years

My Stepfather was Ariston Bicaldo. He was born on February 22, 1911 in Nabua Camarines Sur, Luzon Island, the Philippines. His nickname was Cy. He was the youngest of seven children and had two brothers, Fernando and Felix, and three sisters Susana, Eupemia, and Teborsia. His family were subsistence farmers on their own land. Cy left school after completing the 7th grade. From that time on he was required to help with the plowing and other farm chores. He disliked farming, especially plowing behind their bull Ox. He was always thinking of leaving Nabua. In 1929, at age 18, Cy and his compadre went to the city of Capite to enlist in the US Navy. From there they traveled by ship to Manila and began their Navy careers. Cy was the only one of his family who went to school and the only one to leave the Philippines.

Luzon the Philippines

He joined the Navy to "See the World". When asked what it was that he liked most about the Navy he answered, "I just liked being in the Navy, farming was not fun." His wish to see the world was fulfilled. His travels took him to China, Korea, Japan, Australia, Panama, Cuba, Puerto Rico, New Guinea, Guantanamo Bay, Guadalcanal, Guam, and the United States. He crossed the equator many times.

During his 30 year career (1929-1958) in the Navy, Cy served on several Navy ships and had numerous assignments. The ships he served on were the USS New Mexico, USS North Hampton, USS Honolulu, USS Bremerton, USS Electra, and USS McCord (1943-1946).

USS New Mexico

USS N. Hampton

USS Honolulu

USS Bremerton

When the Japanese bombed Pearl Harbor on December 7, 1941, his ship was stationed in Pearl Harbor, but fortunately was out to sea on a training session. Had his ship been in port on that day, there is little doubt it would have been sunk along with the many others that went down.

While serving on the USS North Hampton, his ship was hit by a torpedo and sunk. Somehow, the crew members got so excited that they cut all the life rafts loose before anyone could get into them and they floated away empty.

Everyone jumped overboard and were kept afloat by their lifejackets. It was in the nighttime hours before dawn. His watch stopped when he jumped into the water. It was 2:00am and he spent several hours in the water before he and other survivors were picked up by an escort destroyer. When asked if he was scared that sharks would attack while he was in the water, he said he didn't even think about sharks.

Loss at the Battle of Tassafaronga

The Battle of Tassafaronga began 40 minutes before midnight on 30 November, when three American destroyers made a surprise torpedo attack on the Japanese. All American ships then

opened fire, which the startled enemy did not return fire for seven minutes. Two of the American cruisers took torpedo hits within the space of a minute, and 10 minutes later, another was hit, all being forced to retire from the action. The *Northampton* and *Honolulu*, with six destroyers, continued the fierce action. Close to the end of the engagement, *Northampton* was struck by two torpedoes, which tore a huge hole in her port side, ripping away decks and bulkheads. Flaming oil sprayed over the ship; she took on water rapidly and began to list. Three hours later, as she began to sink stern-first, she had to be abandoned. The survivors were all picked up by destroyers. While a tactical defeat, as three cruisers had been severely damaged and *Northampton* lost in exchange for the loss of only one Japanese destroyer, the Japanese had been denied a major reinforcement, turning the action into an American strategic victory.

Cy was aboard the USS Honolulu when it was hit by a torpedo blowing a huge hole in the bow, but it did not sink. During most of the war he was assigned to a small aircraft Carrier which ferried planes and supplied from the US to the South Pacific Theater. Cy was decorated with citations for his combat experiences.

The USS Honolulu was in the South Pacific early in December 1943. For the rest of that year and into 1944, she took part in the Bougainville operation and other actions intended to isolate the Japanese strongpoint at Rabaul. In June 1944, she steamed northwards to participate in the Marianas invasion, during which she bombarded Saipan and Guam. The *Honolulu* also covered the landings in the Palaus in September, and at Leyte in October. While off Leyte on 20 October 1944, she was the victim of an aerial torpedo attack. Hit amidships, the *Honolulu* required repairs in the United States. This work, which included extensive updating of her secondary battery and an increase in her beam, was not completed until after the end of the Pacific War. After brief duty as a training ship, the *Honolulu* was decommissioned at the Philadelphia Navy Yard in February 1947. She remained in the Reserve Fleet there for twelve years and was sold for scrapping in late 1959.

His ship was being loaded for another trip to the Pacific when the Japanese surrendered and the war ended. Cy recalls that he was bowling at the time and everyone went "crazy". He stated that the city closed all the bars and liquor stores.

Cy rose to the rank of Chief Steward. His responsibilities included all matters concerning the Officers Mess. He was an Admiral's personal steward for a few years. He also had shore duty assignments. He spent eighteen months in Alaska on Kodiak Island and finished out his career by supervising the Officers Mess on Terminal Island in Long Beach California.

Cy received two letters of commendation. On May 30, 1951 for his continual devotion of duty and example of leadership, and August 25, 1956 for his ship being awarded the BATTLE EFFICIENCY COMPETITION.

He began bowling in 1944 on Treasure Island in San Francisco and continued as an avid bowler until a bad knee forced him to retire from bowling at the age of 86. During his 53 years of bowling, he won some fifty trophies.

The story of how he got the nickname of "Cy" is interesting. It seems that when he was a young man he and his friends went dancing. Cy wanted to dance with this one pretty girl, but couldn't get up enough nerve to ask her. Later the evening she asked him what his name was and his friend said "He's shy". The girl thought they said Cy, and called him Cy the rest of the night. From then on, his shipmates called him "Shy Cy". Well, the Shy eventually faded but the Cy stuck forever.

In 1946, Cy married my Mom Ethel. They were married in Tijuana, Mexico. He was the very best step father you could ever hope for. My two older brothers were already out of the house, but he raised my two sisters and me as if we his own flesh and blood. I will be forever thankful for all he did for me and our family.

Cy retired from the Navy on October 1, 1959. He and Mom spent their time maintaining their home and rental properties. Mom passed away in 1983 at the age of 73. Cy continued to live in their Long Beach home which they owned for over fifty years. It took me five years to talk him into selling the house and move into a smaller place. In 1988, he sold that house and bought a condominium in Signal Hill. In 1995 he sold the condo and purchased a house in Murrieta Ca. to live close to

his companion, Jovita (Vita) Salcido's family. His grandniece, Rosie Soribello and her husband Billy lived close by and made sure that Cy and Vita were safe and comfortable. It was a 60 mile trip to visit him but I didn't mind and went as often as I could.

On September 17, 2000 Cy passed away from natural causes. He became ill in early August, and was given a pace-maker to control his heart beat. He recovered from that problem but in early September he just seemed to fade away. I believe he was ready to let go of life and begin his next voyage and adventure. He is buried next to my Mom in All Souls Cemetery in Long Beach, Ca.

ID Card No. 561-54-8226
Retired Navy

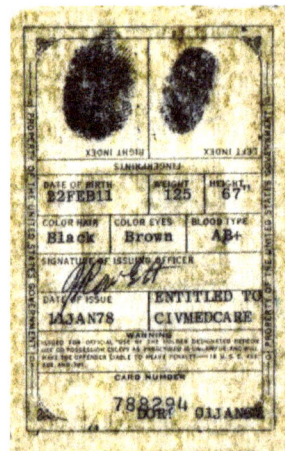

Back of ID Card

Cedula Certificate

Immunization Record

American Defense

Asiatic Pacific

Good Conduct

WW II Victory

Authorized Ribbons

BICALDO, A.C.Std. U.S.N.
Authorized to wear following
ribbons in addition to any al-
ready authorized:
DEFENSE: With star.
ASIATIC PACIFIC AREA: With one
silver star & the numeral "2".
AMERICAN AREA.

C. MOORE,
Commander, U.S.N.

Korean Service Medal

United Nation Medal

Navy Unit Citation

American Theatre

Chief Petty Officer

US Navy Service Strips

Service Strips

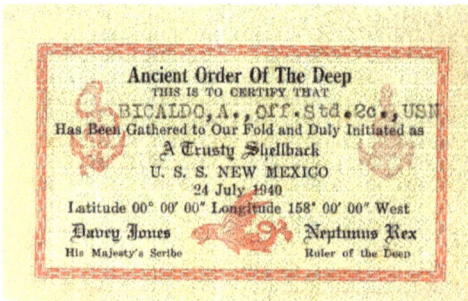

Ancient Order of the Deep 1940

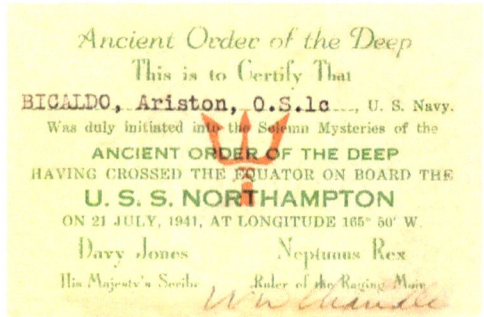

Ancient Order of the Deep

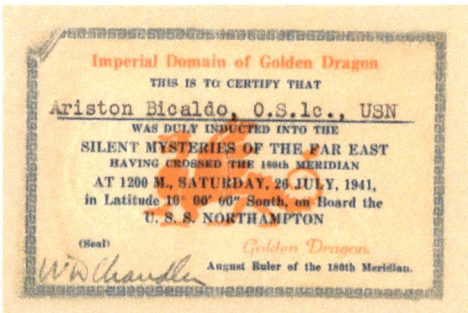

Imperial Domain of Golden Dragons
1941

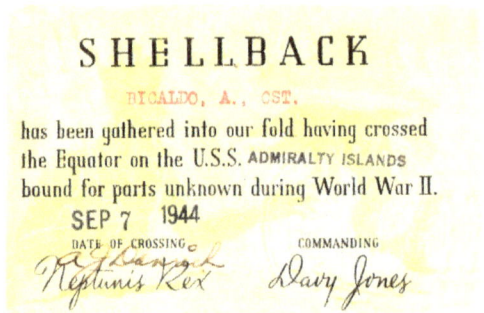

Shellback 1944

Domain of the Golden Dragon 1950

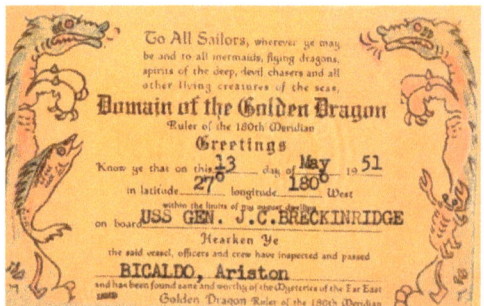

Domain of the Golden Dragon 1951

Domain of the Golden Dragon 1956

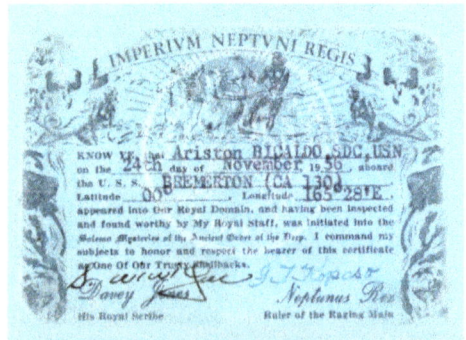

IMPERIVEM NEPTVNI REGIS
1956

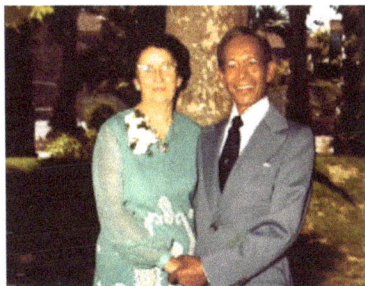

Cy is buried in all souls Cemetery Long Beach CA. Between curb markers 115 & 125 16 rows back.

Julia McCormack Brunner
March 16, 1889 - September 1, 1979
90 years

I don't have any history about my Grandmother Julia. She was born in Brooklyn, New York in 1889. She had two daughters, Ethel and Viola. Her maiden name was McCormack and her married name was Brunner but there's no information about my Grandfather anywhere in the family that I know about. She came to live with us in California when I was about twelve years old. She lost her eye sight not long after she moved to California. She was not a "lovey- dovey" type grandmother, but we had a nice relationship. I would sit beside her and have long conversations about what was going on in my life. I wish I would have had the foresight to ask her about her life. As an adult I would always spend some time with her whenever I would visit my parents. She spent the last year or so in a nursing home and sadly I didn't see her as often as I should have. Even after all these years I miss our chats.

Julia is buried in All Souls Cemetery Long Beach CA. At curb marker 115. 5 rows back

William George Bisnar
March 19, 1925 - April 22, 1997
72 years

Bill Bisnar 1941

My brother Bill was born in Brooklyn New York in 1925. He moved with the family to California in 1934. He attended St. Mathews Grammar School and St. Anthony's High School in Long Beach. Although he was ten years older than me we had a wonderful relationship.

Bernie and Bill 1930

Bill's confirmation   Bill - right side bottom row third from the right

When I was young, he was the one that made sure I was always safe and sound. Of course, my other brother and sisters were there for me too. When I was about six or seven he bought me set of tin soldiers. I can remember playing with them every day for a lot of years. He also bought me an Electric Train Set and an Electric Steam Engine.

Bill Hank Ethel Bozo Dot Bernie

At age seventeen he joined the US Navy.

George William Bisnar
United States Naval Service
Service Number 564-99-88   Rate S2C V6S
January 8, 1943 to January 21, 1946

Bill enlisted in the Navy on January 8, 1943 at the age of 17 years and 9 months. He was 5' 3½" tall and weighed 188 lbs. He was sent to Farragut Idaho for his training before being assigned to the USS McCord. He spent 24 months at sea and was on the USS McCord from October 15, 1943 to July 23, 1945.

The USS McCord was a World War II Fletcher-class Destroyer. She was named after Commander Frank C McCord. Length-376' 6", Beam- 39' 8", Speed- 35 knots, with a Range of 6500 nautical miles. She was commissioned on August 19, 1943 and decommissioned on June 9, 1954.

Bills Action at Sea

Feb. 1944   Participated in the invasion and occupation of the Marshall Islands. (Tinian Island)

Mar. 1944   Qualified for Shellback, crossed the Equator. Long.172 E.

Jun. 1944   Participated in bombardment of Fangelawa Bay.
New Ireland Island, Bismark Archipelago.

Jul. 1944   Participated in the invasion of Marianas Islands (Tinian Island).

Sept. 1944   Participated in the invasion of Palau Islands.

Oct. 1944   Participated in the invasion and occupation of Layte Island and the second battle of the Philippines.

Dec. 1944   Participated in the support of Mindoro Landing and against enemy held airfields in the Philippines.

Jan. 1945   Participated in the invasion and occupation of Luzon Islands. The first carrier task force strikes against the South East Cost of China (Siagon, Amoy, Swatow, Kamranh Bay & Hong Kong) Attack against Nansei Island (Okinawa Shima.

Feb. 1945   Participated in carrier strikes against Tokyo Area of Japan and support of Iwo Jima operations

Bills Authorized Ribbons and Medals

World War II Victory Medal

Good Conduct Medal

American Area Ribbon

Asiatic – Pacific Area with a Bronze Star 5-29-44

Philippines Liberation with two Bronze Stars

Marshall Island Operation

One star for occupation of Kwajalein and Majuro actions 1-24-44

Occupation of Emiwethk Atoll 2-17-44.

Anti-Submarine Action one star 5-24-44 and one star 4-7-44.

Marianas operation one star 7-20-44. Capture and occupation of Tinian.

Western Caroline Island Operation one star 9-6-44.

Capture and occupation of the Southern Palua Inlands.

Special Operation one star 5-22-44.

American Defense

Good Conduct

Asiatic – Pacific

Philippine Liberation

Bronze Star

Southwest Asia Serv.

Combat Action

WW II Victory

Henry Anatolio Bisnar

Bill was honorably discharged on January 21, 1946. He chose not reenlist because he could not get the training and job he wanted. He claimed that he was a cook only because his records showed he was Filipino which is where all Filipinos were assigned in those days. I don't know what kind of job he wanted, but he said that's why he got out of the Navy.

Bill was called by many names. William not so much, George by few, Bill by most, and Mo by those who knew him from his Boy Scouting days. For a short time he was my Scout leader. I think he was a bit harder on me when it came to the merit badges just because we were brothers.

He like to hunt and fish. One time he brought home four ducks. We had roast duck for dinner but no one liked it because it was too greasy. Another time, he went deer hunting and didn't get a deer but hit one with his car. The whole front end was pushed in. He repaired it himself and painted it Kelly Green with a paint roller. He did have many successful hunting trips. He also had the first motor bike I ever saw. It was just like a regular bike, but it had a small gasoline engine on the back that powered the wheel. I don't think it could to more than 25 mph.

He married a girl name Ann. I don't know much about her, only that she was eighteen years old when they married. They had two sons John and Tom. John is an attorney in Newport Beach, Ca. and Tom past away at a very young age of forty-five. Bill and Ann divorced when kids were around four or five.

She moved away and I didn't see her again until Tom was hospitalized just before he died. Bill married two more times. I don't remember his second wife, but the marriage only lasted a few months. He and his third wife Eunice were married for many years. They had five children. John and Tom from Bill's first marriage, Patty form Eunice's first marriage, and Susan and Mike from their marriage. They divorced after all the children were on their own. Bill worked at the Naval Weapons Station in Seal Beach Ca. and was a munitions expert. After 30 plus years, he retired only to move to Hawthorn, NV and take a job as a contract munitions expert. He was receiving his Civil Service pension and getting paid the same salary he made at his C.S. job. He worked and lived in Nevada for four or five years. It was a great place for him because his true love was fishing and hunting. Walker Lake was only a few minutes from his house and when he retired the second time, he went fishing nearly every day. Bill suffered from diabetes and eventually he lost his eyesight and had to give up fishing. Every few weeks, I would make the eight hours trip to see how he was doing and visit for two or three days. He was seventy three years old when his right big toe turned black. His local doctor told him that he would lose his toe and maybe his foot, and at his age he didn't think it was worth the trouble. Can you imagine any doctor saying that to his patient? Sylvia and I decided that he should move back to Ca. and live with us. At first he didn't want to move, but he soon realized he would need help recovering from any surgery he was going to have. I drove him directly from his house to Veteran Hospital in Long Beach. They were not sure if he would lose his toe or his foot. They said the first thing was to place a catheter so he could receive dialysis treatments. Feeling he was in good hands, I left for a weekend photo shoot. On my way home I received a call from my son Andy saying that Bill passed away during the placement of the catheter. The doctor said that something happened that caused him to bleed out. He offered a longer and technical explanation but I chose not to hear it. No amount of explaining would bring him back. I wish I could have done more for him and I miss him a great deal.

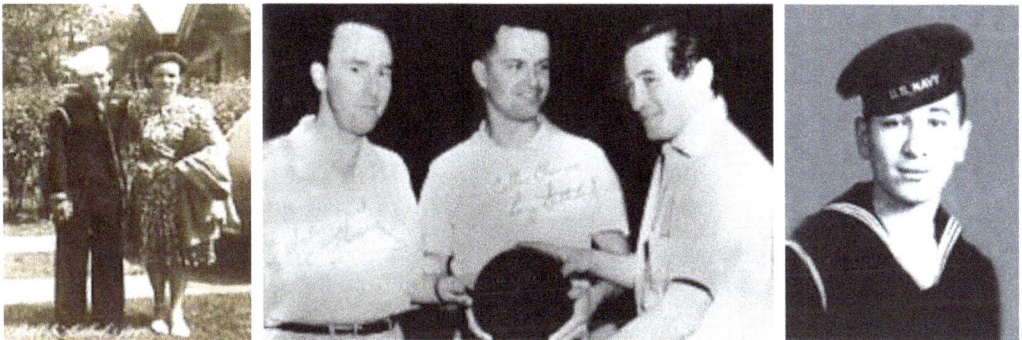

Per Bill's wish, he was cremated and his ashes are in Veterans Memorial Cemetery in Riverside Ca. Buried May 15, 1993. Plot: 46A 0 1135

Bernaldo Francis Bisnar
April 8, 1927 - September 19, 1995
68 yrs.

Bernie was born in New London Connecticut on April 8, 1927. He was eight years old when the family moved to California. Bernie was without a doubt everyone's favorite in the family. He was good looking, funny, a great athlete, and people just love to be around him. He and his friend Jerry were the first to call me Hank. I was about ten or eleven. After graduating from St. Matthews's grammar school he went to High School at Southern California Military Academy in Signal Hill. He was a fulltime boarder and came home on weekends. Sometimes with two or three of his buddies. He was the star football player and received a football scholarship to Humboldt University in Arcata California. He was also the most decorated and honored cadet to have graduated in the school's history.

He only stayed a Humboldt for one year. He didn't like the weather or the coach. The weather in Arcata CA. is typical northern California weather mostly overcast, rainy, and cold. He was always cold even in Southern Ca. He had several jobs throughout his lifetime. One time he worked in a bakery at night, and would come home late and wake everyone up for warm fresh donuts. Once he spent the summer in Lancaster Ca. picking water melons.

Bernie had two cars, a 1932 Ford five window coup, and 1941 Plymouth sedan. Sometimes when he was gone, my buddies and I would take the car he left home and go for a joy ride. We never got caught, but I think he knew what we were doing.

He was a really good dancer. My Mom would take us to San Pedro to a Filipino restaurant and after dinner Bernie and Dot would entertain everybody by dancing the Boogie-Woogie to the jukebox music.

Bernie and Bill Bisnar

142

He got married just before he was drafted into the Army. He married his second cousin Florence Mc Dougal. Her mother was our mother's 1st. cousin. They used to say that cousins shouldn't marry, but they had three wonderful children. Dennis, Chris, and Kathy. The Army sent him to Ft. Bless TX, and then to Germany.

When he got discharged from the Army he took a job as letter carrier for the Post Office. He only carried mail until he got his Barbers license. He owned his own Barber Shop for many years and was quite successful. I worked part-time for him for a few years.

Unfortunately his marriage only lasted for about twelve years. He and Florence never actually got a divorce, but stayed separated for the rest of his life. He was not the model husband and father. Bernie liked to be the center of attention and spent a lot of his time in bars where he knew everyone, and they liked to be around him as well.

He sold his Barber Shop and went back to the Postal Service somewhere around age forty five or fifty. He didn't carry mail, but worked in the main post office in Long Beach. He retired at age 65 and was living in one of his houses in North Long Beach. Bernie was a wheeler - dealer. He always had some hot deal going. He bought and sold cars and houses on a regular basis. Sometime without the proper paper work being processed. That became a problem after he was gone.

He became restless and bored and took a job as shuttle driver for Dial -A- Ride. He normally worked days but occasionally would take groups of people to a Lakers games at night. One night he got home late and when he entered his house he got mugged and robed. They didn't hurt him, but they tied him up and took his money and a few things from the house.

The next day he quit his Dial-a-Ride job. He said he couldn't be coming home late at night anymore. I tried to convince him to keep his job but not to take the night drives. That was the start of his decline. He soon became a recluse and wouldn't leave his house. He got so bad, he wouldn't pay his utilities and ate almost nothing. I had to have his water, gas, and telephone turned on more than once. I would go and

try to take him to breakfast or lunch on Saturdays. He refused most of the time. It took some time but I was able to talk him into putting me on his checking account so I could pay his bills.

I would call him two or three times a week from my office. One day, his phone kept ringing and ringing so I left work and went to his house. He wouldn't answer the door and I finally broke the door to get in. He was lying on his couch and with his shirt off and I saw he was covered with sores on his chest and back. He refused to let me take him to the hospital. That night I called Dennis, his son, and Dale our nephew the doctor and explained what was going. We agreed to meet at his house the next day. All three of us tried to get him to go the hospital and he wouldn't listen. Dale told him he was starving himself and that was the cause of the sores on his body. Dale suggested we call the paramedics because they could take him to the emergency room without his permission. When the paramedics showed up he said, "where the hell have you guys been? These knuckleheads wouldn't take me to the hospital, and that one thinks he's a doctor ". He was joking but he was the only one laughing. When we got to the hospital the doctor asked if he was a street person. They kept him in Downey Hospital for about three weeks until all of his sores were gone, and then transferred him it the Veterans Hospital in Long Beach.

The plan was for him come and live with me after his discharge from the VA. They assigned him to their onsite nursing home. He was there for about one year and never did get healthy enough to be released. I received a call from one of the nurses saying he was getting really sick, and the doctors wanted to do exploratory surgery. She didn't think he could survive any kind of surgery. He died two weeks later, before his scheduled surgery. September 19, 1995. I wish he hadn't gotten sick. He was so much fun to be with. I miss him dearly.

Bernie is buried at All Soul's Catholic Cemetery in Long Beach. Curb marker 115, seven rows back.

Dorothy Effie Bisnar
June 21, 1931 - 1978
47 years

Dorothy was born in New York, New York on June 21, 1931. She was the third child in the family. Her older brothers were Bill and Bernie. She was four years old when the family moved to California. We called her Dot. Always the "Big Sister". She was always concerned in everything that I did, and how I looked and acted. She was full of advice. I listened most of the time. One time, when she was babysitting me and my sister Boots, she got mad and scolded me. I was about 9 or 10 and ran out of the house and down the street to a friend's house. When I didn't come at dark she panicked and she and Boots were looking all over the neighborhood but couldn't find me. Later when I got home, they were crying and hugged me and said "don't ever do that again". I never did

She was a beautiful girl and woman. She had striking auburn hair and dark brown eyes. She loved to dance and be the center of attention. Her Godfather bought her a piano, but she only took lessons for a short time and never did play very well. She did take dance lessons and was very good at tap-dancing and participated in several dance programs. She would put on her records and forced me to dance with her. It paid off when I got older.

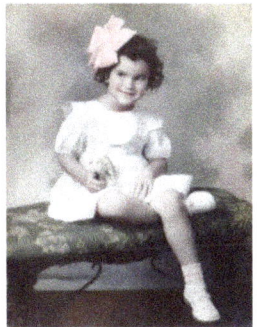

In high school, she was very popular and had many friends, both girls and boys. There were always one or two of friends around the house. She was Cheerleader for two or three years and was some kind of class official. After high school, she went to Long Beach City College and was a cheerleader.

She received an AA Degree and met her first husband Bob Taylor.

She wanted desperately to be an Airline Hostess. She applied to all the Airlines, but they turned her down because at 5' 2" and she couldn't meet their height requirements. Somehow, she finally got TWA to accept her and she traveled to Kansas City, MO for flight training. When she got there, they wanted to turn down again because of her height but she cried and begged and they let her stay. She worked as a Hostess for over ten years. In those days, they were not allowed to be married. She got married about two years before she quit but had to keep it a secret.

She married Bob Taylor who she met at LBCC. He went to Wilson High. He was really a nice guy and treated me as his own brother. Unfortunately, the marriage only last about three or four years.

She married again to a man she had met in Florida and move to Merritt Island, Fl. His name was Harold Van Riper. Everyone called him Van. He flew the confederate flag in his backyard, is a diehard Southerner, and uses the 'N' word quite often. He worked in the space program for Kodak and sent my boys lots of photos of space ships and their blast offs. He treated my sister like she was a queen and seemed to fit into our family with no problem. I really liked him even if he was a redneck.

In 1967, they adopted and baby girl and name her Krista. Krista was only nine years old when Dot got sick with bone marrow cancer. She fought it for two years and made trips to Houston Texas for treatment two or three times. She was only 47 when she died. I feel fortunate that I was able to see her in her last days.

She is buried in Merritt Island, Fl.

I was able to visit Krista in 1990 when I was in Florida visiting my son Brent. In 2003, I took an extended RV trip. When I got Florida I thought I would see Krista but she had moved to Gulf Breeze and I didn't get to see her. We haven't really kept in touch as we should. It was two or three years from the last time we talked when Brent e-mailed me her e-mail address. They connected though Facebook. Now that we have reconnected, I'll try to do a better job of keeping in touch.

Note: In May of 2016 Krista came out to California to the Family Reunion. She stayed at Brent's house and we all had a very nice visit.

It was through one of Dots friends that I met my siblings from my dad's second family. See article below. I'll tell that story later.

Connie, Bill & Dot
1946

1945

1936

1935

1941

1946

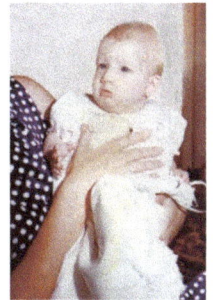

1967

1967

1990

1971

Krista Stein 2011

Van and unknown

1937 Bill, Hank, Ethel,
Connie Dot, & Bernie

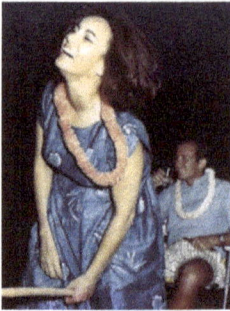

1948

1941

1941 Dot, Ethel,
Hank, & Connie

1949

Bernie & Dot

1948
Prom Night

Dot, Connie & Hank

Dot and Krista 1968

1953

Cameron and Connor Stein

1946 Dot, Bill, Hank, Ethel,
Boots and Bernie

Krista

Bob

Cameron

Connor

Van 2011

Constance Thelma Bisnar
January 14, 1933 - April 2, 1994
61 years

Connie was born in Annapolis Maryland. She was two years old when the family moved to California. She was two years older than me. Her nickname was Boots. I don't why she got that name or what it referred to. She and I were the only brown skin children of the five of kids.

Boots was a quiet soft spoken girl. She always seemed to take a back seat to our sister Dot who was the extravert. You really never knew she was around, but she was always there when anyone in the family needed her. Her younger days and High school years, she was like most of her peers. Not much limelight, but she had plenty of friends and did all the usual things growing up. Once she went to Tijuana Mex. and brought back a puppy for me. He was a small white terry and she named him Tito.

After High School, she went to St. Vince De Paul nursing College in Los Angles. In her senior year she met Jack Ellis and they got married before she graduated. Jack was in the Navy at the time and they lived in San Diego, CA.

My dad and I went to visit her while Jack was out to sea. While we were there, her water broke and she nearly delivered her first born (Dale) in the back seat of my car. It scared the hell out of me. After Jack got out of the Navy he became a salesman. He began selling pots and pans door to door, and also used cars. He went to work for a Big Chevy dealer in Long Beach and did so well he won all kind of sales contests and even did some of their TV commercials.

Boots 1951

Boots and Jack had two more children, David and Danny. They lived in the city of Cypress for a few years and moved to Glendale when Jack got a sales job at Felix Chevrolet in Los Angeles. By this time, he was well under way to becoming a successful and rich Auto dealer. Unfortunately, their marriage didn't last more than twelve or so years. Jack married again a few years later and became the owner of three Auto Dealerships and a much respected man in and around the city of Los Angles. He died at the early age of 60 due to a misdiagnosis while in the hospital for a minor problem.

Boots suffered from Manic Depression which didn't show up until she was in her mid-thirties. She did quite well as long as she took her medications. The problem was when she felt good she wouldn't take the meds and then would go off the deep end. She was hospitalized several times for treatment. Although it was years after their divorce, Jack always paid for all her medical expenses.

Her son Dale is a Doctor and very successful. Her son David owns an Auto Dealership and is also successful. Her son Danny suffers from the same sickness and lives in a home for the medically challenged and is provided for by his brothers. At age sixty one, she became ill with cancer. Her son Dale looked after her in his home until she passed on. Thankfully, she didn't suffer for a long period of time.

She is buried in All Soul's Catholic Cemetery in Long Beach CA. 7 rows back from curb marker 115

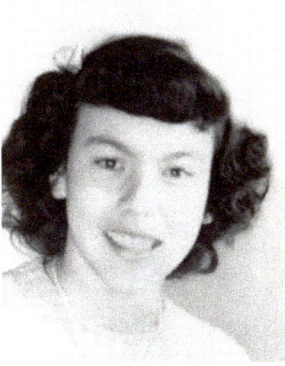

Boots & Dot

Boots & Mom

Boots and Dad

Boosts Prom

Dale Ellis

David Ellis

Danny Ellis

My half Siblings

Evelyn, Elizabeth, and Ferdinand Bisnar

These are my three half siblings. Left to right **Elizabeth, Ferdinand, and Evelyn**. We only knew vaguely of each other's existence and had no information or contact with each other until a miracle happen. (See newspaper article)

Elle, Ferdi, & Evelyn 1963

PEOPLE

Los Altan unites siblings who were strangers

By Michelle Moore

This summer, the Bisnar family reunion in Long Beach will have an unconventional twist when three members meet their California kin for the first time.

For the past 30 years, half-brothers and sisters in California and the Philippines knew vaguely of each other's existence but had no information or contact with each other. Then one day last month Ferdinand Bisnar walked into Citibank in Los Altos to cash a check and walked out with his long-lost half brother's phone number.

The mediator's name is Jo Stone. Currently an employee at Citibank, Stone grew up in Long Beach where she went to grammar school, high school and college with Dorothy Bisnar. After college Dorothy moved to Florida and the two friends lost contact. Over the years Stone tried to reach her on the phone and left messages, but never spoke with Dorothy. She was saddened to hear in 1978 that Dorothy had died of cancer.

Then in January 1993, Ferdinand Bisnar walked into Citibank in Los Altos, where Stone was working as a teller—a job she only does once a week. As a full-time employee at Citibank, her usual duties do not include contact with the public. Her customer Ferdinand Bisnar's name caught her eye, but she dismissed any notion of his being a relation of Dorothy. Ferdinand spoke with a

Dorothy Bisnar

heavy accent and was clearly Filipino.

Stone couldn't resist asking if he had any family in Southern California. Ferdinand exclaimed "yes!" and ran out the door. He returned shortly with a photograph taken in the 1940's of Dorothy Bisnar, her sister and three brothers. "My God, it is your family!" Stone said.

For Stone, it was a surprising revelation; for Ferdinand Bisnar, it was a miracle. She didn't know that Dorothy had half siblings and he didn't think he'd ever meet anyone who knew where to find his brothers and sisters.

After calling a few old friends, she acquired Hank Bisnar's phone number in Long Beach, and Ferdinand called his half brother who wasn't even aware of his existence. Hank knew that after his

Ferdinand Bisnar (third from left) walked into Citibank in Los Altos and walked out with the phone number of relatives he knew of, but had never met. He is pictured here with his sisters Elizabeth and Evelyn, and his new-found half-brother Hank.

parents' divorce, his father, Anatolio, had remarried. Hank received a photo from his father of one-year-old half-sister Elizabeth, but "I wasn't aware the younger two existed."

Hank was surprised and delighted to hear that his half siblings were living in California. A month after speaking with Ferdinand on the phone, Hank flew to San Jose to meet Ferdinand and his sisters, Elizabeth and Evelyn. There they had a festive union as Hank was able to help his half sister celebrate her daughters' birthday.

Dorothy, Hank, Bernie, Connie and George Bisnar grew up in Long Beach where their Filipino father Anatolio served in the U.S. Navy. The youngest of the five children, Hank was 10 years old when his parents divorced in 1945.

The children continued to live with their Caucasian mother in Long Beach. Several years later, Anatolio went to the Philippines on vacation and met and married his second wife there. Together they had three children, all of whom came to the United States before age 21 to claim U.S. citizenship.

Their first stop was Los Angeles. Ferdinand wanted to find his half siblings who his mother had told him about. His father had passed away when he was only six, and even before Anatolio's death, correspondence between father and children in California was limited. Ferdinand had no information to help him in his search, and was unskilled in the English language. Discouraged, he stopped looking.

Ferdinand moved to Daly City

and joined the Army there. After four years, he began working in electronics and eventually took a job as a printer at Harmon Management in Los Altos. He had been in the United States for nine years when he met the woman who connected him with the rest of his family.

Stone was delighted to be a factor in the happy family reunion. She described how emotions ran high when she and Ferdinand made discovery. "He was so emotive, so darling."

One day In January of 1993, upon getting home from work, there was a message on my answering machine. It was from a woman (Jo Stone) who had been my sister Dot's friend through Grammar School, High School and College. She was living in Los Altos, CA and was working in Citibank. She was working as a teller---a job she only does once a week. A young man by the name of Ferdinand walked in the bank to cash his paycheck. His last name caught her eye, but she dismissed any notion of his being a relation to Dot. She couldn't resist asking if he had any family Southern California. Ferdinand said "yes", and ran out the door. He returned shortly with a photograph taken in the 1940's of Dorothy Bisnar, her sister and three brothers. "My God, it is your family!"

Soon after, I called Ferdinand and we made a date to meet. I drove up to San Jose to meet my new siblings. I knew of Elizabeth from letters from my dad, but didn't know anything of Evelyn or Ferdinand. When I arrived, it was also a birthday for one of Elizabeth daughters. They had a big banner with welcome Hank, and a cake. It was really great to meet and talk with them, and our meeting was very festive.

Unfortunately, we didn't keep in touch. Ferdi did move to Long Beach for a short time. He came to the house several times and we were becoming good friends. We even talked about him and me making a trip to the Philippines together. Then suddenly he just disappeared. I tried to contact him by phone and sent Christmas cards, but got no response. I'm going to try to contact them again. I did get an e-mail from one of Evelyn's daughters, and again, when I answered it there was no response.

Hoorah for the Internet! In December of 2009, Sylvia received a forwarded e-mail from my sister Evelyn. She was searching the net for information on me and came across Sylvia's web-site. She sent an e-mail saying she was my sister and was trying to contact me. The e-mail went to Sylvia's web-site manager and she forwarded it to Sylvia. When I saw the message, I immediately e-mailed Evelyn.

From there we exchanged information via e-mail and set a date to meet. Evelyn suggested that they (eight of her family) come to Laughlin, NV for a visit.

On March 21, 2010 Elizabeth, Edgar, Evelyn, Dante, Daisy, Ferdie, Maxie, and Ken came to Laughlin for two days. We spent one whole day together and really enjoyed seeing each other. We went to Havasu to see the London Bridge and to the old mining town of Oatman. We had a nice dinner at the Golden Nugget casino. We talked about going to the Philippines next October. They left the next day to go to the Grand Canyon West and Las Vegas. I'm glad to have made contact with my siblings and their family.

Ferdinand Bisnar
October 21, 1962 -

Ferdinand (Ferdie) is my half-brother from my dad's second wife Maximina. He was born on Oct. 21, 1962 in the town of Inopacan on the Island of Leyte in the Philippines. He has one son named Richard. He was only five years old when our dad died. He came to the US before he was 21 in order to keep his US Citizenship and lives in San Jose CA. He did try to find me when he first got to the US but was unsuccessful. He spent four years in the Army. I did see Ferdi in 2010 when he came to AZ for a visit but have not heard from him since. I send him birthday cards but he doesn't respond.

Note: Ferdie has moved back to the Philippines we keep contact on Facebook.

Ferdi 1993

Ferdi 2012

Richard 2004

Bis, Maxie, & Ferdi

Lt. Bisnar 2012

Jeanette Bisnar 2012

Alexia Joy

Elizabeth Bisnar Nirza

February 7, 1956 -

Elizabeth is my half-sister from my dad's second wife Maximina. She was born on Feb. 7, 1956 in the town of Inopacan on the island of Leyte in the Philippines. She was only twelve years old when our dad died. She has three children by her Husband Edgar Nirza: Edmund, Edgarlito, and Eliza.

She came to the US before she was 21 in order to keep her US Citizenship. She lived in San Jose CA. for many years until she and Edgar retired and returned to the Philippines. I haven't seen her since 2010 but I try to keep in touch on Facebook.

Elle 1993

Elle 2010

Elle 2010

Elle 2012

Elle 2011

Edgar Nirza

Edgarlito Nirza

Edmund Nirza

Eliza Nirza

Evelyn Bisnar Manapsal
July 14, 1960 -

Evelyn is my half-sister from my dad's second wife Maximina. She was born on July 14, 1960 in the town of Inopacan on the island of Leyte in the Philippines. She was only seven years old when our dad died. She has two children by her ex-husband Diospado Manapsal, Debbie and Daisy. She also came to the US before her 21 in order to keep her US citizenship and lives in San Jose CA. The last time I saw her was in March of 2010 when she visited me in Arizona. We keep in touch on Face Book and e-mail.

Note: Evelyn, Debbie and Daisy came to the Family Reunion in May of 2016.

Debbie

Daisy

Maximina Borju Bisnar

Maxie 1966

When my dad returned to the Philippines for a visit in 1954 he met a young girl named Maximina Borju. They were married on December 4, 1954. At 16 years old she was not old enough to get married so they said she was 18 and were married in a Catholic Church in the city of Dulag on the Island of Leyte. Maxie came to visit in March 2010 and we had a very nice visit. She's now married to a man name Ken White. They travel back and forth from the states and the Philippines.

Note: Ken White has passed away 2015.

Maxie 2010

Elle, Ferdi, Hank, Maxie, Evelyn, Dante, & Daisy

Hank & Maxie

Ken White
Maxie's husband

Maxie 2012

Valerie Marie Bisnar

1936-1995
59years

Val was born February 16, 1936 in San Pedro CA.

She was the first born to Art and Valerie Pegg. She had three sisters and one brother. Joanie, Art Jr., Kayse, and Patricia. Her family lived in Alhambra CA. for a few years before finally settling in Long Beach. They lived in the north end of Long Beach in area call Bixby Knowles. She was 14 years old and freshmen at St Anthony's High School. We met sometime near the end of our junior year and became good friends eventually going steady. We had so much fun in high school.

We would go to all the school functions and the activities outside of school. We both like to dance and

were considered one of the best couples on the dance floor. Val was a great sport. She didn't play any sports but was willing to go water skiing, tobogganing, or whatever the group was up to. One of my favorite stories is when she first got her driver's license. I and my buddy Roger were at Val's house and her Mom asked her to go to the store. She asked her Dad if she could use his car. He said yes, and the three of us took off. Upon pulling into the parking lot there was only one other car in the entire parking lot. She pulls into the spot next to the car and sideswiped it. There wasn't much damage but we never let her live it down that with all the open spaces she picks the one next to a car.

After High School, I went to Long Beach City College and Val went to work for an insurance company. We continued our relationship and things were good until her parents thought we were getting too serious and were definitely against her marrying me. They said it was because we were too young but the real reason was they didn't want Val to have a mixed marriage. I confronted her dad on the telephone about him being prejudice, but he denied it and kept to the "too young" story. The funny thing was that Val and I never even talked about getting married. They didn't stop us from dating, but the sad thing was, whenever I picked her up at her house I just waited outside in the car and didn't go to the door the way I should have.

When I decided to go into the Army we agreed that we could see other people and not expect each other to not date and enjoy ourselves. We would wait until I returned from the Army and see where it went from there.

Soon after I left for the Army, Val had a falling out with her parents and moved out to live with one of her girlfriends. She got a job at the Telephone Company. Just before I shipped out for Germany, she and my parents came to Monterey (Fort Ord) to spend the weekend with me. At some point in time she moved in with my parents, but I could tell by her letters she really wanted to move back home. Who could blame her?

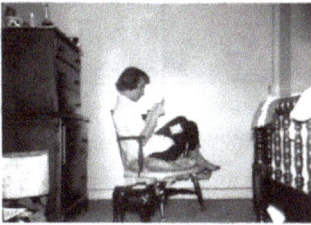

She did eventuality return home. We wrote letters to each other for about a year, but as time went by they were fewer and fewer. She never said she was dating anyone and I never wanted to know. I had a few encounters with women in Germany but it was never any kind of a relationship.

When I got home and out of the Army I didn't contact her for a while because I didn't know if I really want any kind of relationship at that time. About two months after I was home a friend of ours called me said he had seen Val and she wants to see me, but was afraid to call me. We met for dinner and a movie and it was as if we had never been apart.

She soon moved in with another of her friends. Her friend was a girl named Louie who she met at the telephone company, and also just happens to be a girl that lived across the alley from me. I knew her from about age ten or eleven and she was my very first date at age fifteen. We went roller-skating.

I got out of the Army in September '56 and we were engaged in February '57 on her birthday. The wedding date was set for June 1, 1957.

Of course, her parents were still against our marriage so they wanted nothing to do with any of it.

My Mom and sister helped Val with all the details and her wedding dress and all I did was sit back and wait for the big day.

We were married in St Mathew's Catholic Church in Long Beach CA. on June 1, 1957. There were about fifty or sixty relatives and friends at the wedding and the reception which was held at my parent's house. My dad Cy and some of his shipmates spent two or three days preparing all the food and decorations. Sadly, none of Val's family attended the most important day of her young life.

Nine months and twenty four days after our wedding we were blessed with a wonderful baby boy. Brent Anthony Bisnar was born on March 24, 1958 in St Mary's Hospital.

We lived in a single apartment that my parents owned on Alamitos Ave. in Long Beach.

It had a pull-down Murphy bed, a small dressing area, a small bathroom and a very small kitchen. Brent's bassinet fit nicely in the dressing area. We lived there until Brent was about three months old.

There's nothing like a grandchild to change attitudes. One week after Brent was born, Val's Mom came to see the baby. I was at work so I didn't have to deal with seeing her. Val said her dad wanted to visit but wanted to make sure I was ok with it. I really didn't care if I ever saw either one of her parents again, but I knew it was very important to Val to have her family back in her life. I wasn't hateful, but I wasn't real friendly either. We got along find and eventually time healed my pride.

From Alamitos we moved to a duplex on Market St. in North Long Beach. Our second son Andy was born just fourteen months after Brent on May 19, 1959. When Brent was about three years old, we wanted to move into a house.

We found a nice three bedroom house in Lakewood, but I couldn't qualify for a Cal-Vet loan. I was working two jobs (the telephone Co. and Barbering nights and weekends) but they wouldn't allow my part time barbering job as regular income.

I always thought Val's parents felt guilty about not being a part of our wedding but I never said anything. I also think that's why they stepped up to help us buy our first home. Val's dad bought the house in Lakewood for 15,000 and then sold it to us for $12,500 so I could qualify for the Cal-Vet loan. He said he didn't want us to pay him the $2,500, but I did a few years later.

The house in Lakewood was just right for us. The neighbors were great and the kids had friends and plenty to keep them busy. On July 9, 1967 we blessed with our daughter Jacqueline.

We were a typical middle class family. We didn't have a lot of extra money so our entertainment was visiting with family and friends and drive-movies. We would take two cars to the drive-in. Val would drive our ford station-wagon with Jacki and one of the boys and I would drive our VW with the other boy. We would put the two boys in the VW with a big bag of popcorn and drinks, and Val, Jacki and I would be in the other car.

We didn't take many vacations because our idea of traveling was so different. Val liked to shop and gamble, and go from A to B as fast as she could. I liked camping and driving to places unknown and taking photos. As the boys grew up and played sports that became our family focus.

When the boys were playing sports at the park I coached their teams, but Val didn't attend the games because Jacki was too small to take to the games. When they got to little league age she became a regular baseball Mom. When I coached Pony League she not only learned to keep score, but was the equipment manager for the Pony and Colt League. She and her buddy Fran would make poor-boy sandwiches to make money for the high school baseball team. They made enough to buy and customize a motor scooter to drag the diamond and carry the equipment.

In 1977 we moved to Lakewood Village. The house was a little bigger with a huge back yard and swimming pool.

After Andy finished playing college baseball, our common interest was gone. I became deeply involved in my photography and Val became a Bingo addict. I wanted very much for her to become part of my camera club. Even though there were a lot of social activities within the club, she wanted nothing to do with it. She wouldn't even go to a club party. She said she didn't want to stand around and watch a bunch of people take pictures. And I wasn't a bit interested in Bingo.

Maybe "Bingo addict' is an overstatement, but she would go the Bingo Parlor four or five nights a week. She went to school to become a Medical Assistant and took a job at a doctor's office in North Long Beach. As far as I know, she spent all her money and some of ours playing Bingo.

One day in August of 1993, Val said she wanted to show me something. She took me into our bedroom and showed me a mole on her right hip. She had this mole since birth.

It was the size of a quarter and had always been flat. It was still flat but it was loose and had some fluid around it. She knew it was serious but put off telling me or going to the doctor because her dad was having health problems and she was more concerned about him than herself. When she did go to the doctor, he took a biopsy and made an appointment with an oncologist at the UCLA Medical Hospital. The oncologist confirmed she had a malignant melanoma tumor on her hip and had to be removed immediately. I can remember telling her early on to keep an eye on that mole or maybe even have it remove. I wish I had insisted.

It was a long and difficult surgery and when it was over the doctor came to talk to me. He said he was sure he got all of the tumor but the wound was so large and deep that he couldn't close it with normal procedures. He said she wouldn't have to hospitalize if there was someone who could change her dressing three times a day for the next two months. Her wound would have to heal from the inside out. I informed him that I was retired and that changing her dressings was not a problem. He took me to her room and instructed the nurses to train me on how to change her dressings.

Changing the dressings was not that bad, but just seeing the size of the wound was hard. At the beginning it was raw and inflamed and deep enough to hold a baseball. After about six weeks it was completely healed and was just a small indentation on her hip.

162

Val recovered without any complications other than her former employer would not give her job back. She actually sued him for age discrimination and got a $4,000 settlement.

On her one year checkup, the doctor found some small white spots on the site of her surgery. A biopsy showed that the cancer had returned. Because they had removed so much of her hip the first time another surgery was not an option. She struggled with chemotherapy, radiation and interferon treatments for months but God took her from us on September 5, 1995.

Ours was a good marriage that lasted for 38 years. It was not perfect by any means as we had our problems as do all marriages, but we raised three wonderful children and established family traditions that our children will carry on in the future.

Valerie Marie Bisnar
All Souls Cemetery Long Beach CA.
Curb marker 100
Sixteen rows back

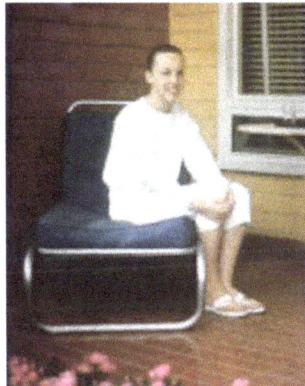

Sylvia Alice Villarreal
February 14, 1935

Sylvia was born in San Antonio Texas on February 14, 1935. She is the third child to Rudy and Hortense Villarreal. The oldest (a boy) died as an infant. Her sister Lydia passed in 2006 and her brother René lives in San Antonio.

I first met Sylvia on a photography field trip to Joshua Tree National Park in 1983. We were both students of the same instructor but in different classes. The classes ended on another field trip to Yosemite National Park. Sylvia and her friend Betty wanted to continue as a group so they took names and said they were going to start a Photo Club.

A few months later I signed up for another class and guess who was in the class. Sylvia and Betty. I asked what happen to the Photo Club and they said they never did anything about it. I offered to have a meeting at my house if they wanted to contact the list of people. Fifteen or twenty showed up for the meeting and that was the beginning of the F-Stop Camera Club. It's been Thirty Three years and the club is still active with twenty five members of which eight or ten are original members.

In 1997 Sylvia and I began dating. My wife Val had passed away in 1995 and I was very comfortable with someone I'd known for fourteen years. After a few months, I asked her to move in with me and she accepted. I told her she could keep working as a legal transcriber or retire. It was a split second decision. She retired and who could blame her.

In September of 1997 nine members of the F-Stops took a nine week photography safari in Africa. It took me a year of planning to find a travel agent and select our route. Sylvia and I had talked about getting married but not in any detail. I asked her if she wanted to get married on the Safari if I could arrange it. Answer, yes!!!

We were married on September 28, 1997 in the county of Tanzania on the island of Zanzibar. We hadn't told any of our friends of our plan to marry. They were very excited and happy for us. Harold was the best man and Betty the maid of honor. Our family members were really surprised when they received post cards signed Hank and Sylvia Bisnar.

The entire story of the safari is told in Sylvia's journal "F-Stops Make Tracks in Africa".

F-STOPS MAKE TRACKS IN AFRICA

By Sylvia Villarreal Bisnar

Introduction

My first trip to Africa. I was so excited and I could hardly wait. Hank Bisnar, my future husband, myself, and seven of our closest friends, all members The F-Stops, our camera club from Long Beach, CA, had been planning this trip for over a year.

Hank Bisnar, the organizer of the trip, is a retired manager for our local telephone company, GTE, and one of the founders of the F-Stops. He and I recently became engaged and this would be our first trip together as a couple.

Harold Basler, married, a retired Long Beach City Firefighter and the youngest of our group by at least 10 years. I knew he would be good to have along because he saved my life once while on a trip to Mexico.

Betty, my good friend, roommate, and traveling companion, that is until Hank and I became more than just friends. She, Hank & I started the camera club in 1883 after a camera class trip to Yosemite Valley.

Ernie Nelson, the most senior of the group, and one of the nicest and smartest guys you would ever want to meet. He is a retired government worker and just a delight to be around. He is quiet, kind, polite and always helpful. He is an expert on birding and has a memory like the New York Times.

Dick and Iris Schutz have been married forever and are wonderful to be around. Both Iris and Dick have PhDs in their respective fields. Iris takes photos with her camera and Dick is good with his video camera.

Dick and Jan Sherman came into the Camera Club well after it was organized. They have been married since their college days. They work together putting on slide shows and love animal and bird life. Notice how many pictures Dick is in wearing a gold shirt.

And of course then there's me Sylvia, divorced, the mother of five, instigator, rabble-rouser, whatever – I've been called it all. I picked up the hobby of photography after moving to Seal Beach, CA from Central California, took some photo classes, met Betty and Hank and rest is history.

All of us live in the environs of Long Beach, CA, except for Dick and Jan Sherman who live in Mission Viejo, CA. We have traveled together on various trips for about 17 years. But none of the trips have been nearly as ambitious or as long as this one.

We had several meetings before we left to discuss the itinerary, tour companies for the African safari and Egypt tour, shots needed, visas, clothes we would take, medications needed in the event of sickness or emergency, airlines, travel insurance, sleeping bags, flashlights, bug repellant, etc. Hank worked for months planning the necessary details of a trip like this and making all reservations. He made several checklists to share with everyone. I was amazed how much preparation is needed for a complicated nine-week trip involving nine people, and how careful Hank was to make sure that nothing was missed.

We soon discovered there are several different ways to "see Africa," depending on how much time and money you want to spend.

Top drawer: you can rent a Land rover, with or without a guide/driver, and tour on your own. Quite a few people travel in Africa this way, and Hank and I want to do this on our next trip.

Next: you can fly by small plane or helicopter from site to site once you arrive in Africa and stay in deluxe lodgings with all the amenities of a first-class hotel, even though you stay in a tent and the roof is made of canvas in the most remote location. For these accommodations you pay megabucks.

A step or two down: you can bus-tour and stay in "permanent tent" lodgings with inside toilets.

We chose the "economy" level: An "Overlander" Truck Tour, where we helped cook, clean and pitched our own tents, riding only with one driver-guide and one cook.

There are several companies who offer this. They tend to follow standard routes because that's where the scenic sights and the campsites are located.

There are cost differences depending largely on the quality of the equipment, food, staff, etc. You get what you pay for. We went low end, so we ended up really roughing it. As you might imagine, most travelers you see on this type of tour are 20ist-30ish folks. We were all 60ish and quite an oddity for this type of trip. In fact, I should mention here that when Hank was making our reservations for the Safari, Tracks International was the only overland company who would take us. All the other overland companies turned us down because they felt we were too old and feared they would have trouble with us on the trip. Later, Destin would say that it was better with us because we always went to bed early and were ready to go the next day. And, it was his first tour where he didn't have to carry some drunk out of a bar.

Finally, the itinerary was set, reservations made, everyone had their shots, packed their bags and camera equipment and were "ready to go." The photo stuff equaled about the same as the other stuff in both size and weight. We were going to visit seven African Countries: Zimbabwe, Botswana, Zambia, Malawi, Tanzania, Kenya, and Egypt. Our Six-week safari in southeast Africa would be with Tracks International. Imaginative Traveler would be our tour company for the 10-day Egypt & Nile Tour.

By the end of the trip, we would travel over 3,300 miles with Tracks International and Imaginative Traveler, in approximately five different accommodations (tents, "under the stars," hotels, trains, and boat), see more than 22 different wild animal species, over 34 different varieties of birds, and ride 19 different transportation modes (airplane, train, cruise ship, local bus, motor coach, overland truck, land rover, metro rail, carriage, Felucca, motor launch, donkey, dinner cruise ship, booze cruise boat, ferry, motor scooter, taxi, helicopter and mokoro, a handmade dugout. Seven of our party got sick, three received minor injuries; three had to go to the hospital in Cairo, one to a clinic in Zanzibar, and two got married. I was the only one who did not get sick, have an accident or lose weight.

When I think of Africa, I think of smiling children, bright colors and burning grass. I fell head over boot heals in love with Africa. I long to go back. It's funny I say that because for years I had no desire to go to Africa. I used to say, "If I want to see animals, I'll go to the zoo." But I started to get enthused as our planning progressed. Seeing pictures Betty and Harold had taken on earlier trips helped too. At this point I wanted to see and photograph the cultures and the people; Hank wanted to see and photograph the wildlife and the scenery. Africa exceeded our expectations.

I think Africa is going to exceed everyone's expectations in the future. Like most Americans, I knew it only as a "Dark Continent – the Land of the Poor and the Home of the Slaves." Nothing could be farther from the truth. The life we saw is less complex or so it appeared to me, but it was no less varied or vibrant. I expected to see a lot of ill-clad, ill-fed and unhappy people. Not so. Many of the people we saw were always smiling and happy. You see many more unhappy poor people in large and wealthy cities all over the World than we ever saw in Africa. Of course, we saw only parts of southeast Africa, and we did get "lost" enough times to drive around on the unbeaten path. I'll bet on Africa's future. It's likely where humanity started in the far, far distant past, it may just be the direction humanity goes in the far, far distant future.

We hauled a lot of luggage. Between Hank and I we had one camcorder, four cameras, and over 250 rolls of film. In addition, we packed enough clothes to last for two weeks, sleeping bags, several books, a Walkman and tapes, flashlights, ballpoint pens and candy to give to the children, my journal, medicines, and toiletries. You name it, we had it – or so we thought. As Hank likes to say, "It's better to have it and not need it than need it and not have it."

Tuesday, August 26, 1997
Long Beach, California

We awoke very early the first day and were ready and waiting for the airport shuttle two hours ahead of time. Hank and I have been so excited about this trip we haven't had a decent night's sleep in over a week. We started laying out "stuff" on the dining room table weeks ahead before the trip for fear we would forget something. My bags had been packed for two weeks, Hank's for one.

The shuttle arrived at 11 am sharp. We then went to pick up the others. By 1 pm, we had obtained our boarding passes at the KLM desk and checked in our luggage. We went to the gate and waited another two and one-half hours. We had a hard time relaxing, everyone talked the whole time. Finally we boarded at 3:30 pm and the plane started taxing to the runway at 4:45 pm. After settling in, I noticed a monitor on the wall in front of the seats which showed a map with a small airplane indicating our route, our current location in flight, and other statistics on altitude, speed, etc. Our route would take us north over Wyoming, Minnesota, Canada, and the North Atlantic Ocean to Amsterdam, where we would stay for one night. We would travel 5,574 miles in 9 hours 54 minutes. Our estimated time of arrival in Amsterdam was 11:43 am the following morning.

The flight was smooth and I read when there was nothing to see from the air.

At one point I was able to recognize Jackson Hole, Wyoming, and the Snake River. We had traveled there the year before, so it was easy for me to recognize. The river is as beautiful from the air as from the ground. Winding in all different directions, the river lives up to its name. I looked for the Grand Tetons, but unfortunately they were on the other side of the airplane.

Wednesday, August 27, 1997

Amsterdam

We arrived in Amsterdam around noon. Rounding up nine independent-thinking people, with our 36 pieces of luggage, in the form of duffle bags, backpacks and camera bags, and then getting agreement on what direction to head next is quite a trick. We decided to find lockers so that we could store most of our luggage while in Amsterdam for the one-night layover. We finally found the lockers, repacked our smaller bags, confirmed our flight to Harare, Zimbabwe, the following day, asked for information and headed outside to find some sort of transportation to our hotel. We boarded a large blue bus to a hotel within one block of the RHO Hotel where we had reservations.

We thought the night in Amsterdam would help us avoid jet lag. Boy was I wrong!! The Amsterdam-Harare flight was another 10 hours, and we didn't want to fly for over 20 continuous hours. The idea was to get some rest, but it was not to be; we were too wound up. We checked into the hotel and found the rooms to be clean and comfortable. But there was no air conditioning and the outside temperature was around 80° F with high humidity. Hank put the fan in an open window to get some much-needed fresh air.

We met in the lobby a few minutes after unloading our baggage. With cameras in hand, we set out to see Amsterdam. We found the city to be very picturesque with lots of colorful flags and signs flying on the old buildings

– and, of course, the famous canals. I was struck by how crowded the streets and sidewalks were with people who all seemed to be in a big hurry. There were fewer cars on the streets than in the US. People of all ages ride bicycles. They ride just as fast as they can, and at intersections, rush in front of cars, taking their lives in their hands. Since pedestrians don't have the right-of-way, we had to be extremely careful crossing the streets.

I noted that most of the bicycles were painted black and had big wheels and wide handlebars. Occasionally we'd see a brightly colored one which really stood out. There were bikes everywhere. We often saw men in suits with briefcases lashed to the bike. Women in short, short skirts rode bicycles. I noticed with envy that all women have long, strong beautiful legs. I saw men and women riding their children on their bicycles either in front or behind them, and twice I saw two children on one bicycle with the parent; one in front the other in back. Hundreds of bikes would park together. I don't know how they recognized their own when they came to retrieve it.

We walked along the streets to the Central Train Station. On the way we came across several mimes and stopped to watch them for a bit. The train station is a huge structure -- impressive and busy. We decided to have dinner there. It was a good choice. The food was tasty and reasonably priced. I don't recall how much we paid, but it was less than we would pay for the equivalent in the US. We remarked that we saw very few old people on the streets. We noticed that cigarette smoking is much more common than in California -- both on the street and in the restaurant (Ugh!). Do you suppose that's why we saw so few oldsters? Probably not, but could be a reason in the future.

Thursday, August 28, 1997
Amsterdam

The following morning after regrouping and having breakfast at the hotel, we headed toward the main canal to take a boat cruise. The canals are beautiful and interesting at the same time. On each side of the streets, above the canals, the buildings are all old. On the canals, there are many

picturesque and colorful houseboats, some with lawn chairs and small gardens. As there is a housing shortage, some people live in houses built on barges. Many of them are covered with colorful plants on deck.

After the hour-long boat tour, we began walking aimlessly through the streets looking at the sights. It was rainy and we got caught in a few showers. Dick Sherman started complaining that he does not like to walk around without a plan. Well, he ended up getting the "Grinch of the Day Award." His unique "trophy" was a pigeon dropping on his shirtsleeve. Oh, My! One of the guys -- I don't recall which one -- said he had it coming for complaining so much. Dick is a good sport and soon started laughing too. He also quit complaining. "Thank you, Mr. Pigeon."

Continuing our walk, we came across a sidewalk café and decided to have lunch. The waitress was very personable and recommended the meat ball sandwiches. Most of us decided to order that with a beer. The waitress was right; the sandwiches were excellent and the beer was cold which quenched our thirst.

After lunch, we continued to wander around old Amsterdam along the canals. Someone suggested we go to the RJS Museum. Since Harold and I are not big on museums, we chose to go to the museum coffee shop while the rest of the group

toured the museum. They reported that it held an impressive collection. Harold and I took their word for it.

After leaving the museum, we rushed back to the hotel, picked up our gear and were at the airport by 6:00 pm to catch the KLM flight to Harare. We made it to the airport with time to spare before take-off, collected our other luggage from the lockers and proceeded to check-in.

At the check-in counter, we were told we could only carry on one piece of luggage. Women were allowed a purse also. Betty was able to consolidate her camera equipment into her backpack, but Hank and I couldn't do that, and we were not willing to check-in our cameras and film or our backpacks. After walking away from the counter, we devised a plan and by being "sneaky" were able to get our two "extra" bags aboard the plane. Here is what we did: While waiting in line, we noticed a woman putting stickers on one bag per person, plus a woman's purse. I put my purse into my backpack and got back in line. That way I could count my backpack as my purse. When I got to the counter they searched my backpack and my camera bag. When I was finished, Hank left his camera bag with me and got in line to get a sticker for his backpack. But we still needed a sticker for his camera bag. Well, I left my camera bag with Hank, took my purse out of my backpack and went back to the lady and told her that she failed to give me a sticker for my purse. I then transferred that sticker to Hank's camera bag and we were all set. There is more than one way to "skin a cat." What a hassle!

We then encountered another problem: Even though we had confirmed our flights and seats assignments the day before, KLM consolidated two flights and gave away the Sherman's and the Schutz's seats, putting them on Stand-by. The KLM customer representative had lousy planeside manners. He started by saying, "KLM takes full responsibility." Well, that sounded good, but it was the last thing he said that did not sound so good. He would have to route all four people – the only four who were bumped – to London and then on to Johannesburg. When Dick Schutz explained that they had a safari leaving from Harare the next day, the man's response was: "Well, you'll miss it." What a Jerk! We were all pretty upset but what can you do in a situation like that.

The rest of us boarded the plane and found our seats. When we finally saw the Sherman's and the Schutz's coming down the aisle, we broke out in loud cheers. KLM is a fine airline, but one person can ruin a good reputation in a hurry and many times screw up someone's travel plans.

The flight to Harare was pleasant and uneventful taking every bit of the scheduled ten hours. I read on the plane and tried to sleep, but couldn't sleep a wink because I was so excited to set my feet on African soil. Finally, the pilot announced that we would be landing in Johannesburg, South Africa, shortly, our only stop before proceeding to Harare. I got so excited then and could not stop looking out the window to see if I could see any wild animals. Our stopover was for an hour and a half, and then we were on our way. Would we ever get there? I was beside myself waiting to get there to see some wild elephants, giraffes and zebras.

Friday, August 29, 1997
Harare, Zimbabwe, Africa

At last, we landed at the small airport in Harare. I was finally on African soil!! I couldn't believe it. However, there were no elephants or zebras waiting for me. The weather was warm but not unpleasant. We made our way to find our luggage, only to find total chaos. The entire luggage from the plane was dumped into a pile on the ground and we had to "hunt" for it. With porters trying to help passengers, passengers trying to find their luggage and arrange for transportation, and everyone speaking in a different language, it was maddening and confusing. Even though, it was very exciting. Harold, bless his heart, came to our rescue. He arranged for three porters and a minibus to take our entire luggage to the hotel where we had reservations. All we had to do was find our own luggage and make sure we didn't forget anything. This was a tough job because of the confusion and the large amount of luggage we had. We went through the security gate, and I got my first Africa stamp on my passport. What a treasure!

Hank had reconfirmed the reservations at the Selous Hotel just before leaving the States through the touring agency, Himalaya Travel. We had booked five rooms and were scheduled to meet with our tour guide the following day for a briefing. The African Safari was scheduled to leave the day after. Well, wouldn't you know it, after our luggage, all 36-plus pieces, was deposited in the lobby of the hotel, we were informed by the very nice clerk that they did not have reservations for any of us and there were no available rooms? WOW! We were nine people in a foreign country with no place to stay. What would we do now? Poor Hank, he had worked so hard and had confirmed and reconfirmed everything. Thankfully, as is his nature, he stayed calm asking the hotel clerk for recommendations.

The hotel clerk, bless her heart, called around and found accommodations at another hotel only a few blocks away and even called for taxis. We put all 36 pieces of luggage into two taxis and walked the two blocks to the Courtenay Hotel, laughing all the way and joking about the situation.

As it turned out, the Courtenay was a much better hotel than the Selous. It even had a swimming pool. The lobby was large and clean and it was funny to see our luggage taking up half of it. The doormen were extremely attentive and helpful, smiling all the time, in their black pants, maroon jackets, white shirts and black bow ties. We checked into the hotel and found our rooms to be very comfortable. Some of the group went for a walk around town to take some photos. Hank went downstairs to use the fax to contact Tracks International and reconfirm the rest of our hotel reservations. I was so tired; all I wanted to do was sleep. Jet Lag had set in already. Bummer!

When Hank returned to our room, I got up from my short nap, and we went for a walk into town with Betty. Harare is the capital and heart of the country of Zimbabwe, population one million. The typical large African city had wide streets and many tall, square buildings. I was surprised to see a Sheraton on the main street. Everything seemed up-to-date in Harare. The people in general were much more dressed up than we were --women in nice-looking conservative dresses and men in conservative business suits – like San Francisco a generation or two ago.

Since it was recommended in the guidebook, we decided to have dinner in the hotel dining room, "Le Escargot," that night. It was a nice Continental restaurant. They had a dress code, so we ladies put on our skirts and the men long pants with their nice shirts. Looking around, we saw that we were the only White people in the restaurant. We ordered bottles of wine and looked over the menu. I can't remember what I ordered, but it was exceptionally tasty and the service excellent. Of course, with all the laughing and joking that went on at our table we attracted a lot of attention from the other patrons as well as the staff. We stood out from the rest of the diners in more ways than one. Wherever we go we always have a good time. Our leisurely dinner finally finished about two hours later. We decided to eat at this same restaurant the following evening because the food and service were outstanding

HARARE
SUNSHINE CITY

The attractive and modern city of Harare was founded in 1890 by the Pioneer Column of Cecil Rhodes. Since independence in 1980 Harare has continued to grow with a wide variety of interesting architecture

An altitude of 1500 metres results in a very pleasant climate. You can expect hot and dry weather in September and October, cool or cold and dry weather between May and August and warm and wet weather in November to April. Flowering trees with vivid colours line many streets at different times of the year. The Jacarandas in September and Flamboyants in October are particularly spectacular.

Harare has a wide variety of shopping centres and craft markets. Shona sculpture is for sale in galleries all over the city. Agricultural processing, engineering, chemicals and tobacco sales are some of the most important industries.

Harare is the major centre for tourism for Zimbabwe and visitors can organise most tours from here. However, bookings for tours and accommodation should preferably be done in good time before arriving in Zimbabwe.

Saturday, August 30, 1997
Harare, Zimbabwe, Africa

Breakfast was in a different dining room downstairs and we ate together. I had cereal, eggs, sausage, juice and coffee. We were given a choice of three different kinds of cereal which were flavorful but different from what we have at home. I particularly liked the coffee – strong, black and flavorful.

Harold took charge of the day and negotiated with a taxi driver to hire two additional taxis to take us to the Cheetah and Lion Park and to other sights in Harare depending on the amount of time we had. We were thrilled as we were all anxious to see animals even if it was in a game park. We divided into the three taxis and were soon on our way.

The Cheetah and Lion Park has been a privately owned park since 1968. It was opened to care for orphaned and injured animals rescued from the wild. We were driven through the park, stopping to take photos, and were able to see lions, leopards, cheetah, elephants, zebras, and various other animals "up close and personal." Our African Photo Safari had begun!

From here, the drivers took us to Chivero Recreational Park. The Lake is a large reservoir on the Manyame River and is a popular weekend spot for Harare residents. It has nice picnic sites, lawns and boat rentals. We walked around and took pictures until it was time to go back to Harare for lunch. In town, we found a Wimpy's and ordered hamburgers and fries. We couldn't find a McDonald's, but Wimpy's was close enough.

We walked over to a Woolworth's store, not because we were familiar with the name, but because I needed to buy postcard stamps and a small notebook to take field notes. Because I am always buying souvenirs, I couldn't resist buying a small stone carving from a street vender on the way. Everyone gave me a hard time about being such a "sucker."

While at Woolworth, I was carrying my backpack on my back as usual when a gentleman came up to me and said that I should always carry the backpack in front because thieves will come by with knives, cut the straps and run off with your belongings. I appreciated the advice. Lesson learned.

We decided that we would go to the National Gallery of Zimbabwe. It has an excellent display of modern paintings and African artifacts, including masks and carvings. Baskets, arts and crafts are sold in the lobby. The garden setting is beautiful and there is a large impressive metal sculpture of a rhinoceros in front. As we were leaving the grounds, I started talking to a young African couple and their friend who were on vacation from South Africa.

They were taking photos of each other, and I volunteered to photograph them with their camera. They were nicely dressed and sweet. We chatted a while and when he learned I spoke Spanish, we started speaking Spanish. He said he had spent some time in South America. He asked if he could take a photo of me with him and also asked for my address. I never thought I would hear from him, but when we got home in October, there was a letter waiting for me! I was later told that they like to know someone in the States who can help them immigrate. Another lesson learned.

Back at the hotel, I took a nap and slept soundly until about 5 p.m. Jet lag, boy, was I tired. Harold, Dick Sherman and Hank started "ragging" on me about sleeping so much. They are always teasing me about something.

We were scheduled to meet the tour guide from Tracks International at the Selous Hotel at 6 pm. When we came downstairs, we saw this "big pink truck" parked across the street, which we recognized from the brochure. We walked over to say "Hello" and introduce ourselves.

The truck which would be our "home-away-from-home" for the next six weeks was a tractor-trailer type Mercedes, approximately 45 ft. long and 10 ft. wide, painted a bright pink. It had black paw tracks and the word "Tracks" in big black letters on the side. It was quite a sight and attracted a lot of attention during our Safari. The trailer was large enough to accommodate 20 passengers including luggage. There were bench seats on both sides, with a

walkway down the middle. Both sides of the truck had canvas coverings which could be lowered or raised as needed. Of course, we kept the sides up most of the time unless it was raining or too windy.

The last 10-12 ft. of the trailer had a caged-in luggage area with a gate that locked. In there, we stored our luggage, camera bags, sleeping bags, foam rubber mats, and tents. The driver and cook rode in the roomy cab up front.

 Waiting in the back of the truck were, Destin, our 28-year-old driver-guide, who hails from Canada, along with our cook, Willie, who hails from Tanzania and speaks little or no English. He just smiles a lot, and when asked a question, always answers "Okay" whether he understands or not and "For sure," whether it's likely to happen or not. Destin turned out to be the authentic "MacGyver." It's a good thing too because the truck broke down several times and he was always able to do the impossible to fix it, using rubber hoses, nylon stockings or whatever.

We climbed aboard the truck, sat down, and had our pre-trip briefing right then and there. I had to laugh when Dick Sherman said that he was so excited about starting the trip he felt like he wanted to sleep in the truck that night. Although the truck usually handles 20 passengers, Destin told us we would be the only people aboard. "Hooray," everyone shouted. We would now be able to move around and have room for all of our "stuff" – which equaled that of the usual twenty passengers. Having the truck to ourselves ended up being a blessing. We spent so much time in the truck that I think we would have "killed" each other by the end of the trip had we been crowded. Also, because we were the only ones doing the tour, we had much more flexibility as to our route and where and when we wanted to stop.

Destin briefed us as to what to expect, and what he expected from us. We were expected to pitch our own tents and help with the cooking and cleaning up. Destin wanted us to learn how to shop in the local markets for food. Everyone agreed as we were eager to do whatever was necessary. It was going to be a thrilling adventure.

Destin said he was late arriving in Harare because he had been arrested and thrown in jail in Tanzania the week before and had just been released. He explained that while staying at a friend's house, he inadvertently let their dog out of the yard. Well, a Black neighbor called the police and said that the dog had "eaten her child." So, the police came and arrested Destin. Of course, after investigation, they found the child was indeed "alive and well," playing down the street. But Destin was still held in custody until the Canadian Consulate intervened. Destin also had to pay a non-incidental amount to the jail officials. Destin said that in Black Africa, the White man is put in jail first and questioned later. We were introduced to what it is like to be White in Black Africa and would witness this for ourselves later during the trip.

At 7 pm, we went to have dinner again at "Le Escargot." Dustin declined our invitation to join us saying he had business to attend to. The food was again delicious and we had a great time, talking all at once about our upcoming Safari. We were in bed by 9:30 pm anxious to start the following day.

Sunday, August 31, 1997
Zimbabwe, Africa

We awoke early, had breakfast at the hotel and after checking out, loaded our luggage into the truck. We were all excited and animated, everyone talking over each other. Hank and I found seats in the back of the truck and kept those seats for the duration of the trip. We each had our cameras at the ready and our own window seat. We headed south, and were finally on our way.

Because the trailer was open, we got a lot of breeze (to put it mildly), but were able to take unobstructed photos. There was a buzzer behind the cab which we were instructed how to use. One buzz, the driver stops for photos; two buzzes, the driver stops for potty breaks; and three buzzes means STOP NOW. Riding in the truck was kind of like riding on a rough road in a jeep. However, it was the roads, not necessarily the truck. By and large, African highways are good although they are deteriorating for lack of maintenance. The farther north we got the rougher the road.

Our first "potty stop" was by the side of the road in the "bush. It was obvious that this spot had been used frequently.

We absorbed the sights as we drove down the highway, and took many photos from the moving vehicle. Dick Sherman didn't take many photos from the truck because he thought with the movement of the truck; the photos would come out blurred. Well, when he got home he was sorry because our photos came out pretty good.

There were hoards of people at bus stops. Many were carrying luggage or boxes. Their homes are round huts built of brick or mud with round cone-shaped roofs made of straw. They were arranged in a circle or group. I was impressed at how clean the yards were. The dirt looked swept. Through an open door of the huts I could see empty rooms with people sitting on the dirt floor. As I learned later, these were sleeping houses as they cook outside. Men and boys carry sticks while tending cattle and goats. We saw several baboons on that first day.

Our first campsite was the campgrounds at the Great Zimbabwe Ruins. The mysterious ruins are remnants of a stone city and it is believe that it was last inhabited in the 13th and 15th centuries. As of present day, archaeologists are baffled as to who lived here and why they left.

This nice campground has showers and bathrooms. There were many gray monkeys in the trees around the campsite and we were told to watch our food and gear as they like to come in like a bolt of lightning, and before you realize what has happened, they are carrying off your camera, purse, lunch or whatever. They have learned to be on the alert for any opportunity.

We arrived about 1 pm, and while Willie fixed our lunch, we learned how to set up our tents. They are blue two-man canvas tents and not hard to set up for two people if the ground is not too hard to hammer in the stakes. There were only two hammers and when we were ready to use one, we had to go around looking to borrow one. Since Betty was alone in her tent, she had to put up her tent alone. Harold, Ernie, Hank and the other guys helped her at first, but then she got to where she didn't need any help at all. Betty has always been quite independent and resourceful. We had 3 inch foam rubber mats to put under our sleeping bags. What a blessing. Since there were enough for 20 people, we were able to use two apiece. It was so much better than sleeping on the hard ground. After a few days, we all were able to set up our tents in no time at all. Destin and Willie slept in the truck every night for security reasons.

For lunch Willie fixed us tuna sandwiches and carrot and cabbage salad. After cleaning up, we started up the hill to the Ruins with cameras in hand. The climb was quite steep, and after a little more than half way, Betty and I decided to come back to the truck. We talked to Destin for a while and then I took another nap. Jet lag? The rest of the day was spent relaxing.

Harold was always the first one to pitch in to help Willie with the cooking. The rest of us helped too, but we were not the first. Willie always made sure that we washed our hands with antiseptic soap before touching any of the food or utensils. I noticed that he always washed the vegetables before cooking them. For dinner that night, we had tomato soup with ginger, fried chicken, white rice and carrot sauce. We soon learned, because we had soup every day, that Willie flavored his soups with lots of ginger and pepper. Once Hank counted how many shakes of pepper Willie used in the soup and told us that he had counted 22. I got to where I would say to him: "Not so much pepper, Willie." And, Harold or Hank would say: "More pepper, Willie." It got to be a joke. Willie's response was always "Okay" and continued to do it his way.

Every night after dinner while most of us sat around the fire talking, Harold took it upon himself to boil water in the teapot to fill the water jugs with sterilized water. He never said a word, just took charge. We always had purified water to drink on the trip when we ran out of bottled water. It was quite a thoughtful gesture on Harold's part and I didn't realized how much we appreciate it until later.

Monday, September 1, 1997
Bulawayo, Zimbabwe

Since nature called before dawn, I was up as soon as it was light enough to find the outhouse. We've been on our trip for a whole week; can't believe it.

After breakfast of cereal, sausage and bread, we left camp and started toward Bulawayo.

Driving toward Bulawayo, the wind was strong and cold early in the morning, and we were glad that we had windbreakers to wear. As we drove along, children would run out to wave at us. When we stopped, they asked for sweets or ballpoint pens or tried to sell us fruit or trinkets. I never tired of looking at the children and taking photos of them; they have such beautiful faces. I was having the time of my life.

We arrived at Bulawayo Camp around noon, had lunch of rice salad and corned beef sandwiches. We laughed because what we would not normally eat at home really tasted good in the Bush.

The city of Bulawayo, formerly called Gu-Bulawayo or the Killing Place is Zimbabwe's second largest city. It is a large, clean looking city and the former stronghold of the Metabele people. There are lovely old colonial buildings along the streets with large houses built behind stone fences. It is more laid-back than Harare security-wise, but we were still warned to be careful when we walk into town and to be sure to stay together as a group. With its one and two-story buildings, it reminded me of anywhere in the U.S during the 1950s.

We walked together into town to look around and find a bank. The walk was only a few blocks long but the weather was hot and humid, so we walked slowly. Dick and Harold, who are in better physical shape than some of the rest of us, kept getting ahead. After several false turns, we found the bank.

Hank and I found that we had to go to a department store to buy stamps for our postcards. Each postcard required three large stamps: two $2.00 stamps and one 20 cent stamp. We got a kick out of the large size of the stamps, which left us almost no writing space. While paying for the stamps we saw the newspaper on the counter with the headline that Princess Diana had died in a car accident on August 31st. What a great loss to the World. Of course, we missed all of the television reports going on in the States.

Back at camp, I again chose to take a nap because I still had jet lag. The rest of the group went to the Natural History Museum and had a great time. After they returned and told me about it I was sorry that I hadn't gone. It is one of Africa's finest natural history museums and has extensive cultural, historical, zoological, geological and botanical displays. Another lost opportunity. Darn!

I took a shower before dinner and felt much better for it. Dinner consisted of soup, spaghetti and green beans. Of course our delicious mushroom soup had plenty of ginger and pepper. The evening was pleasant and I noted that there were a lot of scavenger cats around looking for scraps.

Before going to bed, we were warned that sometimes thieves jump the fences to steal, so to be careful with our belongings. I was a little apprehensive during the night. I always slept with my head toward the opening in the tent and kept looking outside during the night. Seeing guards walking around to keep watch was comforting.

Tuesday, September 2, 1997
Rhodes Matopos National Park, Zimbabwe

The following morning, we were up by 6 am to get ready for a tour of Rhodes Matopos National Park. We were to travel there by land rover with a guide. Peter was promptly on time and gave us a brief overview of what we would expect to see. The ride in the open land rover was windy and we got bounced around pretty much from the rough road. On the drive, we saw baboon, monkeys and several warthogs. This is what we came to Africa for.

Our first stop was to view Cecil John Rhodes' farm from the road. Peter gave us some brief history of Cecil Rhodes. We got out of the land rover at our next stop to climb a very steep hill in order to view the Bushman's rock paintings

The next stop on our tour was to view Cecil John Rhodes' grave, which was located up high on top of this rock out- cropping. I stopped to rest about halfway up and stayed there to wait for the group to return. The climb up was not steep, but again, I was still suffering from jet lag. Anyway, anything physical tired me out. I felt like a "Wimp." Or maybe I was just "out of condition." No, couldn't be.

At our next stop, Peter fixed a tasty lunch, but while eating we were annoyed by tiny bees that buzzed around your heads looking for moisture. At this stop, we spotted a small group of sable antelope. These large majestic looking animals ran off immediately when spotting us.

After lunch, we headed for Rhodes Matopos National Park. The game park is a large area where wild animals are protected and able to roam free. Although it is a national park, there are still poachers. We saw several warning signs that read: "Poachers will be shot."

We saw giraffe by the road, several monkeys, baboons, wart hogs, one hippo, a water buck, and several lizards and birds. Our guide, Peter, took us to a location where a large white rhino was sleeping. Both black and white rhino are the same grey color. The difference is in the shape of their mouth.

The white rhino has a flat mouth because he eats grass; the black rhino has a pointed mouth because he eats the leaves off the trees. Strange; isn't it? The

rhino never budged while we quietly got to within 50 yards of him to take his photo. Ernie leaned up against a tree to get a steady shot with his telephoto lens, but was told not to do that as he might be mistaken for a poacher and shot. Another lesson!

It's amazing how tiring a rough road trip like that can be because when we got back to camp, all I could think of was getting a shower, eating a light dinner and getting to bed. I didn't know jet lag could last so long. I slept very soundly that night.

Wednesday, September 3, 1997
Bulawayo, Zimbabwe

As usual, we were up by 6 am and on the road again by 7 am toward our next destination. Willie had a good breakfast ready for us by the time we got dressed, took our tents down and put them in the truck. I feel well-rested and think that the jet lag is finally gone. After a few wrong turns, we found our way out of town. When we drove by the plaza, we saw venders with their wares spread out before them. We ladies wanted to stop, but the men out-voted us. On our way out of town, we saw many children on their way to school. They were dressed in clean, light gray and blue school uniforms and all carried backpacks. The boys wore ties; the girls skirts. We drove through Francistown, across the Makgadikgadi Salt Pans. The Pan is located along the northern fringes of the Kalahari Desert, home to the San Bushmen and a sanctuary for herds of animals, including lion and leopards.

Since we rode in the trailer part of the truck with the side rolled up, we took the weather as it came. Today it is terribly windy and I'm sure we looked a sight all bundled up. Some of us would put bandanas over our heads under our hats, or put them over our noses to keep out the dust.

Wherever we stopped, there were always children around who would come up to look at us and ask for ballpoint pens and sweets. Some of the children or young men had fruit or crafts and would hold them up to tempt us to buy. I took a lot of photos and liked bargaining with them. But, I later learned not to bargain unless I intended to buy because they get mad if I don't buy. We gave the children pens and candy when we could. Sometimes there were too many and we had to hold back. I can still remember their voices calling, "Pen, pen, pen," and their big smiles when they were lucky enough to get one. The children in Africa are wonderful, always smiling and happy. I couldn't get enough photos of them.

We stopped at Plumbtree for gas and find an outhouse. If you are lucky enough to find a place to relieve yourself in Africa, you take your chances. They run the gambit from dirty to unbelievably filthy. Many times it was preferable to just go in the bush.

Harold walked around and was able to find some long, thin donut-type sweets which he shared with everyone.

The border crossing from Zimbabwe into Botswana went as normal as most border crossings in Africa, except for Willie, our cook. He did not have the proper documents to enter Botswana and was refused entry. We were all pretty worried about him, but there was nothing Dustin could do about it. So, he left with his backpack and agreed to meet us again at Victoria Falls.

Because of this delay, it took us about three hours to get across the border. Our next destination is to be, Nata Bird Sanctuary.

On the highway, Dustin was able to drive fast, so we really got blown around by the hot, dusty wind. But, none of us wanted to put the sides down and sacrifice the view or risk getting car sick. Thank goodness we had plenty of room to move about.

On this ride, I saw my first Baobab tree. What a funny looking tree it is. It looks like it is upside down wearing its roots on its head. We also saw quite a few birds. The lilac-breasted rollers with their colorful feathers are particularly beautiful.

I never tired of looking at the villages with their thatch roofs and children who laugh and wave as we drive by. Some of the children, especially the girls, would stare in disbelief. I'm sure we were a funny sight in our big pink truck. I waved and yelled back. We saw a few cattle and a lot of goats.

We arrived at the sanctuary at about 4:30 pm. After going in, we decided that it would be a nice place to camp for the night. There were clean showers with hot water and actual clean flush toilets. We pitched our tents and relaxed.

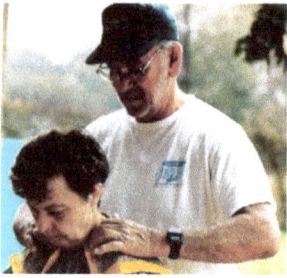

Even though my hair was already short, I wanted it shorter and out of my eyes when the wind blows. Since Hank still holds a barber's license, I asked him if he would cut my hair really short. He did a good job and when Betty and Iris saw what a good job he did, they decided to have their hair cut too. Of course, we had to have our picture taken to memorialize this event. While we got haircuts, Ernie did his laundry and Harold and Dick Sherman cooked dinner. The rest of us did the dishes.

That night I noticed a glow on the horizon and learned that it was a grass fire. Being the "worry wart" that I am, I was concerned that it would come too close to us. I later learned that grass fires are common and this one was pretty far away.

Thursday, September 4, 1997

Nata Bird Sanctuary

Maun, Botswana

The following morning I awoke to sounds of birds singing and the smell of smoke. I was in Africa and happy to be here, enjoying the sounds and smells. Hank did a great job on my hair. After breakfast of bread, jam, porridge, fruit and coffee, we started on a bird drive. The Sua Pan is mostly a single sheet of salt-encrusted mud that stretches across the lowest basin in northeastern Botswana. During the wet season, water birds flock here to nest in the delta. We saw several Kory Busters and ostrich. Kory Busters are large birds resembling the secretary bird.

We stopped in the town of Nada to look for books and maps but didn't find any. Next stop Maun, Botswana. The weather is warm and windy, but not too hot. On the highway to Maun, a tire blew out at about mid-morning, so Destin put on his mechanic's blue coveralls and immediately went to work changing the tire. We stood around and watched. It took him almost an hour. We arrived in Maun at about 4:30 pm. Maun is a dusty little town situated on the south-eastern tip of the Okavango Delta and the safari center of the country's most important tourist region

When we got there, Destin handed Harold some money and said that we needed to decide what we wanted to eat during our 3-day excursion into the Okavango Delta and go into town and buy the food. Since he would not be going with us on this part of the trip, we would be on our own with the local guides. As usual, we depended on Harold to look after us because we knew that he had been on Safari before. Dick Sherman and Hank went with him. The rest of us went into the trading post located next door. Betty and Ernie bought books about animals and birds of the delta. Back in the truck we waited for Destin to buy water cans for our trip.

Back on the road, we saw quite a few goats, ostrich, hornbill and a few Lilac Crested Rollers. I thought they were the most beautiful birds in all of Africa until I saw the Carmine Bee-Eaters.

When we arrived at our campgrounds, I took a shower and got cleaned up for dinner. This would be our last night in a regular campground with showers and toilets for a while. For the next three days we would really be roughing it in the bush. I'm not sure but that evening I think Harold felt we needed to learn how to cook for ourselves because he sat down and watched us fumbling around doing our best to put a meal together. Or it could have been because we ladies decided to go shopping for souvenirs instead of helping him buy the food. Looking back, I can't blame him; we were all depending on him to "take care of us." But maybe he was not feeling good that day and wanted to rest. Thank goodness for Dick Schutz, Jan and Betty because they are very resourceful and took charge. I have never cooked outdoors and didn't know where to begin. After cleaning the dishes, we had to repack our gear into smaller bags for the trip into the Okavango Delta. We would be there three nights and transported to our campsite in dugout canoes made from trees, called Mokoros. We got to bed about 9 pm and I slept very soundly. I think I'm getting used to sleeping in our tent.

The Okavango River, as described in the guidebooks, is "the river which never finds the sea." It surrenders its water to the Kalahari Desert and disappears into a 15,000 square mile maze of lagoons, channels and islands, which is abundant with birds and wildlife, including elephant, zebra, buffalo, wildebeest, giraffe, hippo, lions and kudus.

Friday, September 5, 1997
Okavango Delta, Botswana

We awoke at 6 Am., as usually, and it felt good to just lie in the tent and talk with Hank before getting up. I dressed in bush clothes of shorts, t-shirt and hiking boots, and we finished our packing. Destin and Harold made pancakes for breakfast that were absolutely delicious. It's amazing how good camp food tastes. We were all ready to go by 8 am, but had to wait for over an hour for the land rovers to arrive to take us to the Delta. I didn't know what to expect. Had I any idea of how wonderful this part of the trip was going to be, I would have been beside myself with excitement and anticipation. Hopefully one day Hank & I will be back.

By 9:15 am we were finally on our way. Hank, I, the Sherman's, the Schutz and Betty rode in one land rover with Harold and Ernie in another with a group from Guerba Overland Tours. The trip to the Delta took two hours over very bumpy terrain. It was like a roller-coaster ride, and we held on for dear life for fear of being thrown out. At times the drivers blazed their own trails. We drove through a recently burned out area and I recall looking down on the ground and seeing logs still smoldering right beside the vehicle. I'm sure had we gotten out to walk, the ground would have been hot. It was pretty exciting and Hank and I would often look at each other and laugh. We saw quite a few wild animals along the way. Victor, our driver, was very knowledgeable and told us the names of the animals and birds. Some of them included, baboon, ostrich, zebra, wildebeest, warthogs, crowned hornbill, lilac crested rollers, fish eagles and elephants

Upon arriving at 11 am, what we saw was total confusion. There were two other groups of tourists waiting for their mokoro rides. As they watched, their guides were busy making the necessary arrangements. People were shouting orders, waving their hands, directing which luggage and/or gear to be loaded where. Native women carrying babies were standing around watching. It was all very exciting. I loved taking it all in and taking photos. When I tried to take pictures of the women or children, I was given

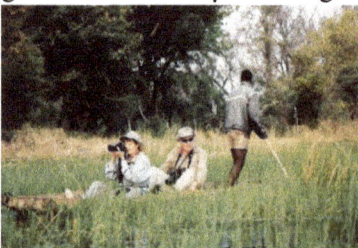

the unmistakable universal signs for "no" or "money." So, we took pictures as unobtrusively as we could.

Their language is "Setswana." It has a very melodic sound. I enjoyed listening to them talk to each other. They are so very black that it's hard to distinguish their features unless you are standing right up close. I watched one woman carrying a naked baby, who was about a year old, on her back like a monkey would carry its own. One old woman, dressed in a red and yellow skirt, kept talking to us in her language. Of course, we couldn't understand but she indicated she just wanted to touch our hands, so we let her.

We were each assigned to a mokoro and poler and had our luggage loaded into the small dug-out canoes. A "Poler" stands up in the back of the mokoro and uses a pole, which is much taller than he is, to push and guide us through the water. Peter was in charge of our group and Hank and I felt fortunate to be assigned to this lead man. Peter packed the bottom of our mokoro with straw to absorb any water that leaked into the boat and loaded our luggage with some of it behind us so we would have a backrest. We still got wet. Once we were settled in the mokoro, I noted that the top edge was only about 1" above the water line. We kept looking at each other, laughing, and taking pictures of each other.

The couples all rode together. Harold had his own boat while Betty and Ernie shared another. We laughed at Iris because she kept shifting around and the poler kept telling her to be still for fear that they would tip over. The polers, who spoke no English, were very polite and considerate of us. Peter, who spoke good English, directed the other polers. He was always helpful and answered all of our questions. Once we were on our way, we crossed to the other side of the canal and waited while the polers ran to their village to get their gear. We were invited to see their village, but since I was afraid I would turn over the boat, I chose to stay put. Some of the group went – another missed opportunity to see African life.

The ride was quiet except when the polers talked to each other in their beautiful language. Hank took out the video camera and filmed them so we could record their language. Ernie was always ready to give us the names of the birds we saw.

I noted that Peter kept looking around toward the center of the canal and steered the mokoro close to the edge through reeds. I didn't know it then,

but he was keeping to the edge for fear that a hippo may be lurking underneath the water. Hippos kill more people in Africa than any other animal. They will come up under a boat, turn it over and with one bite can cut a man in half. Had I known that then, I would have been afraid.

Beautiful water lilies and yellow buttercup-type flowers floated on the surface if the water. There were many birds singing. We also saw several fish eagles sitting on tree branching watching for an opportunity to snatch up a fish. They looked magnificent with their white heads and black bodies.

Midway through the boat trip, we pulled over to the shore, walked to a nice grassy area beneath a tree to eat a light lunch of potato salad. It was so beautiful and quiet just sitting there having our lunch in the middle of the Delta.

The ride to our campsite took two hours. Arriving at our final destination about 1:30 pm we knew what to do first – set up our tents -- we set them up among a group of trees beside the canals. This is really "bush camping." We had no foam rubber pads to sleep on and the ground proved to be very hard. For an outhouse, the guides dug a deep hole with two tree limbs in the ground in front to hold onto so we wouldn't fall in. That was a first for me.

The guides had no tents, only mats and light blankets, so we didn't feel so bad. They slept on the other side of the campfire from us. There were eight of them who laughed and sang enjoying each other's company at all times.

The youngest one was Harold's poler. He was by far the hardest worker of the bunch, hauling water, building the fire, etc. Harold named him "Hercules." We noticed that the older polers made Hercules do most of the work even staying awake at night to keep the fire going

I took quite a few pictures of Hercules. Because he was so cute I just couldn't take my eyes off of him. He is absolutely beautiful with his black, black skin and big smile. He soon became my favorite. The t-shirt he wore was a charcoal black. I'm not sure if it was the original color. Although it didn't look dirty, it looked as though it hadn't been ever been washed. It was way too big for him and the bottom hit him almost to his knees. The collar was stretched out and fell over one shoulder. His pole was twice as long as he is tall, and I watched as he put his pole into the water, walk a couple of steps back, jump to take

hold of the top and pull on it with all of his weight. He got full measure out of each stroke. I wonder if he is still there taking tourists out and having his photo taken.

That afternoon, we got back in the Mokoros for a short ride to the swimming hole. The cool, refreshing water was a strange red color due to the vegetation underneath. There were some young people traveling on the Guerba tour already in the water when we arrived. They were from England, Australia and New Zealand and were interesting to talk to.

At about 4 pm. we went on our first game walk. It was really hot so we drank a lot of water we were wise enough to bring along with us. We saw a young hippo in a pool or water. We saw some lion spoor, but no lion. It's one thing to ride in a land rover or truck to see wild animals close up, but quite another experience to actually walk where some of the most dangerous predators in all Africa walk. The feelings are indescribable. Peter told us to keep in single file directly behind him and be very quiet. You couldn't hear a peep out of us. Peter tried to find elephants for us, but couldn't locate any. We did, however, see wildebeests, impala, wart hogs, zebras, some antelope and some giraffe.

We got back to camp at around 6 pm. It was getting dark and I'm sure we must have presented quite a show for the guides while making dinner. We were disorganized and didn't know what we were doing. Our leader, Harold, must not have been feeling well because that day he decided to take a break and rest. I don't remember what we ate, but again, thanks to Jan, Betty and Dick Schutz, we were able to enjoy a tasty meal. We finally fell into bed at about 8 pm but had a hard time getting to sleep because of the hard ground. The guides built up a large roaring fire to keep the animals out of our camp. Hercules kept watch and fed the fire the entire night. It was all very exciting. This is animal territory, and had we not had the fire, they would have just walked through our camp where we were sleeping. We are the intruders. Sleep was intermittent and we heard our first lion roar in the distance. It was pretty thrilling. We also had a few "snorers" in our group and teased them quite a bit the following day. I think the loud snoring would keep any wild animal away.

Saturday, September 6, 1997
Okavango Delta, Botswana

I woke up at daybreak excited and ready for the day. I don't believe I've been this dirty since I was a kid. There is no thought of getting clean. Putting on the same dirty shorts and t-shirt I had on the previous day, I "peed" in the hole the polers dug as a toilet, and brushed my teeth with bottled water. Although we try, keeping sanitary is difficult. We are washing dishes in cold water from the Delta and drinking water from the Delta that thankfully Harold boils for us every night.

It's amazing we didn't get really sick, although I think a few did get "the runs." We breakfasted on cereal, fruit and coffee. The milk is not agreeing with me, so I ate only a banana and a slice of bread with my coffee. I keep thinking that I will lose weight on this trip, but it never happened.

At 7 am we started on our next game walk. We were told that this walk would take about three hours and to bring plenty of water. It was our best game viewing yet. Peter pointed out spoor and tracks of various animals. We saw two large giraffes among some trees staring at us. The giraffe eat leaves off the tops of trees. We also saw zebras, wildebeests, warthogs, five elephants, Tsesebes and a heard of water buffalo. Peter

made sure that we kept downwind of the animals so they wouldn't smell us and run off or charge us. The water buffalo we saw were really big and mean looking, just standing there staring at us. Peter told us not to move because if we did they were very fast and could charge suddenly.

Back at camp, we rested for a while and I tried to catch up on my journal. Betty and Jan made tuna sandwiches with apples and cucumber, which were very nourishing as well as good. After lunch, I put a tarp down under a tree to sit on while writing in my journal and listening to jazz on my Walkman. It was so peaceful. I read a little and soon fell asleep. At about 2:30 Peter asked if we wanted to go swimming again, so we got into the Mokoros and went to the swimming hole for another swim. It was refreshing and I began to feel clean again.

Later in the afternoon we went on another game tour. The guides took us in the Mokoros to another island. It was so beautiful and quiet on the way over, with just the sounds of birds singing and the Mokoros gliding through the water; the only unnatural sound was the clicking of the cameras. We saw a lot of birds, egrets and fish eagles. Again we saw beautiful water lilies and yellow buttercups. Listening to the birds sing is like a symphony in the wilderness.

All of a sudden we made a turn in a bend of the canal and saw a heard of zebras standing in the water. Beautiful! Zebras are magnificent large and majestic looking animals, much larger than in the zoos at home. When they heard us coming, they took off running out of the water but stopped a little way off to stare. We beached the Mokoros and walked as close as we could to them to take pictures. I didn't take my camera long on this walk because I just wanted to enjoy the day without the burden of taking photos. As usual, I was sorry that I missed so many good photographs. We saw several low flying airplanes carrying tourists to view the animals from the air. Hank said that he wanted to do that someday.

By the time we got back to camp it was dinnertime. There was no Willie to make it for us. But Betty, Jan and Dick Schutz had planned ahead and made some preparations during the afternoon. It was just a matter of putting on the corned beef, cabbage and potatoes to cook. The meal was very good, but needed more of Willie's pepper. We had fruit for dessert. Hank and I did the dishes and Jan put them away. Since we still had some daylight left after dinner, Iris, Betty, Jan and I took our camp chairs down by the river and sat until dusk and talked about what a wonderful time we were having. What a great way to spend an evening! I read for a while before going to sleep in my tent. About midnight, we awoke to a loud noise that was frightening. I didn't know what it was at the time, but it was definitely in our camp. The next morning Peter told us it was a baboon. Of course, if nature called during the night, I had my coffee can or Ziploc bag ready. There was no way any of us would go outside in the dark in Africa.

Sunday September 7, 1997
Okavango Delta, Botswana

The following morning several of our group went on another early game walk. My feet were hurting from the previous walk because I made the mistake of wearing my new hiking boots, so I chose to stay in camp alone. It felt good to have some quiet time. I cleaned up the tent, had breakfast and went down to the water's edge to watch the sunrise and put my sore feet in the water. It was beautiful. Listening to the guides talking in their melodic language and the birds singing was absolutely heavenly. I love it here. After a while, I put my sandals back on and walked over to see the owls in the tree that the guides had spotted the day before. There were two; a mother and her baby, grey in color. They just stared at me in silence. When the group returned to camp, they were raving about what they had seen and said it was the best viewing yet. Another missed opportunity! Darn. Of well, I needed to rest my feet and enjoy the solitude.

We were scheduled to leave this wonderful place at approximately 9:30 am. I didn't want to leave even though I was dirty and sleeping on the hard ground was uncomfortable. I don't believe I have ever been this dirty or uncomfortable sleeping on the ground. My hands look like I have been working as a mechanic for years. My fingernails are broken with black dirt underneath them. My feet look like the feet of an African native – black with dirt. I know that I smell. Of course it goes without saying that all of us were dirty too. After a while I found myself looking forward to a hot shower and clean clothes.

The guides packed our gear in the Mokoros, and we were soon on our way. The two-hour return ride was, again, pleasant and quiet. When we got back to the site where we would meet our land rovers, were not there yet, so we stood around watching the activities. I noticed Harold talking to Hercules' father, so I went over to say "Hello." I wanted to let him know that I thought his son was very polite and a good worker. His father looked proud. And Hercules smiled; he probably understood. I think I took another roll of pictures of him.

When the land rovers arrived, one driver brought out an ice chest with beer and cold drinks for us to drink before heading back. What a blessing! We all grabbed a drink that quenched our thirst. The driver didn't know that Destin had packed sandwiches for us too. The ride back to our base camp was rough, long and hot. We saw giraffe, wildebeest, zebra, red buck and baboon. The giraffe were the closest to us yet; just beside the road. When we got back to the campground, we told Destin that we were "starving." He asked why we hadn't eaten the sandwiches. He found them for us and we ate as if we hadn't eaten in a week.

Our base camp this time was the Island Safari Lodge, which had a swimming pool. After putting up our tents, we took a swim, showered and reorganized our clothing. Our dirty clothes are stacking up. Destin cooked hamburgers with Dick Schutz and Betty helping. I think we all are looking forward to sleeping in a clean sleeping bag on foam mats tonight. Well, Mother Nature had other ideas. While we were having dinner, the wind started blowing dirt and by the time we went to in to check our tents, our bedding was covered with a fine layer of dirt. We cleaned it out as best we could, and I crawled into my sleeping bag at about 8 p.m. to read and get some peace and quiet. The guys are always teasing me about going to bed early. They don't realize that I prefer to read than sit around the campfire to "shoot the breeze." In the middle of the night, after we all were sound asleep, some joker decided to begin revving-up a motorcycle and kept us awake until the wee hours of the morning. It was a long night. You can go into the bush but you can't get away from jerks and their toys.

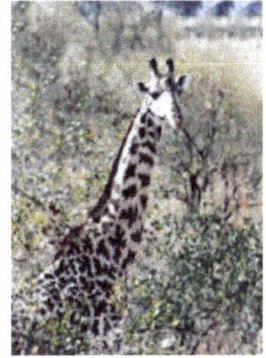

Monday, September 8, 1997
Maun, Botswana

Two weeks into our trip and I feel like we have just arrived. Despite the inconveniences and my previous feeling about being content with seeing animal in zoos, I have fallen in love with Africa. It is a wild and wonderful country despite its poverty.

We arose again at daybreak. Destin made French toast for us. I didn't eat any because I am trying to stay away from greasy foods so as not to get sick. So far, it's working. Ernie, who is a real trooper and never complains, caught a cold and has a sore throat. At 73 years of age he is the oldest of our group. I don't know how he has the stamina. I am 11 years younger and know I could not take a trip like this at his age. He is to be admired.

By 8:30 am we were in Maun to shop for souvenirs and postcards. Between, Hank and I we have eight children with spouses, and 15 grandchildren, friends and other relatives to buy for. There's a lot of shopping to do on this trip. Maun is a dirty little rural town with not much more than an airport and a few shops. I had been looking forward to coming here since I read about it in a book written by a young couple who went to Africa to study the Brown Hyena. We went to the bank where we had to wait in long lines to exchange money. While there we saw three women dressed in period Colonial Clothing. They wore long, full skirts with long aprons and long-sleeved blouses. Their heads were wrapped in cloth with a wide flat brim only in front. All of them were tall and regal looking, and I couldn't help but stare. I asked someone who they were and was told they were "Herero."

Nata was our next stop. While Destin filled the truck with gasoline, we walked across the street and bought some ice cream. Continuing on our way, we spotted an eagle, ostrich and some elephants. We next came to a makeshift village in the wilderness where we saw only women and children bundling reeds. We stopped there for a moment while Destin asked if they knew where the elephant water hole was. They told him it was along the narrow dirt road to the left. The women chatted with us as best they could and one woman pointed out her twins. She was very proud of them. Before we left we saw a man with a couple of women coming in from the field with reeds loaded on a wagon pulled by one or two oxen. They stared at us too.

We took the narrow dirt road to the left and along the way began to see the destruction that elephants make to trees in order to pull the top branches

down. We also saw a lot of elephant dung and spotted some elephants back from the road. This confirmed that we were on the right track. Since the water hole was set back from the road, we passed it up at first and had to backtrack after a couple of guys walking along the road gave us more directions. We were really out in the bush by now and it was kind of intimidating with wild animals so close.

We set up our bush camp close to the truck and about 100 yards from the water hole. Iris was concerned to be camping so close to the elephant watering hole. Dick Sherman expresses some concern too. Iris thought the elephants might walk through our tents. Someone suggested they could always sleep in the truck.

For dinner we had soup (without too much pepper), white rice and a soy mix which tasted like chili. At dusk, we began to see dark gray shadows moving toward the water hole. They are so quiet when they move, appearing out of nowhere. It is quite a sight to see. We couldn't take pictures because it was too dark and didn't want to use our flash for fear of startling them. In all, we saw about 15-20 elephants. What a thrill to be that close to their habitat. The sky that night was clear and it was very, very quiet.

Tuesday, September 9, 1997
Chobe National Park, Northern Botswana

I woke up at about 5:45 am and immediately looked out for elephants. I saw only one and as soon as he saw movement, he took off running into the bush. We did, however, see some fresh dung about 25 yards from the truck. We breakfasted on porridge, eggs and toast. It was really good. Amazing what tastes good when camping.

Our next stop would be Chobe National Park, which is in Northern Botswana. Harold had been here before and told us that there weren't many tourists here and we would see more animals than in other parks. He was right. He usually is even though I like to argue with him.

It took us four hours to get there. Along the way we saw elephants crossing the road and several ostrich. We arrived at the campgrounds at around noon. Destin checked us in, made arrangements for us to go on a game run that very evening, and then fixed lunch of avocado sandwiches and cabbage salad. He also served sardines. The guys loved them, but there weren't too many women takers.

There was a laundry in this campground, so Betty and I walked over to check it out. The prices were a little on the high side, but we didn't want to do the laundry ourselves. For 52 Pula, or $17 US dollars we had only half our dirty clothes washed and ironed. It was well worth it at the time as Hank and I had run out of clean clothes. Harold did his own laundry every week. As soon as we got to a campsite, out would come a small bucket and laundry soap. He would put on his bathing suit, wash all his clothes, and hang them in no time at all.

After lunch, some of the group went for a swim in the swimming pool; others just took a shower and relaxed. I wrote in my journal and listened to jazz on my Walkman. There were monkeys all around in the trees, but they left when they found they could not steal any of our food or belongings. The weather is hot and humid. There is also an annoying bird somewhere in the trees that keeps making a noise like a child blowing a horn. Every 2-3 seconds it blows a soft, mournful sound. Before the game run, we went to find a bank to get more money as we were running low again.

The evening game run was the best yet. Couldn't believe it only cost us 30 Pula or $10 US dollars each. The two land rovers and drivers arrived promptly at 4 pm and we loaded up. Our driver's name was also Peter. He was well educated on the names of birds, trees and wildlife and readily answered any question we asked, even the stupid ones. He took us immediately into the bush. I noticed that the color and texture of the sand had changed from the white powdery sand in Maun to a thicker rust color. I still can't believe how close to the wild animals we were able to get. The water bucks were only 25-30 feet away. They aren't afraid of tourists at all. We also got within 15-20 feet from one large elephant.

The guides know exactly where to find these animals and took us right to them. We saw two female lions with five cubs. Three of the cubs were only 3-4 weeks old and still quite small; the other two were a little larger. We photographed and watched them for a long time and they could have cared less.

One of the lionesses came out from behind the bush carrying a kudu leg and a cub soon began chewing on it. We were very quiet taking our photos and in awe of being so close to lions living in the wild.

We saw hundreds of elephants crossing the road right in front of our vehicle. We had to stop for them to pass and some of them stopped in the middle of the road to "mock charge." This is their way of trying to scare us away. To intimidate their enemy, they flap their big ears; pick up their trunk and "trumpet" loudly. It is quite a sight to see and hear. After they crossed, we followed them to the river and watched as they sprayed water with their trunks over their backs to wash themselves off. Then they roll in the mud to remove the parasites. One baby elephant fell into a mud hole and couldn't get out. When he started to squeal, three big female elephants immediately came over and pushed and pulled it out with their trunks. Free at last!! I can still see him, running after the elders with his little trunk flying. It was a sight I will always remember. I recorded the whole event on video. We were told he was less than a year old because he could still walk under his mother's belly.

Across the river we saw large herds of water buffalo and impala. We saw hippos and crocodiles. We saw fish eagles, storks, geese, kites and many other varieties of birds. We asked Ernie what kind of birds they were and he always knew their names. We took his word for it because he has been an avid birdwatcher for years.

For dinner that evening, Destin cooked steak, fried potatoes, cauliflower and cabbage. Absolutely delicious! It started to shower lightly and thunder at about 3:30 am, so we put up our rain fly. We could hear the hippo in the water at a distance. They live in the water by day to protect their delicate skin from sun burning and come out at night to forage for grass.

Wednesday, September 10, 1997
Victoria Falls, Zimbabwe

Harold cooked corned beef, potatoes and egg scramble for breakfast. By 7:30 am. We were loaded in the truck and on our way to Victoria Falls. On the drive we saw a few elephants standing on the side of the road, foraging for food. In town, we stopped at a store and bought bottled water, juice and chips.

Thank goodness for bottled water. It tastes so much better than the boiled water we always had in jugs for cooking and backup.

We arrived at our campgrounds by 11 am, and Willie was waiting for us. Hooray, we had our cook back. This campground is right in town with a bar in the center. These accommodations are the dirtiest we have stayed in so far; however, it is close to town and the Falls. We could see the main street from our tents as it was directly across the street from the camp. After setting up our tents, we walked to town to look around. We bought a couple of t-shirts and souvenirs. We then walked about eight blocks to a craft center. They had some really nice artifacts. Iris and Dick bought some tablecloths.

Destin told us that he could arrange to have t-shirts made for us to commemorate our trip if we were interested. Of course we were. After a bit of haggling and pointing fingers, Betty and I were elected to do the negotiating. We drew up a design and Betty and I headed to their makeshift shirt shop. It was nothing more than a couple of rooms about the size of a bathroom at home. We told them the sizes, colors, and gave them our design. They agreed and promised that the shirts would be ready the following day.

That night we decided to go on a dinner river cruise on the Zambezi River. The river cruise turned out to be kind of corny, but interesting. The meal consisted of small cold hamburgers and warm drinks. The waiters entertained us with singing and dancing. The weather was pleasant and we did see some elephants on the shore very close to our boat. All in all, it was a pleasant journey. When we got back to town, the guys were still hungry, so we went to Wimpy's to get something to eat. The ladies had ice cream. I slept wonderfully that night despite the music and noise from the bar. I couldn't believe it when I heard them singing "La Macarena." I hate that song. It had been popular in the States a few years back, and I hated that song even then. I counted and heard it sung a total of four times while traveling in Africa, including on a dinner cruise in Cairo. The melody haunts me for days after. The next morning, Betty mentioned that she could hear the Falls during the night when it got quiet. I guess I slept through that.

The Zambezi River runs along the border between Zambia and Zimbabwe and at Victoria Falls widens to 1700 meters and then plunges 107 meters into the Zambezi Gorge. The force of the water is estimated at around 545 million liters per minute during the rainy season, sending clouds of spray up to 500 meters into the sky.

According to the guidebook, white-water rafting trips through the Zambezi Gorge are among the wildest and safest thanks mainly to the deep water steep canyon walls and lack of rocks midstream. I don't believe it can be the safest for one minute. Hank wanted to go rafting but no one would join him. I certainly didn't want to go and run the risk being eaten by a crocodile.

Wednesday, September 11, 1997
Victoria Falls, Zimbabwe

Even though we were up at 6 am, we took our time because we couldn't get into the park to see the Falls until 9 am. Dick Schutz was happy that morning because he likes to sleep later than the rest of us, and didn't like it that we always got up so early. They kept teasing me about liking to sleep late, but I was usually up right after Hank, Harold and Betty who were always up before the rest of us. But it didn't matter; I got teased about one thing or another. For breakfast, Willie tried to make pancakes, but failed, so Destin took over.

When it was time to go to the Falls, we walked along a nice path. Victoria Falls is without a doubt one of the greatest natural wonders of the world. The Falls are twice the height of Niagara Falls, ranging in height from 61 to 108 meters. You could hear them thundering from a good distance. As soon as we went through the gate, you could feel the fine mist on your face. We had to be careful because all of the sidewalks and steps were slippery. We walked around the grounds and took photos from every direction. I know I went through a whole roll of film; Hank must have gone through two or three rolls. It was amazing. Betty had been there before during the wet season and said the difference was amazing. Oh by the way, there are only two seasons in Africa, the Wet and Dry. We talked about wanting to see the Falls during the wet season sometime.

As I was walking on top of a bluff looking at the Falls, a young girl, who looked 15 but was actually a college graduate, approached me. I was wearing the hat Hank was given the last time we went whitewater rafting in California. It had "Whitewater Voyages" written on it. She asked if I went whitewater rafting with Whitewater Voyages. I told her; "Yes, I've been two or three times". She said that her father manufactured the boats that are used by Whitewater Voyages. What a small World!! She added that her father was one of the sponsors of the girl's rafting competition going on that weekend on the Zambezi River near Victoria Falls. She and her father have rafted all over the world. He came over and introduced himself. The U.S. Girls' Team won the event. Yeah, for the US girls!

We walked over to the tall bridge to see the bungee jumpers. It looked so hazardous. I'm told it is the highest bungee jump in the world. Anyone who does that is nuts. We never did see anyone jump.

By the time we returned to the campsite, Willie had sandwiches ready for us. We were happy to have him back. And he looked happy to be back. Some of us had reservations for a helicopter ride over the Falls that afternoon at 2 pm, so we walked to the helicopter office and from there they drove us to the pad. After a short wait, we boarded the five-passenger helicopter. I was lucky to get to sit in front with the pilot. Not only was I able to see out front and to the side, but I could see down between my feet as well. The view was indescribably awesome. It was my first helicopter ride and I loved it. I took videos of the Falls while in the air instead of still photos. Harold, Dick and Jan Sherman went up in the helicopter after us and while they were airborne, the rest of us viewed the video.

When we got back to town we stopped for an ice cream and then Betty and I walked over the get our t-shirts. They were really going to be "nifty" with all our names on them, a map of Africa and the dates of our trip. Well, only one shirt would have fit any of us; all the rest were way too small. I felt sorry for the guys who made the shirts because they lost money on the deal. They put a lot of work into the job, but, as I demonstrated by putting one on, the shirts were all too small and we couldn't possibly wear them. They had used the shirts they had on hand instead buying the sizes we asked for. So, we refused the order. I think they were a little upset, but were gracious enough to give us our money back. Destin and Willie got a t-shirt free of charge.

That evening we had big plans to go to dinner at the old colonial Victoria Falls Hotel. Harold had been there before and told us about it and how much he enjoyed it. The hotel is for the elite and shows it. I'm not sure when it was built, but would guess before the turn of the century. We were really looking forward to going and having a real sit-down dinner after living so long in the bush. There is something to be said about getting dressed in skirts and putting on make-up in a tent, but we cleaned up pretty good. We strolled leisurely to the hotel as the weather was warm and pleasant. The large, bushy Bougainvillea along the path sparkled in a profusion of reds, pinks, oranges, yellow and white. It was beautiful!!

We were told that many famous people have stayed here and we believe it. On the walls are many stuffed animals heads. It is a beautiful place. After Iris came out of the ladies' room she told us to be sure to go in there because it is very elegant. She was right. It is most certainly the nicest and cleanest I had visited while in Africa.

Service that night was rather slow, but dinner was superb. It was an all-you-can-eat buffet and the men were thrilled. The main courses were wild game such as impala, crocodile, kudu and ostrich. I played it safe by having only the beef and ostrich. The ostrich was very sweet and moist. For entertainment, there was tribal dancing. The men and women in their colorful costumes were all well-built and beautiful dancers. We had a great time. Even though no one said so, I think we all wished we had rooms in that hotel for at least one night

Friday, September 12, 1997
Lusaka, Zambia

Our usual routine, up at 6 am and off by 7 am. We rushed through breakfast because we anticipated a long drive ahead. Destination: Lusaka, the capital city of Zambia. Getting through the border was slow, as usual. We had to get off the truck and wait in lines. We also had to go through the process of buying visas at $25 U.S. dollars each. It seemed a bit costly.

The drive was very cold and windy. I was torn between staying where I was to see the scenery or move to the front to get out of the wind. I marveled to see Dick Schutz reading in the truck regardless of the motion. The terrain had changed in that there were more trees, and the sand now is a beautiful bright rust color. We saw quite a few villages, the children continuing to wave and shout as we drive past. As we got closer to Lusaka we began seeing people on bicycles for the first time and large farms with cultivated fields.

I was surprised to see how big the city is. It appeared to be the largest city thus far. We saw many high-rise buildings. When we got into the center of

town, we saw young men walking around with belts, pants, watches and various items in their hands or their arms, hawking them for sale. There were also young women sitting on the sidewalk with their wares spread out before them. I was amazed at how many people there were and about 95% of them were young Black men under the age of 25. They were all clean and neatly dressed. Some even wore ties.

The streets were narrow and cars were parked diagonally. While creeping past a string of cars, a Mercedes began backing up and stuck our truck. Destin and the driver of the Mercedes, a large Black man, got out to inspect the damage. The truck sustained no damage, but the Mercedes had a slight dent. Everyone on the street began to congregate around. At first we were taking photos, but soon stopped as we began to get a little concerned. Here we were, White tourists with thousands of dollars' worth of camera equipment as well as cash in the midst of hundreds of young Black men shouting and waving their arms. We, of course, didn't know what they were saying, but they could easily have overpowered us and stolen everything.

A policewoman soon came to investigate. The driver of the Mercedes was irate and began telling her that it was Destin's fault and wanted him to pay for the damage. She listened to both sides and before we knew it, Destin was driving the truck to the police station. He told us that the policewoman wanted to take both drivers to the police station to try to get things straightened out. When we got there, Destin went inside the police station while we waited in the truck. To kill the boredom, we did what all photographers do, we took pictures. After

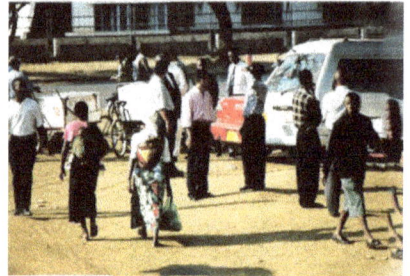

some time, Destin, the policewoman, and the driver of the other car came out got into the police car and left. We just sat there. What now? When they returned, Destin explained that they had to return to the scene of the accident to try to determine whose fault it was. Destin went back inside and again, we waited. After what seemed like a long time, Destin came out and told us that they wanted him to pay a fine of $55 U.S. dollars or spend the weekend in jail. We told him we would gladly pay the fine, but he is a very determined young man and wanted to win his point. He said that because he was White and the other man Black it was going against him. Finally, he went back in and paid the fine with the money we gave him. We couldn't get out of Lusaka fast enough.

The campgrounds where we stayed that night was, thankfully, a good distance from the city and by the time we got there it was well after dark. There was a house on the grounds and a bar in an A-framed building next door. On the grounds was a large grassy lawn with trees all around. Everyone was happy that the tent stakes went into the ground with ease and our tents could be placed on grass instead of dirt. We put our tents up quickly and while Willie cooked dinner, we went to the bar for a drink and listen to the music. Inside were tables and chairs, and a long bar. We had some local wine, which wasn't very good but palatable, and talked to a group of people from England staying in rented rooms in the house. Two families with young children were staying in vans in the campground.

After dinner of spaghetti at around 9 p.m., we finally got to bed. I decided to wait until morning for my shower; I was that tired. Sleep came quickly.

September 13, 1997
South Luangwa National Park, Zambia

We were awakened at 5 a.m. to get an early start because we had a 10-hour drive in order to get to South Luangwa National Park before dark. Willie was making porridge but it would not cook, so he took the almost-cooked porridge with us still in the pot -- no Tupperware here. Willie finished cooking the porridge the following morning and we had it for breakfast then. Nothing goes to waste in Africa.

The early morning drive, again, was cold and windy. We did not want to put the sides down because we would lose the view and Dick Sherman and I were afraid we would suffer from motion sickness. We are the only two of the group affected. I decided to sit away from the wind toward the front of the truck and read as the view was not that great. I was reading "The Last Elephant" by Jeremy Gavron. I am fascinated with this book written by an English Journalist who writes about the elephants. He traveled all over Africa visiting various national parks and interviewing elephant experts to study their habits and family life. After reading this book, I look at elephants in a totally different light. I highly recommend it to anyone concerned about the welfare of elephants in Africa.

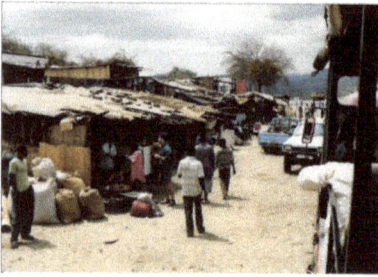

At about 11 am, we came across a shack-town along the side of the road. It is a collection of lean-to shacks made from poles or branches with roofs made of scrap lumber, sheet metal or straw mats and held down with bricks. We saw people everywhere selling clothes, bananas, fruit, vegetables, cooked food, straw baskets, and other wares. Destin wanted us to buy some sweet potatoes and bread, so Harold and I went into the maze of shacks as the buyers. There was no bread to be found and they refused to bargain on the sweet potatoes, so we left without purchasing anything. When we got back to the truck, there were dozens of young people and children around the truck. They were all dirty but when they look at you with those big bright eyes and smiles, you just melt. The boys all want to have their picture taken, while the girls just stare at you. The women won't let you take their picture at all. One boy had a shirt on with

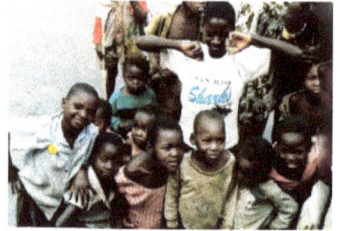

"Alhambra Pool Tournament" written on it, while another boy had a shirt on with "San Jose Sharks." Small World! We learned on this trip that the clothes we give to Goodwill or other agencies that are not sold are packed in bales, like cotton, and sent to Africa to be sold at local markets.

For lunch we made peanut butter and jelly sandwiches in the truck while driving down the road at about 60 mph. As we are driving, I notice that the terrain is changing again. We are starting to climb some hills or small mountains. The dirt is still a beautiful copper color. Looking out at the trees, I am reminded of fall in New England. We passed quite a few villages. As usual, the children ran out to shout at us and wave. In many of the villages we saw pigs wondering around loose. We also saw boys and men on bicycles.

At one point, Destin stopped to tell us that he knew of a short-cut to South Luangwa National Park that would save time, and if it was okay with us wanted to try it. We said, "Go for it." So off we went, off the main highway at a small town named, "Petauke." Well, take my advice; don't take short-cuts if you don't know what you are getting into. What we ended up on was a very, very rough road with huge ruts in the middle. Although, the truck can take a lot of rough roads, it couldn't take this one especially when it looked like there was no road at all in front of us. So, we turned back. And, I'm sorry to say that when we backed up, we drove over someone's cultivated field. We felt bad because we're sure we ruined his crops. This four-hour detour, however, ended up being one of the most memorable drives of the whole trip.

While the truck was stopped so Destin could ask for directions, a group of about 25 children gathered by the truck and asked for, pens and sweets. Although many of them were dressed in raggedy clothing, they all had beautiful faces and big smiles. One shy girl, dressed in nice clothes, stood back from the group leaning on a tree. I got some good photos of her. I also couldn't get enough photos of the children. We gave them M&M's and after a while, Hank started taking Polaroid photographs. We could tell that they had schooling because when Hank asked them to line up, they immediately got into a line and just stood at attention. They really got excited when Hank gave them a photo.

After taking about two rolls of prints, I began shooting videos. I asked them to move around and sing. They knew how to sing a Christian song and it must have been the only song they knew, because they sang it over and over and over. We gave them the last of the candy and some ballpoint pens. The children in Africa may be poor but they don't know it, always ready with a smile and laugh. This made the trip rewarding.

On the main road again, we were tired and began dozing. Someone rang the buzzer twice and Destin stopped the truck for a potty break. His favorite phrase was, "Boys in front; girls in back." It was so funny; Iris, Jan, Betty and I lined up in a row and "did our thing." While "squatting," a couple of local men walked by and waved. We waved back. ." Modesty had long been forgotten

Even though we were trying desperately to get to the campgrounds at Chipata before it got too late, the truck had other plans. The power steering broke between 10 and 11 that night. We would have to sleep right there by the side of the road and repair it in the morning. Hank, Dick and Jan Sherman, Ernie and Betty decided that they would take their sleeping bags and foam pads to sleep outside on the ground. I was too tired to move and carry my stuff outside, so decided to sleep on the seats inside the truck, as did Harold and Dick and Iris Schutz. It was really uncomfortable trying to sleep on the four-foot long seat while being kept awake by the two biggest snorers in the group. I was sorry that I chose to stay in the truck. In the morning when I heard about how beautiful the sky was that night with all the stars so bright you could almost touch them, I deeply regretted my decision to stay inside the truck. Another lost opportunity! Darn!

Sunday, September 14, 1997
Chipata, Zambia

We are now beginning the 15th day of our Safari. Time is going by so fast, I can't believe it. We awoke as soon as it was daylight. Of course, there is no thought of showers or clean clothes. We just kept the clothes on that we slept in. My, how priorities change when you are on Safari. Destin began working on the truck immediately and by 8:30 am Willie had cooked us two breakfasts. The first was the leftover porridge from the morning before; the second was delicious fresh potato pancakes. We ate them as soon as they came out of the bubbling hot oil. We sat around drinking coffee and talking, while Betty inspected the engine.

The first person to come by the road was a young man of about 15 years of age driving an ox-driven cart, but he just stared and continued on his way. A little while later, he came back with a friend and a load of wood on his cart. Soon, we saw three boys on two bicycles. They stopped at a distance, did a little jig and stared at us. Before long, there were more children standing at a distance and staring too. Slowly, they kept getting closer and closer. Since we were bored waiting for Destin to finish with the truck, we started taking pictures. Hank and his Polaroid camera were big hit. Iris had some stickers and started putting them on the children's foreheads. They just laughed and laughed. One young girl, using sign language, wanted

my earrings. I felt bad telling her no. She just kept asking, and looking at me with a look that said, "Poor me, you have so much and I have so little." It was my only pair of earrings. Had I had another pair, I surely would have given them to her, but she still made me feel guilty.

Destin told us that we shouldn't give them anything because it makes beggars out of them. He has a good point but believe me, they didn't learn to beg from us. They already knew how to beg long before we got to Africa.

Before long a couple of women came to see what was going on. It's funny. You couldn't see a hut or a village from the road, but there were certainly a lot of people living around there somewhere and word got around quickly. The women were dressed in bright colored blouses and skirts and one of them was balancing a can of beans on her head. Surprisingly, she allowed Hank to take a picture of her. When he gave it to her she broke out in a wide grin, showing how proud she was. But, as boys will be boys, one boy of about 16 years of age, grabbed the picture out of her hand and ran off through the brush. She got angry and yelled at him, chasing him for a while, but gave up shortly because she knew she could never catch him. Hank was out of film or he would have taken another picture for her. We really had fun that morning, and no doubt, we were their Sunday morning entertainment. They stood around and watched us until we left at about 10:30 am. Everyone waved goodbye when we left.

We arrived at the campground in Chipata about an hour later. While Willie immediately set about to make us lunch, we took showers, set up our tents, and put on some clean clothes. There was a sink at the end of the building where the showers were located, so I decided to wash some clothes. Hank put up a clothesline. After lunch, I crawled into the tent to catch up on the sleep I lost from the night before.

The campsite, Wildlife Conservation Camp, was nothing to brag about, but there was a bar with an adjoining patio. I'm beginning to think that Destin picks out campgrounds that have bars. On the patio were tables with chairs. It felt good to eat lunch at a table while sitting in a chair with a back. Small things seem to be a blessing at times.

Destin continued to work on the truck. Jan, Iris and I took a walk around the village and saw several young people wearing their rosaries around their necks. Willie took the afternoon to scrub the pots and pans really clean and cleaned out the food storage area. Since the food is stored below the truck bed, it gets extremely dusty and dirty. No wonder Willie washes the vegetables good before cooking them. Destin had purchased tablecloths in Maun, so we used them for the first time. Everything looked clean and nice. It felt good to sleep in the tent again after a hot shower.

Monday, September 15, 1997
Zambia

Today marks the end of three weeks of our trip and two weeks and two days of our Safari. We have a good routine going in setting up our tents. We are comfortable sleeping in sleeping bags, so we are all sleeping well. It is beginning to feel like "home." Oh, dear, have we been in the Bush to long? We are getting along good as a group and having a wonderful time. How fortunate indeed to have such good friends to travel with.

When we got up, Willie was already busy making French toast for breakfast. While having breakfast, Destin started to laugh at us because we were all eating standing up; none of us had bothered to sit down. Another sign that maybe we've been in the Bush too long?

Our plan today is to stay here until Destin can find parts to fix the power steering in the truck and buy some extra belts. While waiting for the stores and bank to open, Destin got his guitar out and played a few songs. He wanted us to join in, but none of us would so he soon quit. We begged him to continue, because we all thought he was quite good, but he wouldn't.

Soon it was time to go, so Destin left, and Betty, Iris and Dick Schutz and I walked down to the bank to exchange some US dollars into local money. What an experience that was. We waited nearly an hour for anyone to even wait on us. They weren't at all busy, just unorganized. All we wanted to do was change $100 US dollars into Zambian Kwacha. When they finally waited on us, they first had to do some paperwork and walked back and forth between offices several times. Who knows what for? And then, the machine that they use to check for counterfeit money would not accept our bills. Obviously, something was wrong with the machine but they would not admit it. Finally, after a long wait, someone recognized the problem and gave us our Kwacha. In all, I think it took us about two hours. It is always a challenge to be patient in a foreign country.

Back at camp, Destin wanted someone to go with Willie to buy groceries, so Iris, Dick Schutz, Betty and I volunteered. Willie did not know how to bargain and, as we learned later, didn't know about money in other countries. So that's why Destin wanted us to go with him, but he failed to tell us. We went to the store and bought our groceries. After we had a box full, I chose to go back to camp. It was a strange experience being the only White person walking on the streets in Africa. Soon, a couple of little boys started following me at a distance. They were not allowed through the gate into the campground, so they watched me through the gate for a long time. When I got close to where Hank and the Sherman's were sitting, I tried to balance the box on my head to imitate the local women. I managed a few steps, but dropped the box when we started laughing. The boys laughed with us. We enjoyed relaxing the rest of the day.

Destin continued to work on the truck and go to the shop for more parts. After lunch of leftovers from the night before, plus peanut butter and jelly sandwiches, and corned beef, I spent time updating my journal and reading. We were waiting for Destin to finish working on the truck so we could continue to South Lilongwe National Park.

When Destin returned with more parts and repaired the truck as best he could, we were finally on our way at about 3 pm. The road was extremely rough. The dirt was very fine and a red-copper color. It covered everything; brush, trees and even the pigs in the villages were red. The children run towards the truck waving and yelling at us. I began to feel like the circus coming into town. The trip only took about three hours but seemed longer because the road was so rough. On the way, we saw several monkeys in trees next to the road.

We finally got to Mad Dog Camp at about 6 pm and Willie immediately started getting dinner ready, however, it wasn't ready until 9 pm. We set up our tents along the banks of the Lilongwe River, which is about 300 yards wide during the rainy season. Since this is the dry season, there was only enough water to run through about one-third of it. We saw some elephants on the opposite bank, but it was dusk and we couldn't get their picture. We know there are hippos in the water because we could see their prints in the mud on the banks. This was really exciting to be so close to wild animals. We were told that sometimes the elephants come into the campgrounds. After all, this is their territory, not ours.

That night we could see the almost-full moon peeking through the clouds. It was really beautiful. Hank showed the video of the previous day's shoot while we waited, waited and waited for dinner. It was worth waiting for however. The fried chicken, fried potatoes, eggplant stew with peppers and tomatoes were delicious. We went to bed immediately after dinner since we were scheduled to get up at 5:00 am for a morning game run. We were told that we would see wild animals "really up close and personal," and were pretty excited.

Tuesday, September 16, 1997
South Luangwa National Park, Zambia

I woke up a 4:15 am to the sound of something "big" walking through the water. I knew that it must be hippos, but couldn't see anything. I put on my clothes and went outside. I thought I would be the first one up, but Willie, Destin and Betty beat me to it. Willie was already preparing breakfast of cold cereal, eggs and toast, and we were ready to go on our game run by 5:30 am.

The guides arrive in their land rovers on time. There were two vehicles for all of us. We rode with Allen, our guide. He was extremely knowledgeable about the area and wildlife. He briefed us on what to expect and told us that we would be very close to animals and under no circumstances were we to get out of the vehicle unless he told us it was okay. Cameras at the ready, we were on our way.

Early in the run as we were driving through a thicket of trees, Hank spotted a lone elephant back from the road. The driver stopped and backed up a little for a better view. It turned out to be a mother and baby as well as a few other elephants in the trees. We started taking photos and shooting some video. Then all of a sudden there were elephants in front and in back of us. There was action in both directions and we didn't know which way to turn.

The driver all of a sudden started to back up and revved his engine. I guess he did this so we could get better photos. Anyway, the elephants in the back got excited and the mother started her "mock charge." Then the elephants in front got excited and did the same thing. As soon as Dick Sherman took a couple of pictures, he said in a quiet, shaky voice, "We can go now." They were getting really close to the back of our vehicle. Even though it could have been a dangerous situation, we all laughed.

The next highlight was when Allen spotted the leopards. He knew exactly what to look for. Allen spotted the first leopard while we were looking in the other direction at a group of three elephants. The leopard, however, ran under the brush before we could get a picture of him. The second leopard, Allen spotted asleep high up in a tree with his legs dangling. None of us would have ever been able to recognize it as a leopard if he hadn't pointed it out. It was too far away for most of us to get good photos, but I think that Harold and Hank with their 300mm lens got at least one.

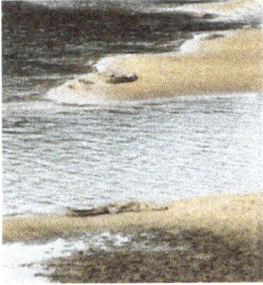

Later, we saw two hippos in a small pond of mud and water. When they saw us, they got out and went to hide in the bush. We saw five hippos in another small mud pond. It is sad to see these large hippos in shallow muddy ponds half submerged. In the dry season, they don't have enough water to cover themselves. Their skin is very sensitive to the sun and if exposed, it will harm them. We also saw several large crocodiles sleeping on the banks of the pond.

By the end of the run we had seen impala, warthogs, kudu, puku, hippos, zebras, giraffe, crocodile, hyena, elephants, and two leopards. Leopards are very hard to spot and get pictures of because they are nocturnal and do a good job of hiding during the day to sleep in peace. We were fortunate indeed to see any at all. Destin was really surprised when we told him, and mentioned that he has taken many groups on Safari and never before had they seen a leopard. We also saw monkeys, baboons, and a mongoose. The birds we saw that day were so numerous it was hard to keep track. We saw Flat-billed storks, cattle egrets, ibis, weavers (birds who make round nests in bare trees that look like balls), Lilac Breasted Rollers and Carmine Bee Eaters. The bee eaters are a magnificent sight. Thousands of them dwell in holes on the banks of dry riverbeds. When they take to the air, they fly in a group and turn the sky red. They have long red, blue and black tails. They were spectacular to watch. Allen let us get out of the land rover to see them since there were no large animals around and we spent quite a bit of time watching them fly around. Unfortunately, it was hard to get a photo because they fly fast and the sky behind them is bright, so all you get is a blur. We also saw some beautiful small emerald green birds that are members of the parrot family although we could not identify them.

It was very hot and humid back at camp while having lunch. The bugs, mosquitoes and flies bothered us, so we got busy putting on bug repellant. You can get Malaria from Tsetse flies.

Some of the group went swimming in the pool that was next to the adjoining hotel. I chose to stay in camp and write in my journal. I must need more quiet time than the rest of the group. The guys are starting to "rag" on me about my journal. They don't understand why it is so important that I write in it daily. They will find out one day. I took a shower after the morning run and it is so hot and humid that by 3 o'clock felt that I needed another.

Allen arrived punctually at 4:00 pm for our evening game run. During the briefing, he told us this run would take about four hours, and we should dress warmly. He brought along a young man who would hold the night light. Allen said that we should be able to see some lions and leopards tonight because another group had seen lions and leopards the night before. Unfortunately, all we saw were some baboon, monkeys, impala, puku, kudu, water buffalo, guinea fowl, storks, sacred ibis, a rabbit and two genets. We spent some time looking for wild dogs reported in the area

We returned from the run late, cold and hungry. For dinner we had sweet potatoes, fried white potatoes, a vegetable stew and a cake for desert that Willie cooked in a skillet. As we were cleaning up, we heard a noise behind us in the park like a large animal thrashing through the thicket. Without getting too close, we watched three large elephants came into our campgrounds looking for something to eat. We watched as they ripped bark off trees and ate the leaves. They moved on after a little while. I can't express enough the feeling I got as I watched these huge wild animals. Later, we sat in a circle around the video camera and watched what we shot during the day. Of course, there was a lot of joking and teasing.

Wednesday, September 17, 1997
South Luangwa National Park, Zambia

During the night, I heard light sprinkling on the tent. I looked at my watch; it was 4 am. I got up quietly so as not wake Hank who was sleeping soundly and started to put the rain fly over our tent. Then I started hearing the hippos walking through the water. About half-hour later, Hank woke up and thought we might as well stay up and take the tent down. Harold, Betty, Ernie and a few of the others did the same thing. Poor Dick Schutz, as much as he tries to sleep in, we always wake him with all the noise we make, so he gets up for fear that he will keep us waiting. We made a plan the night before to leave at about 8 am, but since we were already up, and getting ready, we thought we'd leave about 6:30 am and head for Lilongwe. We anticipate another long drive. We left at about 7:30 am.

We were cold in the truck, but still did not want to put the sides down for fear of missing something. When we drove back through Chipata, we stopped for something sweet to eat. All we could find was some cookies in a store, and we were happy to have these. Harold did manage to find some English chocolates, which he shared.

Going through the Zambia-Malawi border again took us a long time. We had to get off the truck, go through to have our passports inspected and answer questions about where we were headed, how long we had been in Zambia, etc.

Immediately after crossing the border, we began to notice a big difference in the two countries. Zambia is a somewhat poorer country than Malawi. The houses in the villages in Zambia were round, made of adobe and have a reed or straw roofs. In Malawi the houses are square, built of brick or cement with thatch roofs. And, the people are much better dressed. We saw quite a bit of well-cultivated farmland. I took many photos of girls and women carrying baskets of clothes, buckets of water or even bundles of wood balanced on top of their heads. It is amazing to see a little girl of about 4-5 years of age balancing a small tin of water on her head. I never tired of photographing the people we saw on the side of the road.

At times when we came across people selling something on the side of the road, we stopped to see what they had for sale. Destin always thought they charged too much. He bought some charcoal when he began running low on propane. He ended up paying about $2 US. for a large burlap bag of charcoal. We thought it was a bargain; Destin thought it was a rip off. It's all relative. We also bought some casaba melons. They didn't have much taste when we cooked them that night for dinner.

We arrived at our campground in Lilongwe at about 1:30 pm, had lunch and immediately set up our tents. Hank and I have a good routine going now. Betty has her system down pat too and no longer needs help. Destin told us that we should go into town and bargain with the sellers at the carver's market, but not to buy anything because we would be able to find the same items cheaper at other stops on our trip. We walked the five or so blocks into town, first to exchange the amount of money we thought we would need while in Malawi. Each country has different currency. We walked out with a huge stack of bills. Looking back, I suppose it wasn't safe to be standing outside of the bank with this large stack of bills, trying to count it. We soon gave up and walked to the carver's market as people were beginning to watch us.

Bargaining at the carver's market was fun and I we got carried away because the items they were selling seemed pretty inexpensive. Hank and I ended up buying 10 letter openers for gifts and a set of coasters. We had fun, but the rest of the group teased us for being "big spenders." While walking back to camp, we saw some teenage boys playing Cricket at a school across from our campground. They appeared to be all White except for a few East Indian boys.

While waiting for dinner, Destin talked to us about our options for the following days. After a long discussion, we decided that we would spend a few days in Senga Bay, which is on Lake Malawi. We would skip visiting the lower part of the lake in order to spend more time in Zanzibar. Destin really likes Zanzibar and said it was a great place to visit. He also said that he thought we would enjoy getting out of our tents for a while. Boy, was he right!

Willie again was really slow fixing dinner so we didn't get to eat until about 7 pm and it was already dark. I gave him my flashlight so that he could see what he was doing. After dinner as soon as Hank got into the tent, he let out a big "gas explosion" that was heard by everyone outside who immediately starting laughing out loud. I rushed out of the tent so I could breathe. Hank laughed more than anyone else and we giggled about that long into the night. Boy, did Hank get teased about that the following day.

For the first time on our trip we began to hear Muslims chanting their prayers. The leaders sing prayers over loudspeakers. It is loud, begins at 4 am and continues every hour on the hour all day long. I suppose if I was of that faith I wouldn't mind it at all.

Thursday, September 18, 1997
Lilongwe to Senga Bay, Lake Malawi

The chanting of the Muslims woke us all up at 4 am. We went back to sleep only to wake up at 5 am to more chanting. We didn't know it then but we would hear that every morning for probably the next two weeks. Not being able to sleep any longer, we got up at around 6 am. There was no rush this morning, because Destin needed to get some money that his office had promised to wire him. (I'm sure Dick Schutz was happy about that.) Destin said it would probably take him all morning. So, we took our time with breakfast, took down our tents, and I again rearranged my suitcase. Things sure get messed up fast on these trips.

We walked into town to buy postcards, stamps and bottled water. When we got back to the campground, Betty, Iris and I asked Hank if he could cut our hair again. Hank wanted to charge us for his services, and we said we would "owe" him. Of course, there was a lot of teasing going on while the others sat around supervising. Destin returned to camp at about 1 o'clock and we left immediately. He did not get the money. Later, we learned that Tracks

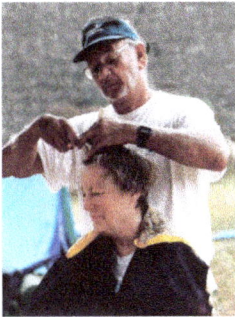

International was in the process of closing its operations in Africa due to financial problems. Although Destin told us that he did not get his money, he did not reveal to us the fact that we were on Tracks' last tour in Africa. We felt fortunate that they honored their obligation to complete our tour. We made several stops in the newer section of Lilongwe so that Destin could send a fax and try to determine what was going on.

Lilongwe is the capital city of Malawi and the Embassies and county offices are located in the newer section of the city. They are housed in beautiful tall, modern buildings that could be downtown anywhere USA. However, among the modern buildings there are street vendors on the grounds selling anything they can get a price for. We saw one enterprising lad polishing shoes. Destin returned to the truck pretty frustrated, so we finally left without his money.

The drive to Senga Bay, which is on Lake Malawi, was extremely windy because Destin was driving fast on the roadway, and I'm sure it was because he was pretty frustrated. There was a lot to see along the drive and we continued taking photos from the truck. We saw a lot of people just walking down the road, large and small plots of cultivated farm land, chicken ranches, and quite a few factories. The people seemed to be walking with more purpose than in other countries. There were more people riding bicycles. And for the first time, we saw bicycle repair stands along the side of the road. We saw many more women carrying baskets filled with laundry or produce or metal buckets full of water balanced on their heads. One memorable scene was of about six or eight women with children washing their laundry in a creek with their bright colored laundry drying on bushes all around them. The children were playing in the creek and seemed to be having a great time. Another was of three young teen-aged girls balancing large baskets of laundry on their head walking in a row alongside of a fenced plot of land growing green vegetables. They were dressed in bright colored blouses and skirts. The scene was so colorful. You could always spot people in the distance by their bright clothing. They seemed to like reds, gold and purple.

At one spot on the road we came across an open market and there were hundreds of people congregated there. We drove by so fast that all I could see was black heads and bright colored clothing. It's hard to photograph or take it all in when you are zooming down the highway at 60-70 mph, so we missed several photo opportunities

After a while, we came to beautiful mountainous terrain. It was quite a contrast from the rough flat wilderness of Zambia. Malawi consists of a thin sliver of densely populated land running the whole length of beautiful Lake Malawi with the southern extension of the country dipping down into Mozambique, almost cutting that country in half. It is a very picturesque country with amazingly friendly people. Almost everyone speaks some English.

When we arrived at Senga Bay, we stopped at another open market to buy food for the next couple of days we would spend on Lake Malawi. Dick Schutz and I enjoyed walking through the markets bargaining and buying food from the locals, so we were usually the ones who volunteered first to go do the shopping. Some of the others in our group wandered around the open market, and some stayed around to guard the truck and entertain the youngsters who came around just to look. We bought some eggs, produce, fruit, bread and beef. The eggs are sold individually and you have to buy a plastic bag to put them in. Of course, there are always young boys at your elbow willing to sell a plastic bag. The beef we bought was from some young men who had a hindquarter just hanging by the leg in a small, dusty open shack. There were flies all around but we ignored that. When I asked for one kilo of beef, one of the young men took a dull knife and hacked off a few pieces. He weighed them and handed them to me just like that. Of course, then he wanted us to buy a bag to put the beef in, but Dick Schutz said, "No, the bag is included in the price." The young man didn't like it, but he gave us a bag anyway. On this buying trip, we bought 2 papaya, 12 ears of corn, 1 cabbage, some potatoes, 2 loaves of bread, 10 eggs, 13 casabas, (which tasted like potatoes when cooked) and one kilo of beef for 155.8 Kwacha or about $9.00 U.S. It was quite a bargain.

Although we looked all over, there was never any ice. Everything we bought had to go without refrigeration. Oh well, we were in Africa, weren't we? We put the cartons of fruit juices in the ice chest, but they were always lukewarm. At one point, the ice chest got so filthy that it made me gag. Harold, bless his heart, took everything out of the chest and cleaned it thoroughly. What would we do without Harold? Willie put the produce we bought in open boxes under the bed of the truck over the wheels. It got very dirty and did not stay fresh very long. Willie was very careful to wash everything before cooking it.

We arrived at the Livingstonia Hotel and Campgrounds about 5 pm. We set up our camp in a beautiful spot on a sandy space close to the beach. There were several other campers in the campgrounds when we arrived, including one large, imposing-looking vehicle, which looked like an armored truck. On the side was painted a map of their intended tour. We later learned that the three adults in the all-terrain vehicle were from Australia on a two-year journey from South Africa to Singapore. They would travel through Africa, Europe and Asia and planned to be in England at the end of their first year. What a trip!

Malawi Lake is so large that you cannot see the other side. We put our tents up about 50 feet from the water. There was an open bar by the beach and after getting settled and taking a walk along the beach, we stopped to have a cool drink at the bar.

That night for dinner Betty and Willie made beef stew and mashed potatoes. Betty jumped for joy. She loves mashed potatoes and missed them during the trip. The beef in the stew from the meat we bought the previous day was pretty tough but the potatoes were delicious. We knew that Destin had to go back to Lilongwe to see about the money he needed to complete our trip and find a power steering pump. That evening he told us that we should take what clothes and gear we thought we would need off the truck until he returned. For the first time, I began to get a little concerned about maybe getting stranded in Africa. Some of the others felt the same way I did and expressed their feelings. But, my Darling Hank said that he knew Destin would never leave us stranded. He convinced us that we had nothing to worry about as Destin had demonstrated thus far to be very responsible and cared about our welfare. We really had no choice but to take our chances and trust him. Beside, we were covered with travel insurance, weren't we?

He left Willie with us and told him to take all of the food off the truck. Although I knew that Destin would return, I still wanted all of our gear off the truck because even though Destin might have good intentions, you just never know what might happen to him on the road. After all, he could have an accident or the truck may breakdown totally.

Destin began working on the truck immediately upon arriving at Senga Bay. Somewhere while driving on a very bumpy road, a spring leaf slipped out of place. Destin had to jack the truck up and hammer the spring leaf back into place. It took him a long time and even though the guys tried to help, there was nothing much they could do. So, they just assisted by handing him tools and "supervising." I couldn't watch for fear the truck would slip off the jack and hurt him, so I left to take another walk on the beach. Destin He continued to work on the truck until 12:30 that night. I went into my tent at about 8 pm to read and write in my journal

Friday, September 19, 1997
Senga Bay, Lake Malawi

Destin left for Lilongwe at daybreak. The sound of the truck woke us up and again I got concerned. "What if something happened and he could not return. What then?" I could not keep these thoughts from my mind, but then after thinking about it a while, knew that everything would be fine. We had travel insurance and knew we would be okay, but it was the unknown that made me feel apprehensive. It would be an unanticipated adventure and we would cross that bridge when we came to it. I kept these thoughts to myself.

During the night, Hank and I were really crowded because we had all our camera equipment and luggage inside our tent for fear that someone would steal it if we left it outside. There was no air circulating in the tent and it was rather warm. We laughed when we tried to get comfortable and go to sleep. The next morning I woke Hank up and reminded him that he wanted to take photos of the sunrise. I stayed in the tent and tried to get some more sleep, but finally gave up and read until Hank returned. He was a little glum because there was no sunrise that morning.

When we crawled out of the tent, the others were already having breakfast. I walked to the showers but there was no hot water. The cool water, however, felt good and washed off the mosquito lotion and night's perspiration. I had cereal and toast for breakfast. We talked and joked about Destin being gone. Hank, ever the optimist, stayed positive and kept reassuring the "Doubting Thomases." While we were eating, a man came by to ask if we wanted to have some laundry done. I gave him ours. He charged us 150 Kwacha or $8.40 US, but it was well worth it.

After cleaning up, we decided to walk to the carver's market, which was about one-half mile outside the gate to the campgrounds. Hank and I, Betty, Ernie, and Iris and Dick gathered together and waited to see if others would join us. Since Harold, Dick and Jan didn't show up, we thought they didn't want to go. So, we went ahead.

Just outside of the gate, there were several young men and boys waiting for us. Destin had warned us about local young men who hassle the tourists. He said that they try to make you think they just want to be your friend, but they really want to steer you toward a certain vender who will give them a cut of what tourists buy. When they started walking with us, we told them that we didn't need them to go with us. Of course, they learn early not to take "no" for an answer, so they just continued to walk with us and "chat." Charlie and

George, who are brothers, walked with Hank and I, and James began talking with Betty. We slowly began to enjoy their pleasant, friendly conversation as we walked along the dirt road. They told us about their fishing village where we would see fish eagles fishing from the lake. We made arrangements through them to meet Jeffrey at 2 pm to go to the fishing village. While we walked they asked if we had old t-shirts and socks we could give them.

When we got to the market, I bought a small wooden bowl, a bracelet, four small carved masks which I had hoped to make necklaces out of, and four pieces of cloth, called Kanga, to be used as wrap-around skirts over bathing suits. I also couldn't resist buying two very heavy heads carved from ebony. Hank bought two masks. Of course, George steered us in the right direction, and I'm sure he was rewarded. Dick Schutz was not happy about their hanging around, but Hank and I enjoyed chatting with them. Harold came around us and began to make fun of me for buying the heavy carved heads and asking Hank if he was going to carry them.

Dick and Jan caught up with us and asked why we hadn't waited for them. They were under the impression that we knew they were going to the hotel to send a fax to their daughter who was expecting a baby and would go with us when they returned. We apologized and said that we didn't know. It was just a misunderstanding. Later that day, they received a reply fax informing them that they were indeed grandparents again; their daughter having given birth to a little girl they named, Carley. We could tell that Jan was sad not being with her daughter for the birth of her first child. Dick just looked proud.

For lunch, Willie fixed Casaba with sauce and corn. The casaba is firmer than potato, and has no flavor whatsoever. The sauce was good, but the corn was tough. While sitting in the shade, having lunch, I could hear the fish eagles in the hills behind us. I also saw monkeys who are ever diligent, waiting for an opportunity to steal something, anything, we would take our eyes off of for a second. After lunch, I caught up on my journal, read a little bit, but soon my eyes began to close.

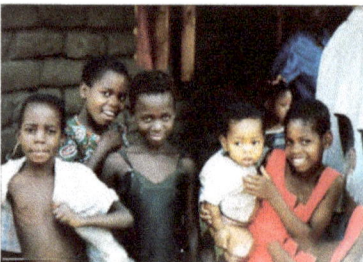

At 2 pm Betty, Hank and I walked to the gate to meet the boys, take their photos in exchange for t-shirts and socks, and tell them that we had changed our minds about going to the village because it was too far. Iris told us that someone told her the village was about 4 km away. Charlie,

George, Jeffrey, James and Phillip were waiting for us. When we told them of our plan, they said, "No, the village is just over this hill. It's not far, and, you can take all the photos there you want." The boys had beautiful features and enjoyed having their photos taken. We took several pictures of them and then began to walk up the hill to their village.

In the village, we were introduced to their chief, who was quite old, and was busy making a house with mud bricks by hand. The boys showed us where they bake scones for their breakfast and to sell. They showed us where they smoke their fish and where they make liquor. They showed us their outdoor kitchens where they cook their meals and their outdoor bathhouses where they bathe. It was all very interesting. They took us to the small grocery store to meet Charlie and George's father. I loved his face because it has so much character, and took several photos of him. The boys also took us to meet their mother and the rest of their family, including beautiful children. I was in my glory because I like nothing better than to take pictures of children and people. And, of course, they all wanted their picture taken. We grouped them up and took their picture many times. One of the boys, I don't recall which one, wanted his picture taken with his bottles of homemade liquor. He had an assortment of about 8-10 bottles of different sizes and color filled with "moonshine." He was so proud. Along our walk, we met a young man who was painting on metal water buckets. He also wanted his picture taken. We came across another boy who was in the process of building his house. There was a fairly new nylon tent beside the unfinished house where he told us he slept until his house was finished.

Much to our surprise at the end of the tour, they told us that they expected a fee for the tour. They said that their chief would expect us to pay for the privilege of touring their village. He would share the money with the villagers who are very poor. Another lesson learned!

Betty gave them $20 US and Hank and I another $20. We didn't begrudge the money at all as it was well worth it. Not only did we have a good time but we took lots and lots of photos.

Back at camp, I went to take another shower and Hank decided he wanted to go to the hotel to take photos of birds. While I was in the shower, a young woman approached me, identified herself as a guide with the Guerba Tour, and asked if I was with the group who had come into the campgrounds on the Tracks' truck. I told her I was. She then asked where the truck was. I explained our situation and said that we were waiting for Destin to return. She expressed her surprise and wished us Good Luck because she had been told that Tracks International was no longer in business. I really got concerned then, but decided to keep this information to myself so the others would not worry.

When I got back to camp, the others were talking about what we were going to do about dinner. Willy had misunderstood Destin and left most of the food on the truck. All we had to eat were potatoes and cabbage. Harold mentioned that there was a snack bar on the grounds, so we decided we would buy dinner there when it opened and give Willie a break. Either Willie didn't understand us or felt it was his duty to make dinner for us, because he took it upon himself to approach the New Zealanders who were on the two-year tour and borrow some food. They gave him some pasta and garlic. So, Willy fixed dinner of pasta, potatoes, cabbage and soup with garlic. Harold went to the snack bar and brought back a couple of tacos. He also ordered fresh bread for our breakfast the following morning. Before going to bed, Hank and I sat on the steps by the beach and talked for a while. I told him of my conversation with the girl from Guerba, and he insisted that Destin would be back. Ever the optimist!

Well, he was right. Destin returned about midnight. What a relief. He had his money and had fixed the truck. We were all set now to continue our Safari.

Saturday, September 20, 199
Lake Malawi

I woke up about 5 am and read until Hank woke up about an hour later. We then walked to the water's edge to take pictures of the sunrise. It was so beautiful and peaceful there.

We had breakfast and then loaded the truck. Next stop, Nkata Bay! Although Malawi is a small country, the lake is huge; the fourth largest in the world. It runs almost the whole length of the country and is absolutely beautiful. We traveled north along the road that parallels the lake, through the town of Nkhotakota. I could not get enough of the countryside and the people along the road. The scenery is wonderful. The houses are built better and we begin to see row houses instead of villages. Most houses had windows with shutters made of reeds. A few had corrugated tin roofs and some even had glass windows. We saw a beach and there were white caps on the water. It's hard to believe that this is a lake and not an ocean because it is so big.

We stopped at a small fishing village and Destin looked for a road to the beach to have lunch. Failing that, we stopped by the side of the road and put the lunch table under a tree. Within two minutes, we had 15-20 people around us just looking. It is amazing. They seem to appear out of nowhere.

After lunch we walked down to the beach. We ran into a couple of guys who wanted their pictures taken and one asked if we would take their picture and send them a copy. We said we would and he gave me his address. He then wanted my address and said he would write to me. He spoke English very well and was a friendly young man. Walking a little further taking pictures of some boats on the beach, we saw a couple of guys swimming in the nude. One of them stood up and waved his arms for us to take his picture. He was "naked as a Jay Bird," as the saying goes. We laughed and took his picture. We also saw some women doing their laundry in the lake and children swimming. The women had some of their laundry spread out to dry on the sand. It is amazing that we think we can't wash clothes unless we have an electric washer and dryer.

When we returned to the truck, Dick and Iris were giving their empty film canisters to the children, who were having a fun time with them.

Continuing on our way, we stopped at a market on the side of the road to buy vegetables. Betty had a Frisbee in her luggage and Dick and Destin began playing with the children while Harold, Iris, Hank and I did the shopping. It was wonderful. This is one of the things I like most about Africa. The people seem to derive a great deal of pleasure out of the simplest things.

Before getting into Nkata Bay, we climbed into the mountains and I was reminded of being in Chiapas,

Mexico, where the terrain is very lush. Betty said it reminded her of Maui. We drove through a rubber tree plantation and stopped to examine the trees with their rubber oozing out of cuts in the trees into cans.

Destin stopped at a place where there was a hot springs and suggested that we walk down to it and maybe get into the warm water. He is trying very hard to give us as much African experiences as we are willing to absorb. There were two sections of the hot spring, one for men and one for women. Jan, Iris, Betty and I walked down the narrow muddy path. When we got there, we saw naked women and girls in the water, as well as clothed women washing their clothes. One old woman motioned for us to give her money and get into the water, but we slowly backed out. The men in our group decided they didn't want this African experience.

We arrived at Nkata Bay about 3 o'clock. Destin parked the truck on a narrow road just south of the beach and we all got out and walked through the little village. There were wooden lean-tos where people were selling their wares. I bought some more cloth for Kanga, or wrap-around, to give as gifts.

When Destin went to the Backpackers Camp to book space for us, they told him that they were full. So, we made our way up a hill along a narrow, very bumpy road to the Nkata Lodge. It was not a campground, but a lodge with rooms to rent and a restaurant. They did, however, allow us to camp on their lawn. Some were unhappy about this location because there was no fence around the grounds and we were concerned about our security. Destin wanted to stay for two nights, but Betty, Ernie and I were worried, so told him that we really didn't want to stay there. Well, we had nothing to worry about. It turned out to be one of the more pleasant stays of our trip. We ended up staying the two nights.

Once we got settled, Destin, Jan and the two Dicks walked down the hill to try to find fish to cook for our dinner.

There is a bar in the lodge, and someone is playing the song "La Macarena" which seems to be following me all over Africa. I dislike that song immensely. It is maddening.

Jan and the guys came back with Butter Fish. Dick Sherman and Destin cleaned it, and Willy cooked it. It was light and delicate, and absolutely delicious. I didn't realize how much I missed eating fish.

After dinner we sat around and talked. There were some misunderstandings that had to be aired out. I won't go into them here, but it was good that we cleared the air. I had to laugh at Destin, because while we were talking, he suddenly got up and left. When he returned, he told us that it was not uncommon to have misunderstandings on a long trip like this. He also expressed his amazement that we all got along as well as we did. He said that some people in other groups he took on tour sometimes got into fights and refused to talk to each other for the remainder of the tour. We laughed and reminded him that we had been traveling together for a number of years. With that behind us, we had no more problems. We decided to go ahead and stay two nights rather than break camp in the afternoon and drive for only 3 hours or so.

We talked for a while longer and I finally retired to our tent about 8:30 pm. I thought that maybe the noise from the bar at the lodge would keep us from sleeping, but they were pretty quiet. Then, about midnight, two men outside of the bar right by our tent woke us up. They were in a very heated argument. Someone finally came out of the lodge and made them leave. After that, I slept very soundly. The tent feels more and more like home all the time.

Sunday, September 21, 1997
Nkata Bay, Malawi

Hank and I woke up about 6 am, as was our custom, but we did not rush because there was no reason to. We dressed, had breakfast of toast, bananas and coffee and just sat around and talked for a while. It felt good not to be in a rush to go someplace.

The Sherman's walked into town to look around. After chatting a while with Destin he suggested that we do the same in order to get to know the local people and the town. So, Betty, Hank, Iris, Dick and I walked down to the carver's market we missed yesterday. It was fun chatting and bargaining with the vendors. I bought a carved comb for my granddaughter, and Hank bought a model fishing boat with "Malawi" carved on it. He also bought two carved faces he wants to frame when we get home. While looking at a carved African chair, the vendor said that he would trade the chair for my Teva sandals. I told him that he couldn't have these but I had another pair back at camp I would let him have. So, Hank and I left the others shopping and walked back to camp to get the other sandals. Well, he doesn't call himself "Mr. Smart" for nothing. When I got back with my

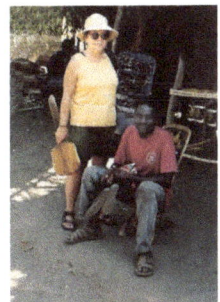

older, more used sandals and said he could have these, he refused. He wanted the newer Tevas. We dickered a while more, so finally I got the chair for $5.00 US, my cheap bracelet from Mexico, and the bandana I was wearing around my neck. Of course, the chair is made if ebony and very heavy. Hank kept asking me how I was going to get it back home. I said, "I'll find a way." And, I did just that, packing it in my bag with my clothes. Of course, it made my luggage that much heavier and I already had the heavy carved ebony heads too, but what the heck, they are still among my favorite treasures.

While we were waiting for the others to return to camp, Hank began to talk to some kids who were selling postcards that they had made by hand. Hank got out his Polaroid camera and said he would trade them a photo for a postcard. They didn't know what he meant. So, he took their picture and showed them how it developed. It was fun watching them as they stared at the picture in fascination. They laughed and laughed, and one of the boys got so overcome that he actually fell to his knees. What an experience that was!

When we regrouped, we started our walk to Chikale Bay, which is a small bay located about 2 km south of Nkata Bay. It was a pleasant walk and we talked to some of the people along the path. Harold and Dick Sherman are accustomed to walking and soon outdistanced the rest of us. While passing some bamboo, I heard music and turned around. There was a young boy of about 10 years of age making music on a hollow bamboo stalk. When he saw me he stopped immediately. I wanted him to continue, but he was too shy. His father who was on the other side cutting bamboo just smiled at us.

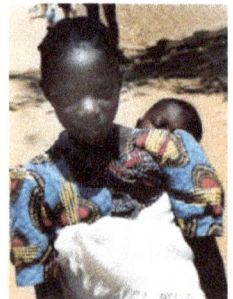

We passed some young girls, who looked to be about 12 years old, carrying babies on their backs. I learned that many of the young girls look after their siblings for their working mothers.

When we came to a fork in the road, we took the left fork when we should have taken the right fork. I'm not saying we got lost, because we didn't. It just took us longer to get there. We ended up way to the right of the bay and had to climb down a steep narrow path. There were small houses on the hill overlooking the bay. We were really hot, tired and thirsty when we finally arrived.

The scene of people enjoying their time by the water playing on the sand and rocks was absolutely magnificent. There were dugout canoes beached along to one side. There were several women doing their laundry and spreading it out to dry on the sand. There were several young tourists interacting with the native children.

We cooled off rather quickly because of the wonderful breeze coming in off the water. After resting a while, we went swimming. I stayed in the water only long enough to cool off and then sat on a large rock to dry. We stayed about an hour before starting our walk back to camp. We took the more direct route this time.

After lunch some of the group decided to do their laundry, while others just read and relaxed. The two Dicks, Jan and Destin decided to take another walk into town. Dick and Jan happened across a group of young men playing soccer in a field. He said it was undoubtedly the best soccer match he had ever seen as the young men were really skilled.

Destin came back first and brought us some local beer. He insisted that we try it. It is made from a grain and is thick and sour tasting. Absolutely ghastly! I didn't enjoy it at all. But many of the locals like it so much they get drunk from it. It was indeed an African experience.

For dinner that night we had spaghetti with potatoes and cabbage with sauce. I retired to my tent to write in my journal and read earlier than usual that night, about 7:30. The guys continue to rag on me.

Monday, September 22, 1997
Nkata Bay, Mzuzu, and Chtimba, Malawi

When you go to sleep early, you can't help but wake up early the following morning; I was awake by 5 am. Hank and I got dressed and joined some of the others to walk down to the bay to take picture of the sunrise and early-morning happenings in Nkata Bay. I can't explain what a memorable experience that was, or how beautiful watching early morning life unfold.

Outboard motor launches bring locals from other villages into Nkata Bay to work or sell some of the wares. I saw someone with a small table, and others were empty handed. I sat on a rock and watched with great interest life in Nkata Bay. One man washed himself from lake water, brushed his teeth, and changed into a white suit there in front of everyone. One beautiful young girl of about 11 years of age, brought pots and pans down to the beach to scrub in the sand. She polished those pots until they gleamed. I kept taking photos of her, and she began to watch me too.

Hank, Dick and Jan went further on the rocks while I was content to just sit and watch the people. They came back to tell me of their memorable experience. They ran into a gentleman who lives in a house by the bay who was the former Prime Minister of Uganda. They said he was highly intelligent, articulate, and extremely interesting to talk to. I was sorry that I had missed meeting him.

Back at camp, we had breakfast, broke camp and left this small piece of heaven on earth. People live such simple lives here and appear so happy. I almost envy them.

We headed northeast to Mzuzu on our way to Chitimba, which is on the northeastern side of Lake Malawi. On the drive we passed brick homes, cultivated farmland and banana groves. The cultivated farmland still has the tree stumps protruding because they have no way to pull them out. The terrain is mountainous with magnificent views of lush green trees and plants with plenty of red dirt all around. The road we are traveling on is very good so we don't get bumped around at all.

At Mzuzu we stopped at an open market. Hank, Betty, Dick Schutz and I accompanied Willie to shop for produce. We went into a supermarket to stock up on other necessities.

Further along the road, the power steering on the truck went out again. Although it was early for lunch, we made most of the opportunity. While we were stopped, an old woman came out all excited because she thought we were going to feed her.

Although feeding one person is not a problem, we had to deny her because then others would want food too. Before long, there were several children of all ages asking for pens or sweets. We chatted with them and gave them the rest of our ballpoint pens.

Continuing on our way, I never tire of looking at the scenery. It is all so beautiful. Jungle, mountains, terraced farmland, banana groves, and even some pine trees. The houses in the villages are square now, as opposed to round, with thatch roofs. We saw more and more people in Western-style dress with the traditional Kanga over their dresses. I spotted several old clay water pots lying around on the ground. Sadly, they have now been replaced with metal and plastic buckets. We see young girls balancing water-filled buckets on their head filled with water from the community well or a river nearby. We also see little girls balancing small pans filled with water on their heads. It is quite a sight. The view from the top of the mountain down to Lake Malawi is spectacular. The lake is so big that it's still hard to believe it is not an ocean. Coming down the steep mountain road is slow, and everyone in the truck is quiet, but the brakes and clutch held up. Thank goodness!!

We got to our extremely rustic campsite at about 4 pm. We are again on the beach and there is an open bar. Is Destin bar hopping?

Destin showed us the showers and the 50 gallon water drum where water is heated by a wood fire. Although there was no fire going under the drum, they soon started one. They fill the drum with water from the lake by hand, carrying bucket after bucket. We are to fill a bucket from the heated water in the drum, and then fill another bucket in the shower stall. The bucket in the shower stall has a spigot and handle fashioned at the bottom. When you are ready to take your shower, you just turn the spigot -- and Voila!! -- A camp shower, no less. Although the water is lukewarm, it felt good to get the perspiration and dust off.

In the trees around the camp, there were many Yellow-Breasted Weavers flying around and I enjoyed watching them eat blossoms from the sausage trees.

Before dinner, we went to the bar for a beer and sit on the patio facing the lake. The beer, like the shower, was lukewarm. Dinner of rice and peas and carrots with sauce was very good. Willie is big on sauces. For desert, Willie made banana fritters. I sat around the campfire for a while until I heard one corny joke too many, and decided it was time for me to go to bed even though it was still early. The music and laughter from the bar went on until late into the night.

Tuesday, September 23, 1997

Chitimba, Malawi – Tanzania Border – Mkumi

During the night I heard dogs barking, peeked out of the tent and saw some guards walking around. Even though it was a little unsettling, it felt good to know we had protection if bandits came into camp. I woke up again around 4:00 am. During the night we could hear the blooms from the Sausage trees landing on our tent. I love the sounds of the birds singing in the early morning hours. The Weaver birds' nests in the trees overhead resemble unpainted Christmas balls hanging from the limbs.

After breakfast of sausage, toast and coffee, we broke camp and left about 6:15 am. The weather is warm and we are finally on the way to Dar Es Salaam. Dustin says it is his favorite place in all of Africa, so we are looking forward to seeing it. It is the gateway to Zanzibar where Hank and I are planning to be married.

The terrain changed dramatically once we left Chitimba. Along the road we begin to see frame houses. It is interesting how they are made. First, they make the square frame with bamboo lashed together. When that is completed, they plaster both inside and out around the bamboo with mud. Some of the plaster is brown and some black. Using the resources available, nothing is wasted.

Nearing the Tanzania border, we begin to see brick houses with actual glass windows. Surprising!!!

When we reach the border, we were first directed to the border offices, which are by far the most rustic we have seen so far, and I note that the officers are very relaxed. We were then directed across the deeply rutted street to a building where a nurse was waiting for us. She examined our

Health Immunization cards. But that wasn't enough; she had to know who was married to whom. We got a big laugh out of that. Along the street, the money changers were very aggressive so we hurried back to our truck.

We drove along climbing hills and passing quite a bit of farmland on the sides of the hills. There were big coffee and tea plantations as well as banana, orange and avocado groves. I am impressed by how beautiful the scenery is with its red earth against the green trees and plants and how well-cared for the groves are. There is no way to capture this beauty on film. As we neared the town of Tukuyu, we begin to see more and more people walking along the sides of the road, and notice children in very white shirts. I don't know how they get them so white.

I was surprised when I saw the town of Tukuyu. The cement houses were all built close together and had tin roofs. There were people all along the roadside either walking or selling produce. We saw mounds of green bananas still on the stalks, large burlap sacks of potatoes with straw on top, trays of oranges and what appeared to be sweet potatoes. We saw women in bright colorful skirts and shawls which is the usual Muslim attire. Other women wore bright colored blouses and the colorful wrap-around skirt, which is called a Kanga. It is exciting to see all the bright colors and activity. I saw one woman walking with a whole stalk of green bananas balanced on her head; I don't know how she could do that.

This appears to be the agricultural center of this area. I would love to spend more time here, but we drive on because we have a long way to go.

Eventually we climbed to about 5,500 feet and houses become sparse. When we stopped for lunch by the side of the road, there were no people around, but soon a crowd of about 30 children and adults gathered to watch us. It is strange how they just stand and stare, talking about us in their own language. As we had a long way to travel this day, we just made our lunch and ate it in the truck.

We climb down the escarpment and soon are in the dry savannah and the weather quickly turns hot. An escarpment is a steep slope or cliff formed by erosion or, less often, by faults. It soon began to get cold, so one by one we got jackets out of the locked luggage area. At a distance we see many brush fires. They are something to see at a distance.

At about 5 pm, we came across a camp where Destin thought we might be able to buy some steaks and have dinner. The owner of the camp was from England and wanted to charge us $5 per head just to stop and eat in his camp. He was trying to "rip us off" as the charge to camp there at night was $8 per head. So, we made our usual corned beef sandwiches and ate them in the truck. It would have been heaven at this point to have a good steak.

At about 10:30 pm, we finally arrived at the small town of Mikumi, and stopped at a rest house. They had a total of six rooms, but only four were available for the night. Destin negotiated with the manager and tried to get him to reduce his price from $10 per person for the night, but he wouldn't budge. When he told us the price, we almost knocked him down in our rush to register for the rooms. Betty stayed with Hank and I in our room. We were all too tired to shower and just "fell into bed" under the mosquito nets. Destin and Willie slept in the truck. The next morning we had a good laugh because the rooms were so poorly constructed, they fell apart during our stay. In Harold and Ernie's room, Ernie leaned on the bathroom sink and it literally tumbled off the wall; Dick & Jan's bed fell from its frame; and in Dick and Iris' room, the toilet seat fell off. Our room was the only one that was intact the next morning.

Wednesday, September 24, 1997
Mkumi to Dar Es Salaam

It was hard to get up at 6 am because of the time changed at the border. There was no water at the hotel for showers, so we just dressed in our same dirty clothes. The water from the tap was brown, but I brushed my teeth in it anyway. Ugh!!!

Soon we were in Mikumi National Park and immediately began to see wild animals alongside the road. We saw giraffe, elephants, wildebeests, zebra, and a baboon. How exciting!!!

The next town we got to was Mokogoro where we saw our first Masai. They are so tall. The men carry a stick and when standing lean their hip against it.

Willy, Dick Schutz, Hank and I went to the market for produce and change money at a local bank. We purchased a pineapple, papaya, grapefruit and other food items. It is always fun interacting with the locals.

Upon leaving Mokogoro, the drive is fast and furious to Dar Es Salaam. The busses are all overloaded with people and twice we were nearly run off the road. Destin said that there are many accidents along the road where people get killed because the drivers go so fast. He also said to be sure to keep our heads and arms inside the truck.

The scenery begins to change again. We begin to see the change in women's clothing to the Muslim influence. The houses are built of cement blocks and we see many coconut and banana groves and plots of vegetable gardens on the hills around the houses. As we neared Dar Es Salaam the streets became increasingly congested.

Dar es Salaam, which means "Haven of Peace," began as a humble fishing village in the mid-19th century when the Sultan of Zanzibar decided to turn the inland creek into a safe port and trading center. Now the capital of Tanzania, it is a city of about 2.2 million people. It is a colonial city with red-tiled roof buildings. In the harbor are many Arab dhows and dugout canoes mingling with huge ocean-going vessels.

Destin parked the truck along the ocean front and he, Hank, Iris and Ernie walked to get maps and snacks. Dick Sherman and Dick Schutz went to buy the tickets we would need the next day for the boat ride to Zanzibar, and Betty, Jan, Iris and I did as women do everywhere; we went shopping. The waterfront is very congested with people coming and going, selling their wares and just shouting. What fun!!! I love it.

When the guys returned, we drove to our camp site for the night. I might say here that prior to our trip to Africa, Hank and I had talked about the possibility of getting married in Africa. We decided that if we "could pull it off" we would go ahead and do it. Well, at the first opportunity of getting Dustin alone, Hank told him that we wanted to get married during this trip and asked his help. Destin, smiling broadly, said he would be delighted. He would ask people along the way and see if he could come up with a plan. We asked him to keep it a secret from our friends for the time being. After a few days, he told Hank that the best place to get married would be Zanzibar and asked us what kind of wedding we wanted. Hank said he would not drink cow's blood, so a village wedding was out. I said I did not want to intrude on someone else's religion, so a church wedding was out. That left only a civil ceremony, which was good for us. Destin said he would make it happen.

Our first stop would be the American Embassy to seek information and assistance. As we drove through the city we passed the American Embassy. I got nervous and started shaking when I saw the Embassy because our plans were actually becoming reality. By the way, this is the same Embassy that was bombed by terrorists the following year.

We arrived at Silver Sands Camp at around 6 pm. Willy immediately started dinner, but it was 9:30 before he finished, we were all famished and ate like we hadn't eaten in a month.

Silver Sands Camp is adjacent to a hotel on the beach near the harbor; a beautiful location. But to our dismay, there is a sign next to the campgrounds which reads: "Muggers Beyond this Point." I looked around but saw no muggers.

One time, I walked to the hotel alone to look around and was immediately intercepted by a clerk from the hotel. He escorted me back to the camp and said that I should never be alone in this area, even in the hotel. Okay? That was interesting. Another lesson learned. It wasn't as safe here as it looked.

As we were waiting for Willy to finish making dinner, Destin briefed us on what to expect in Zanzibar; what to do and what not to do. He said that there would be many beach boys who spend their time hassling traveler, peddling everything from dope to boat rides or just wanting to guide us somewhere. It is best to simply ignore them as they are extremely aggressive. He also warned us to watch our belongings, as they can disappear before we know it.

At the appropriate moment, Hank said: "Sylvia and I are doing something special in Zanzibar and we would like you all to participate. (pause) We are getting married." After a moment of stunned silence, our friends cheered, congratulated us and expressed their happiness. There were hugs and kisses all around. And, of course, then the jokes started. You can always count on jokes in our group. It's great to have such good friends.

After dinner we packed our bags for the three to four day trip to Zanzibar and went to bed in our tents. The tents are beginning to feel really good by this time – so much better than the rest house we stayed in Mikumi.

Thursday, September 25, 1997
Dar es Salaam to Zanzibar

We were up before 6 am as usual. After breakfast, we finished packing. Our first stop that day was to be the American Embassy to seek advice about getting married in Zanzibar. Destin drove us all in the truck and, of course, there were jokes again. Dick Schutz made a big deal out of filming with his video camera. However, when we arrived outside of the Embassy, American soldiers immediately stopped us and wanted to confiscate his video camera for security reasons. Dick quickly explained why we were there and they let us go, saying, "Okay, but no more filming." Immediately we put our cameras away.

Destin dropped Hank and I off and made arrangements with us to meet later that morning. He suggested that we ride the bus into town alone, but we were rather intimidated by the thought of being on our own in that large foreign city where we didn't speak the language to ask directions if we got lost. Destin agreed to return to the Embassy for us.

After being thoroughly examined and questioned at the gate, we were allowed to enter the Embassy. It was an awesome experience. Once in the waiting room with others, I began to relax a bit. Hank is always relaxed. Next to us I noticed an American man with a young African woman who was very nervous. He kept assuring her that it would be okay. I wonder if they were going to get married too, or if she was going to the US to become a Nanny.

When our names were called, we explained our situation to the two ladies behind the counter. They were very nice and after copying our passports, gave us a letter of introduction. They said that there was a hotel in Stone Town by the name of The Emerson Hotel owned by an American who would know about the procedures to follow for permission to get married. They wished us good luck and we were on our way. Step 1 completed.

We waited for over an hour for Destin to arrive. He came by bus to meet us as he would be leaving the truck at Camp during the days we would be in Zanzibar. The three of us boarded a bus into town. It was a strange feeling being the only Whites in a busload of Blacks. Although I never felt threatened, it was still an unsettling experience. Once off the bus, we made our way through the throngs of people, taking care of our belongings as there are many pickpockets and tourists are definitely the minority here. We grabbed some food along the way and soon were at the docks where our friends were waiting for us.

We boarded the Catamaran at noon and were finally on our way about an hour later. The pleasant Catamaran ride across the Indian Ocean took about 45 minutes. Onboard we bought meat rolls and drinks for lunch. It was all very exciting!!

Once onboard, we found a lounge where we sat together and looked around. Soon we noticed some Muslims in very dirty robes rolling their prayer rugs out on the floor before them to begin their prayers. A man on television overhead is leading the prayers. We would hear this almost every hour on the hour beginning at 4 am during our stay in Stone Town.

The Island of Zanzibar, once called "The Spice Island," was once the slave capital of the World. It is a mixture of Arab, East Indian and African culture. Stone Town is the hub of Zanzibar, and one of the most fascinating places in the World. It is a maze of narrow streets lined with tall white washed houses and shops. Many have balconies and large beautifully carved brass-studded doors. There are people everywhere. There is noise and confusion the minute we get on the streets.

Destin encouraged us to go our own way and find a hotel, but we follow him in single-file, like a row of children following their father along the narrow streets to his destination to The Riverman Hotel. After some haggling with the manager, Destin agreed to pay $8 per night per room, including breakfast. He thought it was too high, but we didn't. That is, until after we saw the rooms. Because we were hot and tired and didn't know where else to stay, we decided that we would stay here. It couldn't be that bad!! We found out later that there is a power shortage on the Island and water, which of course runs off power, ran intermittently.

After depositing our luggage in our room, Hank and I went in search of the Emerson Hotel. Harold went off exploring alone and the rest of the group followed Destin.

After walking around a bit on the main streets, not knowing which way to go, we decided the wisest course of action would be to hire a taxi. Of course, he would know where the Emerson Hotel is; Right? The taxi driver indicated that he knew the hotel but with his accent and limited English, we were not so sure. After driving for about five minutes, he stopped before a narrow street his taxi could not navigate and told us to go down this street and turn down that one and it was right there. Well, we weren't convinced because it didn't seem like an American would own a hotel in such a poor section. So, we said, "No, no, the Emerson, The Emerson." "Oh," he said, The Merzon, with such a heavy accent that we thought he said Emerson, and we responded "Yes." He turned around and took us to another hotel by the name of the Merzon where he let us off. Once inside, the clerk told us that Tom Green, the American, was at the Emerson, not the Merzon. He gave us directions, but we could not make sense out of what he was saying. Sensing our confusion, he suggested we use the "street urchin" Ahmed, who was just outside the door and he would take us there. And, he did, running ahead at a brisk pace.

Stone Town is a maze of multi-storied buildings and it is almost impossible to find your way around without a guide because all the buildings look alike.

Ahmed is a small young man, barefoot, dressed in shabby, dirty clothing and has very bad teeth. It was impossible to tell his age. He was nice and respectful and knew exactly where we wanted to go. When we got to the Emerson, we were told that we needed to go to the New Emerson Hotel, not the old one. That's where Tom Green lives. So, Ahmed quickly guided us there. Believe it or not, it was exactly where the taxi driver tried to tell us it was the first time

Once in the lobby which had a dirt floor and no furniture except for a desk and a couple of chairs, we had to wait for over an hour for Tom as he was taking a bath. While waiting in the lobby, a young couple came in with a little girl. As they were heading toward the stairs, I asked if they were staying here. He said they were, and we asked if the rooms were nice. They replied they were and asked if we would like to see theirs. Of course we did. So, we followed them to their room, about four stories up the narrow stairway. The room was huge; the size of an apartment in New York. It was tastefully decorated in Moorish motif and quite beautiful. They told us that Mr. Emerson had bought the hotel a few years back and was re-decorating it from the top down. Hence, the dirt floor in the lobby. We thanked them for their cordiality and chit-chatted a bit about our Safari trip and upcoming marriage, before returning to the lobby.

When Tom Green finally came down to meet us he informed us that his partner, Mr. Emerson, who usually handled weddings, was in London, but he would be happy to help us. He agreed to meet us again at 7:30 the following morning to help plan the wedding. As it was almost dinner time, we asked for a suggestion for dinner and he recommended The Spice House.

Ahmed took us to the Spice House and agreed to return for us at 8 pm. Dinner was very nice even though there was no electricity. We had drinks and dinner by candle light. They must have cooked our meal over an open fire because it took forever. But, we were in no hurry, enjoying each other's company in the candle light. Hank ordered white fish and I had shrimp and calamari. Ahmed was there as instructed and walked us through the dark to The Riverman Hotel. What fun to be alone in this foreign country and planning our wedding. I couldn't believe this was really happening.

Back at the hotel, we had to wait for almost an hour for water to begin running again so we could take a shower. After the shower, we crawled in between the damp sheets where we quickly began to perspire again. Not only was it hot but it was very humid. We couldn't even snuggle.

Friday, September 26, 1997
Stone Town, Tanzania

We have been gone from home a whole month now, but it seems like we only arrived a couple of days ago. Didn't get much sleep but we survived due to anticipation. Today was the day we would get our license to be married.

The next morning Destin, Hank & I found – after several wrong turns – the New Emerson Hotel and met with Tom Green. Ahmed, who had agreed to meet us there, arrived a few minutes later. Tom was excited to be arranging our wedding and was agreeable to everything we asked. We worked out the details for a roof-top wedding at the hotel restaurant. As the restaurant would be open to guests at night, we agreed to an afternoon wedding with appetizers and drinks and be out of there by 4 pm so they could get ready for their dinner guests...

Tom then spoke to Ahmed for a few minutes and we were off to the Regional Commissioner's office for the license.

Again, no one is on schedule in Africa. After having to wait for over an hour for the local commissioner, we were shown into his office where we were asked to sit down in front of the desk of Mr. H. S. Ahmed a large, obese, very stern looking African man. We told him what we wanted and his first question was: "Why do you want to get married?" What a question! We looked at each other, and Hank answered him. He then asked "Why do you want to get married in Africa?" Another silly questions; although I don't think he thought so. Now, he said, "How do I know you are not already married to someone else?" We answered that we weren't. He then asked "You need to be a resident of this Island for three weeks before you can get married here? Say What? Hank answered, "But we'll only be here a few more days as we are on a Photo Safari Tour." The Commissioner, looked puzzled, but then answered, "Oh, that's okay, just pay the additional fee and that will be waived." I guess money talks everywhere you go. After he was satisfied with our answers, or else he couldn't think of any more questions, he told us that we needed to go to another location and pay a fee at the tax office. He handed us a paper to be stamped as a receipt that we had paid the tax.

Ahmed said he knew where that office was, so off we went again, walking quickly through the busy streets to keep up with Ahmed. We were told the tax was $10,000 Schillings, which is about $18.00 US. OK, we could afford that.

We ran into our camera club friends who were on their way to take a Spice Tour and talked about what we were up to. Once at the office, we saw several long lines of local people patiently waiting their turn. Hank & I thought "Oh, no, this is going to take forever." But that didn't stop Ahmed, our street urchin. He elbowed his way to the front of the line, immediately paid the fee for our license, and off we went. With the stamped paper in hand, we made our way back to the commissioner's office, only to be told that he was out and would be back later. Oh, My! Now what?

However, he soon returned and we were immediately ushered into his office. Now, his office reminded us of the old Sidney Greenstreet movies of the 1940's. It was a big, long room, devoid of furniture or decoration except for a large old-fashioned desk at one end, old curtains, a florescent light hanging from electrical cords in the middle of the room and tall windows.

Again he asked, "Why do you want to get married." When we answered to his satisfaction, again he asked: "Why do you want to get married in Africa?" When we answered that questions, he asked: "How do I know you are not already married?" What? Why would we want to get married if we were already married to someone else? Do people really do that in his country?

Hank told him that we were both unmarried and we had seven friends with us who would testify that we were not already married. He replied, "Well, that won't be necessary, just give me an affidavit that you are not already married and we will accept that. Unbelievable! I asked where we could find a notary. He said that will not be necessary, just write on a piece of paper that you are not already married to someone else and sign it. I tore two pages out of my journal and Hank and I wrote out our affidavits. He looked at them briefly along with the stamped paper, put them aside and then nodded. He also needed copies of our passports and a copy of the letter from the American Embassy. So, we were all set.

All this time Mr. Ahmed had been very serious and gruff, never making eye contact with us or smiling. As we rose to leave, impulsively, I asked if we could take a picture with him. His demeanor changed immediately as if I had offered him a million dollars. He smiled broadly, motioned for his assistant to take the camera and put his large arm around me. With Hank and Ahmed at my side, the picture was taken. The photo didn't turn out very good, but it is a great memory.

Since Mr. Ahmed would be conducting the wedding and was busy on Saturday, he agreed to meet us at 2 pm on Sunday at the New Emerson Hotel to perform the ceremony.

By 10 am, we were done. All was set. We had two whole days to make the final arrangements and do a little sightseeing. When we met Destin, he took us to a local restaurant for lunch; a "hole in the wall" really. It was dirty with a sink hanging off the wall for patrons to wash their hands. But we ate there anyway, not wanting to seem squeamish. We had their typical white fish, a samposa, which is a cold drink, and tea. It was worse than eating off the streets in Mexico, but we were able to get it down.

Ahmed guided me back to the New Emerson Hotel to tell Tom what we had accomplished and finalize our plans. The wedding would be held at 2 pm in his beautiful roof-top restaurant.

Hank went with Destin to get some money. Back at the Riverman, I was hot and sweaty, so stripped and tried to take a nap. There was no thought of taking another shower as there was no water. We regrouped at the Riverman for our next adventure.

We needed wedding rings and find a nicer hotel for our honeymoon. After checking a couple of jewelry stores, we decided to take a break at the Fort for refreshments. Destin joined us briefly, but then went off on his own. Hank & I wandered the streets looking for a nice hotel. We found that the rates were either $135 US or $8; no mid-range. We tried The Tembo Hotel, which was beautiful with a clear pool in the center of the lobby, but there were no vacancies. Destin recommended the Chavra, but we couldn't find it. Where was Ahmed when we needed him? Tired of walking and lugging camera equipment, we returned to the Riverman to unload. On our way out again and after several wrong turns, we ran into Destin. Of course, he knew where the Chavra was and agreed to take us there. He knew we would really like it. Well, can you believe that even Destin got lost? But with the help of another "street urchin" we finally got to our destination. The hotel and honeymoon suite was wonderful, decorated in Moorish decor and would cost us $113 per night. After telling the young gracious hotel manager of our plans, he asked "Where are you having dinner after the wedding?" We hadn't thought of that. He suggested that we could have dinner there for the 10 of us at the hotel and he would give us a reasonable price. We agreed. So, we would have two receptions that day. It would cost us $100 US for the wedding at the Emerson and $400 US for the two nights and dinner for 10 at the Chavra; seemed reasonable to us. It was done. All the plans made. We then went up to the roof-top bar for drinks, relax, enjoy the view and bring Destin up to speed with our plans.

Now all we had to do was find some wedding rings. We would wear clothes we had with us. After all I did have a skirt. We then headed toward the main street and as we were meandering along, Destin spotted an East Indian Curio Shop and suggested we go in because they had a good selection of postcards. And, would you believe it, in the counter right in front were silver rings; how lucky we are. Hank & I selected one each, forgetting about the postcards. We told the nice lady in her native dress that we were getting married on Sunday. She mentioned that she had heard that Americans were getting married at the Emerson– small town. She then asked if I had a dress to wear. I told her that I had brought a skirt with me and would wear that with a t-shirt – nothing fancy, after all Hank & I often talked about getting married in jeans and sweatshirts back home. She said that she had a Muslim style dress that she recently purchased but hadn't worn yet. She would be willing to sell it to me for her cost -- $33.00 US. I tried it on and it was perfect. Soft peach colored pants and top with a beautiful sheer flowing scarf of the same color. I loved it. We looked for a shirt for Hank, but found none.

Thankfully, back at the Riverman Hotel, there was water and electricity, so we took showers and got ready to go to dinner at the Emerson Hotel, the location for our wedding on Sunday. Walking, we found the old Emerson okay, but looking lost, someone from there offered to guide us to the New Emerson Hotel.

We climbed the four or five flights of stairs to the roof top and what a pleasant surprise. The open area was decorated in a Persian motif with cushions around small tables and billowing silk for a ceiling. Custom dictated that we remove our shoes before entering. There were about six or seven local men waiters standing around the bar. We chose a table next to a White couple from South Africa and introduced ourselves. They introduced themselves as Shirley and Edward Pysden. Shirl is extroverted while her husband is quiet and shy. Isn't that always the way with couples? We talked throughout the dinner and felt I had known them all my life. I impulsively invited them to the wedding on Sunday. Tom Green sat down and joined us for dinner. We had a grand time.

The well-cooked white fish, and delicately spiced rice and mixed vegetables were delicious. The appetizers were unique as well as tasty. Along with the ten other guests, we were fortunate enough to see the beautiful sun setting.

Between food courses, Tanzanian dancers -- two women and one man -- sang and danced to music by men keeping the beat on drums. It was wonderful and quite a unique experience. Finding out way back to the Riverman Hotel in pitch black was memorable. I don't know how Hank did it, but he went right to it as if he could see in the dark. We were in bed by 10 pm and slept soundly.

Saturday, September 27, 1997
Stone Town, Tanzania

We awoke at 4 am, 5 am and again at 6 am to the sounds of piped Muslim music announcing the time. Finally giving up, we arose and sat on the porch outside of our room. Our friends came out one by one to catch up on our plans for the wedding. They were as excited as we were.

We packed our belonging as we would be sleeping tonight in a $113 dollar a night hotel instead of the $8 dollar a night hotel. Hopefully, we would be able to take showers when we wanted and not when the electricity made the decision for us.

Downstairs at breakfast, everyone talked about their plans for the day. The rest of the group would be going snorkeling, but Hank & I decided we had to take care of a few things before the wedding -- mainly get some more money, which is not as easy as going to an ATM on a street corner in the US or Europe. We also wanted to check into the Chavda Hotel and get settled there.

Destin came by and decided to come with us. We again got lost. Finally, Hank took the lead and we were able to find the hotel. We checked in, dropped our luggage and with only our cameras in hand headed out on a new adventure. At Destin's suggestion, we agreed to rent Vespa motor scooters to explore the northern and rural parts of the island. After checking the prices at a couple of rental shops, our guide said he could get Vespa's for $15 each per day. So there again, we followed a guide clear across Stone Town to a shop, which was nothing more than a small dirty garage, probably owned by a relative. Before taking off on our scooters, Hank suggested that I ride behind Destin until he got used to riding the Vespa. It turned out to be a very wise decision.

Destin and I took off first. We turned one corner, then another and looking back found that Hank was not behind us. So I asked Destin to stop and wait for him. Two young men also on a Vespa rode by and one shouted "He's dead." Oh! I would be a widow before I was even married. I just started running. In the middle of the block, a gentleman stopped me and started talking in Swahili -- which sounded like gibberish. But every now and then he said the American word "husband" and pointed. My heart stopped -- I continued running. When I got to the corner, I saw Hank was standing, and laughing and talking to the men of the shop with a crowd of locals around them. What a relief! Upon getting close, I saw that he had quite a large gash on his leg.

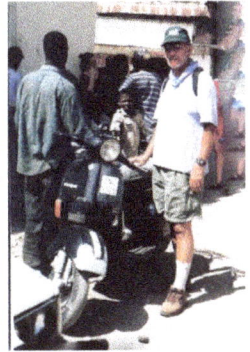

He told me when he rounded the first corner, the bike slid on some gravel into a ditch pinning his leg between the bike and the drainage ditch. Not much damage to the scooter, but some to his leg.

The owner of the shop insisted that Hank go to the clinic around the corner for treatment. I agreed because with all the debris in the gash, it could easily get infected. At the clinic, which was not much more than a room with a dirt

floor, Hank was attended by a beautiful young girl, who wore an all-black gerba. All you could see were her eyes. She looked like a teenager. The doctor, who spoke very good English, asked Hank when he had his last Tetanus shot. Even though we had gotten ours in the States just before coming to Africa, he insisted Hank get another. We had been told that whatever happens; do not get shots in Africa as many of the needles are not sterile. Hank was ready to decline, when we saw that the injection needle was sealed in plastic and appeared completely sterilized. So he let her give him the shot. She then poured iodine on the wound, which hurt like crazy. Then, she took some sterilized cotton and put it on the wound. Sounds nuts, Huh? But it completely sealed the wound and kept it from getting infected. When it dried, it became hard like a scab and Hank was then able to peel it off when the wound healed. What an experience! The fee for the medical service was $5.00 US.

We went on our way with me behind Destin and Hank behind us. Needless to say, I kept looking back to make sure he was still there.

We drove through some of the most beautiful lush areas we had seen thus far. There were tropical trees, banana and cocoanut groves, and plants surrounding the small villages. The homes of the villages were red as they were built of bamboo and red mud. The local men all wore kangas (native skirts) instead of pants. At the north end of the Island, we came upon a beautiful white sandy beach. The water was a beautiful turquoise color and very clear. There was a small open bar selling beer and drinks, so we each had one and just sat there enjoying the view. It was so colorful, white sand, red dirt, turquoise water, bright green foliage all under a bright blue sky. It was like a picture postcard. Beautiful!

After a while, Destin went off to explore alone. I rode behind Hank from then on. Unfortunately we had another spill while riding through a village on the way to the beach. Hank did not see the bamboo pole across the path at about eye level. Too late to stop, he laid the scooter down before hitting it. Only his pride and camera lens filter were hurt. As we left, we saw an old man come out and remove the bamboo pole. We enjoyed our time there taking photos of the scenery and locals.

Back in Stone Town, we needed to get more cash to pay for the wedding expenses. We knew exactly where this bank of sorts was, drove directly there through the maze of traffic dodging pedestrians, bicycles, and scooters, parked the Vespa and went inside. The place, which looked like an old-fashioned bank, with tellers behind iron bars, was busy. After waiting our turn, I pushed my credit card toward the clerk, saying "Cash." He said a few words in Swahili, which I didn't understand and pushed the card back toward me. What? Hank & I looked at each other, and I pushed the card back, saying again simply, "Cash." He again said something and pushed the card back. Realizing we were getting nowhere I asked a blond gentleman, who happened to walk in, for help. After talking to the clerk the man told us that on Saturdays they only cashed travelers' checks. What kind of business is this? The man said that he knew of another money business where we could get cash on our credit cards.

So, we left following him on our Vespa while he rode his bicycle very fast. We had a hard time keeping up with him what with all the weaving in and out of traffic, but Hank managed. The man stopped at the opening of what looked like an open-air market and told us to go down one block and it would be the last building on the left. We thanked him for his help and he then proceeded on his way. Hank walked the Vespa very carefully through the throng of people and parked in front of the last building on the left. Inside the store, we were told to go back outside and up the side stairs. This was spooky and reminded us of going into a Speakeasy in an old Humphrey Bogart movie.

Anyway, we went back outside, up the stairs then into a large room that was like a very nice banker's office. There was a pretty young African girl sitting behind the desk. After telling her why we were there, she had an African man escort us into another large room empty of furniture except for a large old desk with two chairs in front of it. Behind the desk was an elderly African gentleman. When we told him that he needed $500 US off of each of our credit cards, he asked for our passports. After writing down our names, my passport number (Hank's was with the Vespa shop), and the amounts we wanted on a yellow legal pad, he asked the first man to escort us to the "money room." We were told his commission would be 15%. Is this a loan shark or what? But what the heck, we needed the money.

In the caged money room, another man counted out the money for us. The bills are nothing like ours. The man insisted that we count the money to see if we had the correct amount. This was impossible; so we just left, stuffing the large bills in our pockets.

We now had to go out into the crowded streets. It was scary because I was afraid we could be held up at knife point at any time. Oh, and I forgot to mention, it was beginning to get dark. My heart was going a mile a minute, praying we would get back to our hotel before it got pitch black. Hank, of course, was as ever calm.

We found our way back to the shop to return the Vespa only to find out that the owner would not return Hank's passport until he paid for the damage to the Vespa he "wrecked." Hank tried to bargain as the damage was minor, but we still had to pay the exorbitant amount of $50 US to get his passport out of hostage. Americans get taken advantage of in every country at some time or another.

Glad to be back at the Hotel Chavra, we showered and went to the roof top bar for a much-needed drink. Oscar, the friendly bartender, spoke good English, so we chatted with him. Downstairs in the dining room, we had a wonderful dinner -- huge prawns and lobster. It was wonderful. The manager, Ahmed (almost everyone is named Ahmed) came in and we were able to finalize our plans for the Wedding Buffet Dinner with Habib, the Chef, who came out to greet us. The hotel had only been open for two months, so everything was new and beautiful, and they were eager to please us.

Sunday, September 28, 1997

Stone Town, Tanzania

Wedding Day in Zanzibar, Africa.

I can't believe this is actually going to happen. Both Hank & I were restless during the night and slept little, even though sleeping in a real bed with air conditioning was wonderful. At 7 am Hank dressed quickly and walked to the Riverman to ask Harold to be his best man. I stayed in the room to watch CNN on TV and catch up on my journal. When he got back, we went downstairs and enjoyed a wonderful breakfast. The staff all knew we were the "honeymoon couple" so gave us a lot of attention.

We walked around town to get our bearings and go back to the clinic for another shot for Hank. He thought it was no big deal, but I wanted the nurse to see him again because his wound kept bleeding.

We found our way back to the Chavra Hotel after stopping to buy a few gifts along the way. Hank found a shirt to get married in. Again, we bought postcards for our family back home. Back at the hotel by noon, we showered and got ready for our wedding. We looked and felt everyone was looking at us as we walked along the streets. Arriving at the New Emerson Hotel one-half hour early, we found our friends and Ed and Shirley already waiting. Tom Green and his crew were not ready for us yet. I suppose African time is the same as Mexican time – everyone is always late. So, we relaxed a bit in the lobby with the dirt floor.

Much to our surprise, Ahmed, our "street urchin and guide," came in bathed, hair combed and cleanly dressed wearing sandals. He showed Hank a letter written in Swahili --which of course we could not read and for all we knew had nothing to do with us. Ahmed said that the commissioner had asked him to attend the wedding because since we were foreigners a local had to attend as a witness. We didn't believe that for a moment but were delighted to have here with us. Earlier I wanted him to be a part of the wedding since he had been so polite and helpful, but because of his dirty hands, feet and clothing, thought it would not be appropriate. With Ed, Shirley and Ahmed, we had 10 guests in all, not counting Tom and his five waiters. The waiters enjoyed the festivities as much as we did. Tom showed us a beautiful orange flower he had personally found in the jungle for our centerpiece.

The commissioner arrived shortly before 2 pm in a very jovial mood ready to perform the ceremony. After a cordial drink, Hank & I stood up in front of him with Betty and Harold as witnesses and he began. It was a very strange ceremony. All it consisted of was the commissioner asking a question, us answering it and then signing a document -- about three times. He then pronounced us married. There were no vows or anything. But we did exchange rings and kiss. The commissioner gave us our marriage certificate, which we found out later is good in the US, even though it had my father's

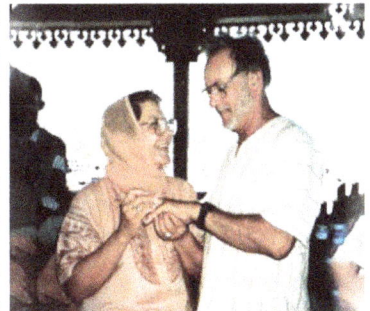

name wrong. He inserted my last name as my father's first name as is the African custom. But, it was too complicated to go about changing anything at this point. Who would know?

The party was festive with wine, appetizers and even a beautiful wedding cake. Ahmed, our "street urchin", enjoyed the reception and the refreshments and I'm sure felt very important. He would have something to brag to his family and friends about for years to come. Tom Green even remarked at one point, "Your street urchin is in his element, look at him, he's having the time of his life." And he was indeed. Hank & I were both happy that he came. Everyone was happy for us and Ed Pysden was the only one who shed tears during the ceremony. I'll never forget that.

The funny thing, about the wedding was that even though we are a camera club, no one thought to bring a camera to photograph our wedding. As an afterthought I had stuck my small "point & shoot" in my bag, so someone used it. Dick Schutz, the only non-member of the club, brought his video camera. So we did have a few photos.

While Iris was taking video, she commented: "Here we are at Hank & Sylvia's wedding, on the tallest building in Zimbabwe." We all burst out laughing because we were not in Zimbabwe – we were in Tanzania. Poor Iris gets teased about that even now after so long a time, especially by Hank.

Ed and Shirl have never failed to send us an anniversary card every year on our anniversary, September 28th. We have remained good friends and email back and forth frequently. In fact, his son and daughter-in-law, Chris and Vicky, immigrated to California in 2003 and we are good friends too-- but that's another story. When Ed and Shirl they came to the US to see their new granddaughter, they went out of their way to spend a day with us in Las Vegas. That was special.

After the reception, we walked in caravan to the Chavda Hotel for dinner. First we had drinks in the roof top bar, laughing and kidding all the time. The sunset was beautiful as only an African sunset can be.

At 7 o'clock we went downstairs to the Garden Restaurant in the hotel for dinner. We had to wait a few minutes so they could add chairs for Ahmed, Tom Green and Ed and Shirl. We had forgotten to add them to our list. Tom even brought over the beautiful orange flower that I had inadvertently forgotten.

The buffet was extraordinary and exceeded our expectations. The prawns were larger than I have ever seen before. There was fried squid, fried fish, chicken and four different salads. I remember that I couldn't eat very much as I was still so excited. We then had another wedding cake along with fruit salad for desert. It was a wonderful day and everyone had a great time, especially the bride and groom.

The guests left about 9:30 and Hank and I went up to our beautiful Honeymoon Suite. But before going to bed, I had to finish the postcards I had planned to send to our close friends and family announcing that we were now married. Hank thought I was "nuts" but helped anyway.

Monday, September 29, 1997
Zanzibar, Tanzania

Rising early, we had a leisurely breakfast on the terrace, talking about how funny the wedding ceremony was, how great the two receptions were and how remarkable that none of our photographer friends brought camera. For breakfast, we had papaya, bread and eggs. The delicious eggs, although called a Spanish omelet were simply scrambled with onion, tomato and bell pepper.

The day before we decided to join the Schutz and Betty for a 3-day trip to the

East Coast of Zanzibar. Harold, Ernie and the Sherman's decided that they would go along for the ride, but would return to Stone Town. After packing our small bag, we met Ahmed downstairs along with the driver of the van we would travel in. We picked up

the others and were soon on our way. The trip cost $50; split between all of us was not too bad, however, they wanted to charge another $50 for half of our group to return to Stone Town. After much haggling, they were able to reduce the return fare.

The roads were terrible with many ruts once you get off the paved roads of Stone Town, so we got bumped around a lot. When we got to the small village we found The Gomani Family Guest House and our bungalows, which were located a row on the cliff overlooking the Indian Ocean. What a spectacular sight! However we were surprised to learn upon checking in that in addition to the room rate, we had to pay an additional $10 for salt water to shower with and use in the toilets that didn't always work. The electricity also went out every couple of hours. Other than that the place was immaculate. A woman continuously swept the dirt pathways. Of course, the first thing we did after checking was have lunch at the very rustic lunch room at the hotel. It was nothing more than a small square room with three of four square tables and one small window through which to see the ocean.

While waiting for lunch to be served we watched the women bring in seaweed they had harvested that morning. We again had white fish and rice with a sauce of some kind. After lunch we just relaxed, some of taking naps, reading or simply sitting and enjoying the view.

While sitting in front of our cabins a young boy came by and asked if we wanted tattoos. It is the Muslim custom for women to have their hands and/or feet tattooed. We asked if the tattoos were permanent, and he said no, they would only last for about six weeks. Betty, Iris and I agreed so he hurriedly went to get his sisters. He brought back two very beautiful girls who appeared to be in their late teens. One carried a book of her designs, so we each picked one each and told her where we wanted the tattoos placed. The prettiest girl was very professional and with a little stick she dipped in black ink, drew the designs we wanted. They were beautiful!!

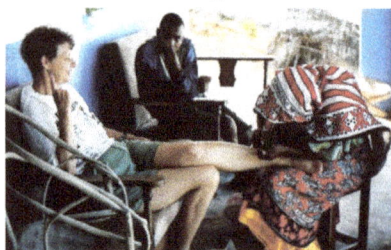

Dick, Iris and I opened a bottle of Merlot given to us by the manager of the Chavda Hotel and enjoyed "Happy Hour" overlooking the Indian Ocean.

Hank took a nap in the afternoon because he wasn't feeling well, but was better by 7 pm, so he went with us to the dining room to celebrate Iris' birthday. Since we did not have transportation, we had to eat again at the guest house dining room. I ordered prawns, which had a strong fishy smell, so ate only the chips. Betty and Iris ordered one dinner of lobster to split, but were charged for two orders. The lobster was not good either so they didn't eat it. Dick ordered Calamari which was chewy. Hank just had a warm soda.

After dinner, Dick & Iris went to the local school to see a filming of folk dancing by the BBC. We later learned that the filming was being done by Henry Gates, a professor from Harvard, who was in Africa tracing his Nubian Roots.

Later that night we heard people laughing behind our cabins. Coming out to investigate, we found that the owner of the guest house had placed a television set on the road behind us and plugged it in with a long cord from the office. That way all the villagers could watch TV. No wonder everywhere we went the young boys would ask: "Do you know Arnold Schwarzenegger or Michael Jordan."

Hank was sick all night running a slight fever and stayed in bed the next day. I saw no cars in the village and worried about how we could get back to Stone Town in case his illness became serious.

Tuesday, September 30, 1997
East Coast of Zanzibar, Tanzania

Hank continued with a low grade fever which broke during the night, so in the morning he felt much better. After a light breakfast, Betty, Iris and I took a day trip South to see dolphins. The car ride took over an hour on extremely rough roads. Although the boat ride was nice, we did not see many dolphins breaking the surface. A few people on our tour swam out over the dolphins to see them underwater. They served us lunch of -- guest what? -- white fish and rice with a sauce. The best part of the trip was meeting a trio of Peace Corp Volunteers from the States. They had completed their tour in Botswana and were on Holiday before heading back home. Tina and Kate were from Seattle and David Otani was from La Palma, California, practically next door to

Long Beach. They were friendly and delightful. David said he knew Harold's daughter Carlene and her husband, Henry from Botswana. What a small world! We exchanged names and addresses and David said he might come for a visit, but as expected, never did. They would continue their African tour towards Uganda and probably leave Africa from Morocco. How wonderful to be young and unattached with no responsibilities. They reminded us that we saw them in Malawi at Nakata Beach. Oh yeah!

We also met a physician by the name of Greg and his companion, Anthony from Manchester. Greg had worked in this area as a physician with the VSO nine years ago and speaks Swahili fluently.

Back at the cottages, we took naps. Hank is much better and the scrape on his leg is healing nicely.

During Happy Hour we finished off the wine and watched Dick's video of our wedding. He did a great job.

That evening Ali, the manager took us in a hired car (didn't know there was one) to the Oyster Hotel Restaurant so we could have a nice dinner. The

service was overly polite, but the food excellent. The hotel had only been opened for a short time and they are trying very hard to please us, their only customers that night. We didn't see any hotel guests either. Their prices were a bit on the high side, but after all it was a classy place with cloth tablecloths and napkins. For dinner I had breaded fried calamari, which was the best I had had in a while. Hank ordered fried chicken; Betty spaghetti with shrimp in tomato sauce; Iris had coconut-covered fried fish and Dick ordered a seafood pizza. The meal made him sick.

After reaching the guest house after dinner, we went straight to bed. I'm am getting used to sleeping anywhere and slept well through the night. The East Coast is certainly primitive with a virgin beauty all its own.

Wednesday, October 1, 1997
East Coast of Zanzibar, Tanzania

Slept with Hank in his narrow bed that night -- after all we are still on our honeymoon. He tossed and turned all night but we made ourselves comfortable.

We packed our bags to be ready to leave when the van arrived. Breakfast was okay, but not that great. We talked briefly with Greg, the doctor before leaving.

Dick Schutz was very sick during the night with his dinner coming out both ends. Poor Dick looked pretty bad and was not looking forward to the drive back to Stone Town over the bumpy roads. However, the van that picked us up was a newer vehicle with nice Captain's chairs instead of benches. Since there were only five us, we were able to spread out and get comfortable.

We drove directly to the docks, arriving at 11 am, to meet the others and make arrangements for the boat ride back to Dar es Salaam. Since the Hydrofoil does not run on Wednesdays, we had to wait until 1:30 pm to exchange our tickets for the Air Bus. Below deck the Captain's chairs were lined up like a big wide bus, and we quickly found our seats together. Dick & Jan stayed topside to enjoy the fresh air.

Unfortunately the ride was rough and quite a few passengers got seasick, including me. Thankfully I don't throw up when I get seasick; just dizzy, weak and shaky. Hank wasn't even aware that I had been seasick during the ride. It was over the minute my feet hit land.

Another chaotic and noisy location when we arrived with barkers wanting you to hire their taxis or guides. The walk through the line of busses was an experience. Someone stole something from Betty's bag, but Harold -- the hero that he is – saw it happening and chased him. He got it back. Destin met us at the docks and, bless his heart, had sandwiches ready for us in the van.

Upon arriving at the Silver Sands Camp at about 5 pm, the first thing we did was set up our tents. Then we all took showers, but before I could finish mine, the water stopped even though I could hear someone taking a shower in the Men's room. How frustrating! But this is Africa, what can you expect? The water came on again at 7 pm and at this point even a cold shower felt wonderful. We had dinner at 7:30 and I went to bed to write in my journal. The men continued to "rag" on me about this, but I didn't care. The wind blew really hard that night. Periodically I would peek out to look at the bright stars.

Thursday, October 2, 1997

Dar es Salaam

Today, everyone needed to do laundry. I woke up around 4 am, but read until about 5:30. Between Hank & I we had a lot of dirty clothes, so first we did only our underwear and a few t-shirts. We would do the rest later. The guys chided Hank because he was helping me. Harold said, "Hey Hank, is this what happens when you get married?"

We relaxed the rest of the day. Breakfast was good, and then Hank & I finished the rest of the laundry, so now everything is clean, just waiting for the clothes to dry.

We took a walk along the beach. The beach was wide because of a low tide and we watched men fishing with nets. They would throw the nets out and pull them in bringing in whatever was caught. We came across a man selling a beautiful large orange seashell. Of course I wanted it so *I* began to bargain with him. I think he started out asking $5 US, but I ended up giving him my Reese' baseball hat. We were both happy with the exchange.

After a good lunch, I put my pad under a tropical shade tree and read. Hank joined me and soon we both were sound asleep. Betty, Jan, Iris, Ernie and Dick returned from a trip to a museum and joined Hank & I in the shade to have their lunch. Hank cleaned his camera and mine -- it's amazing how dusty a camera can get when you are on a trip like this. We took down our dry laundry, folded it and put it away. Dick Sherman was now sick and moped around all day. He looks like he has lost not only 20 lbs., but his best friend too. I tried to make tortillas that evening for dinner with "corn flour" I had found at the market, but failed miserably. Hank saved the day by frying them. Willy liked them, but he had never had a tortilla before. Betty and I made Spanish rice and beans. Willy made a sauce with peas and carrots. (Again Dick Sherman passed on the cooked carrots) For some reason I couldn't get comfortable so didn't sleep well that night.

Friday, October 3, 1997
Arusha, Tanzania

We were up by 6 am and Harold had already cooked breakfast of Hash with potatoes, eggs, onion and bell pepper. What a guy? Willy cooked oatmeal for Destin because he had been sick for a couple of days and did not want to eat the hash. At one time or another everyone has been sick except Betty, Harold and I, but the trip is far from over. (seasickness doesn't count).

We left camp at 7 am and drove through the early-morning commuters in Dar es Salaam with guys hanging out of small busses yelling for people to ride their buses.

When we got to the countryside, we began to see people dressed in Muslim-style clothing and small villages with huts made from the red dirt.

The vista is absolutely beautiful as the road climbs into the mountains with rock outcroppings peeking out of the lush vegetation. We saw dozens of banana groves, coconut trees and fields of maize (corn). We saw jungles, savannas and fires in the distance. We saw Masai warriors walking along the road, walking through the fields, in towns and even riding on the backs of trucks. At one spot, there must have 30-40 of them. The Masai wear only red shawls, wrapped around them. One couple I saw must have been chiefs because they were wearing bright purple instead of red.

Nearing Arusha, we began to see more and more crops of maize, tobacco, bananas and coconut, and it goes without saying, more housing and people. We stopped for lunch of left-over hash, peanut butter and jelly sandwiches and watermelon. There was another Overland truck by the side of the road so Destin walked over to see if they needed help. We took photos while we waited, our favorite pastime. What else?

We were up by 6 am and Harold had already cooked breakfast of Hash with potatoes, eggs, onion and bell pepper. What a guy? Willy cooked oatmeal for Destin because he had been sick for a couple of days and did not want to eat the hash. At one time or another everyone has been sick except Betty, Harold and I, but the trip is far from over. (seasickness doesn't count).

We left camp at 7 am and drove through the early-morning commuters in Dar es Salaam with guys hanging out of small busses yelling for people to ride their buses.

When we got to the countryside, we began to see people dressed in Muslim-style clothing and small villages with huts made from the red dirt.

The vista is absolutely beautiful as the road climbs into the mountains with rock outcroppings peeking out of the lush vegetation. We saw dozens of banana groves, coconut trees and fields of maize (corn). We saw jungles, savannas and fires in the distance. We saw Masai warriors walking along the road, walking through the fields, in towns and even riding on the backs of trucks. At one spot, there must have 30-40 of them. The Masai wear only red shawls, wrapped around them. One couple I saw must have been chiefs because they were wearing bright purple instead of red.

Nearing Arusha, we began to see more and more crops of maize, tobacco, bananas and coconut, and it goes without saying, more housing and people. We stopped for lunch of left-over hash, peanut butter and jelly sandwiches and watermelon. There was another Overland truck by the side of the road so Destin walked over to see if they needed help. We took photos while we waited, our favorite pastime. What else?

Today we drove for about 10 hours -- long ride -- arriving in Arusha at about 5 pm. During the approach to Arusha we were so lucky. Snowcapped Mt. Kilimanjaro was peeking through some clouds and we were able to get some good photos. Mt. Kilimanjaro, like Mt. McKinley in Alaska, is usually covered with clouds.

After a brief stop at an open market to buy meat, we arrived at the Masai Camp to stay the night. Surprise, Surprise!! -- There is a bar at the camp and a restaurant that serves what they call "Mexican Food." Destin informed us that this is a Friday Night meeting place for the ex-patriots that live in the area. So, the place was full of families with children, all visiting animatedly with each other.

While having drinks in the bar, Hank and I left the group because the trip was beginning to wear on everyone, and they started complaining. Hank is such a jewel taking every event in stride, but he didn't want to hear people snapping at each other. Tomorrow would be another day and everyone would be cordial again. After dinner of stew with tough meat and spaghetti, Hank and I went into the bar to have a cappuccino.

For some reason, during the night Hank & I got the giggles and couldn't stop. Of course, everyone heard us and teased us about it the following day.

Saturday, October 4, 1997
Arusha, Tanzania

It rained a lot during the night and Hank was up around midnight to put the rain fly on. In the morning, everything was damp and the sky full of clouds. We had oatmeal for breakfast.

After showering, we packed for our five-day trip to the Serengeti and the Ngorongoro Crater where we were told we would see hundreds and hundreds of wild animals. While waiting, I caught up on my journal and Hank and I worked on our gift list. At noon, while still waiting for Destin, Willy made lunch. Destin finally arrived at about an hour later. Ernie and Harold chose not to join us on our trip to buy groceries in town and gifts in the carver's market. They don't enjoy bargaining with the sellers at the carver's market as much as we do.

At 3 pm we met the rest of the group at the truck. Willy was waiting with a large basket full of produce. Someone mentioned that there were éclairs in a shop nearby, so a few of us took off in a rush. Hank and I bought chocolate croissants, and he had some ice cream. We bought 11 more postcards to send home to family and friends.

As Destin would not be going with us, he introduced us to his replacements -- our cook, Juma, and Wilford, our guide and driver. We had a meeting and Destin told us what to expect. He also told us that Tracks was having financial problems and he had to get that straightened out. He said that we would be going to the Serengeti and The Ngorongoro Crater in the Tracks Truck not in Land Cruisers. He said that the road would be very rough and much slower. He then told us that he did not have the cash to pay for the park fees. We could either advance him the $450 needed now or wait until Monday when he hoped to get the money from London. We voted to advance the money and hoped to get reimbursed. After dinner and popcorn, Destin left. We wondered about our new guide and cook. Would they be any good? It turned out that Wilford was an excellent guide, and Juma was a much better cook than Willie.

I was in bed writing in my journal by 7:30 pm but the group stayed up until after 1 am talking and laughing. It began raining again during the night.

Sunday, October 5, 1997
Mto-Wa-Mbu, Tanzania

Although we were not scheduled to leave until 9 am, we were up early, had breakfast and left camp an hour early. We are always early. As Hank always says, "If you are not one-half hour early, you're already an hour late."

We drove through Arusha, through some very poor sections with people busy with their early morning activities. I will never forget crossing a stream that looked like an open sewer with a tremendous amount of trash in it. Hank actually spotted someone taking a drink from this dirty stream. "Yuck." These poor people!! It's amazing how they live.

The first part of the drive was on good paved roads and we saw a lot of Masai villages, cattle, and Masai in their bright red and purple shawls. The men are very tall and thin and carry a long stick which they use to rest against when stopped. Funny, how it makes them look like they have three legs.

After a while we turned onto a dirt road and the bumps began in earnest. Dusty, rocky, roads with lots of potholes making us jostle from one side to the other. The land is desert with low scrub brush. Dust was all around us, so we put on our kerchief masks. One bus full of people tried to overtake us but then decided to make its own road through the desert. There are no rules. All we could see of them was a cloud of dust as they passed.

The Masai huts are round and made of cow dung with grass roofs. Along the way we began seeing rectangular huts with grass roofs and less and less Masai.

At first the dirt was tan or grey and then began to be red, which made everything red. It was very fine like a powder. The roads, the huts, the trees, the shrubs and even the corn stalks were red. What we thought was a salt pan in the distance was actually dry Lake Manyara. Lake Manyara is the only area where you will find lions sleeping in trees. As we got closer to the escarpment, the vegetation began to green-up and we started seeing banana plantations. We stopped for lunch at a camp in the center of Mto-Wa-Mbu. While lunch was being prepared,

we walked to the tourist shops. I had fun bargaining with the Masai and laughed as Hank allowed two Masai to inspect his leg wound.

Lunch was wonderful. Juma arranged it nicely around the table and he even had paper napkins laid out for us. It was quite an improvement over the past few weeks with Willie.

The afternoon was again dusty and bumpy. Leaving town we began the slow, dusty, bumpy climb up the escarpment. The view was spectacular. We traveled over more hills and soon saw two young boys wearing wooden masks playing homemade wooden guitars. One young boy ran after the truck for a long way, continuing to serenade us. I'll never forget the red dust flying up as his small feet hit the dusty road.

We arrived at Kudu Camp at around 3 pm. We all laughed after the tents were set up because everyone always set up the tents close together, except Harold. Because he knows he snores, he always pitched his tent far away from us. This time, Ernie set his tent up so close to Dick and Jan's tent that they couldn't even get into it. That started a mild-mannered argument, each saying he had put up his tent first.

We showered in cold water, had a beer and took a few photos while waiting for Juma to fix dinner. There is a warm breeze blowing but there are still pesky flies bothering us.

The camp is only one year old and one of the best we have encountered so far. The view all around is beautiful, the grounds clean and the workers friendly and attentive.

Dinner was again delicious. We were getting fed better, since Juma is our cook. We ate chicken in sauce, rice and cauliflower with carrots in a cheese sauce. Dick passed on the carrots again. Juma used a white cheese for the sauce which was very strong.

Monday, October 6, 1997
Kudu Camp - The Serengeti, Tanzania

During the night, the wind blew and it rained. Thank goodness, Hank had the foresight to put the rain fly up before going to bed. I sometimes wish I could stay up later in the evening, but get bored listening to the idle chatter, because I know that I can spend my time productively either reading or writing. With the noise of the wind and rain, we spent a very long night.

Up by 6 am and had breakfast by 7 am; our usual routine. Blue sky is peeking through dark, heavy clouds; hopefully the rain is over. No one was quick enough to catch the sunrise reflecting on the clouds to the west for a moment. It was another beautiful sight in Africa and another missed photo opportunity.

Soon after breakfast we were on our way again. The drive was cold but the dust was not as billowy as the day before because of the dampness. Some of the group wanted the sides down because of the cold, so when I began to get carsick I went upfront to sit next to Dick Schutz. Amazing how he can read even when we are being bumped around. We passed by rolling hills of wheat, colored grass and rows of light green plants with beautiful white poppy-like flowers. There were few people on the road.

At about 8:30 in the morning, we got to the gate of the Ngorongoro Conservation Area. Dense jungle lined the road. The higher up we climbed into the clouds, the colder it got and the lower the visibility. We saw two monkeys in a tree. It kept getting colder, so we began putting on layers of more clothing. At about 10 am, we made a potty stop at Simba Camp; it wasn't too bad. We saw two groups of rangers fixing their breakfast, but they said nothing to us; just stared. As we were leaving, we saw some zebra by the side of the road. Elevation at one point was 7,500 feet.

As we came down out of the clouds, we began to see the desert below and it was absolutely magnificent. We could see two Masai Villages from above. The bright red shawls are easy to spot from a distance. We then saw several herds of cattle with young boys tending to them.

Once on the desert floor, we began to see a few giraffe and ostrich. I spotted a "Dik-Dik" by the side of the road. It is a tiny deer, about 18" tall. We saw quite a few Thompson and Grant Gazelles and two young hyenas by the side of the dusty road. These wild animals are so much more beautiful in the wild than in a zoo.

We had lunch at the Naabi Gate. Juma has flair and serves appealing lunches. We still have one and one half hours to get to the Serengeti from Naabi Hill.

Along the drive we began to see many beautiful Acacia trees and much taller grass, and more gazelle. We stopped to take photos of two Cheetahs sitting on rocks back from the road. Harold and Dick Sherman begin calling me "Eagle

Eye" because I'm the first to spot the wildlife. What beautiful animals the Cheetah are; so majestic and nonchalant. We saw about seven elephants in a group, including a big mother and her tiny baby elephant. They were pulling up grass with their trunks and stuffing them into their mouths. The baby was still suckling. What a sight!! We also saw warthogs, Cape buffalo, Topi, Bushbuck and one big male lion that was fast asleep. He never moved a muscle as we drove by.

We passed a village of black rectangular-shaped house, a school, a couple of small hotels, a grocery store and a bar. We saw Keribu storks. They are really big and ugly. We saw quite a few baboons and monkeys and a tree Hyrax.

The campground was very nice and quiet in the middle of the bush. There were two gazelle foraging when we arrived, but left soon after. There appeared to be no one else in the camp, and we were warned not to wander off into the bush. The showers were as usual – cold

It looks like we will have fish again for dinner, but that's a good thing. And, it was delicious. With the fried fish, we had fried potatoes, peas and carrots in a sauce and banana custard for desert. Dick Sherman passed on the peas and carrots. While eating dinner, we saw many bats flying about.

Tuesday, October 7, 1997
Ngiri Camp, Serengeti Park

Up before 6 am and ready in a half hour for our early-morning game drive. The first thing we saw was two mature female and one juvenile lion. The

juvenile was crunching on bones and the other two were cleaning themselves after their meal. We could still see the blood on their faces and paws. Oh my goodness! I can't believe we are seeing this so close in the wilderness of Africa.

We continued to see gazelle and Impalas all morning, a few waterbuck and a few warthogs and one more Cheetah. Later that morning, we came across a pack of hyenas trying to take a kill away from some lionesses. What a scene from National Geographic's!!! We couldn't be in a better position for viewing this

without getting in harm's way. We were only a few yards away and could see and hear everything. A pack of hyenas will harass lions by making loud noises and running toward them. At one point, one of the lionesses got mad and charged one hyena, but it was just a bluff. Finally, when the last two lions walked away with full bellies, the hyenas moved in. The lions usually will share a feast with each other as they kill in packs. The hyena, however, will fight each other for the food. When the hyenas had the kill away from the lions, they began to fight amongst themselves for remnants. I spotted one carrying the rib cage and while trying to get away was chased by the others. They raise quite a

bit of dust in their struggles. There was also one carrying a zebra tail. Away from this drama we saw seven lionesses resting while digesting their meal showing large full bellies. There was also a young male lion in the distance.

Wanting to see a leopard, we drove round and round looking for the one who had made a kill the day before, but never did find him. On this drive, we saw a large herd of zebra on an open plain, a few wildebeest on one side of the road and three giraffes on the other. We later saw a very large herd of wildebeest with a few Zebra and a huge herd of Cape buffalo.

We came across an area of trees which had been totally destroyed by elephants. When they want to get to the upper branches, they will knock the tree down with their heads. It looked like the area had been hit by a hurricane or tornado. Hank spotted a Dik-Dik, and four Keribu Stork. Back in camp were a few very large Baboons, who are so wicked looking; always looking for an opportunity to steal from you. They have even learned how to unzip a tent.

For lunch we had pasta, tomatoes, beets, potato pancakes and crapes. Juma is outdoing himself with every meal.

After lunch Wilford drove us to the lodge to check on the possibility of taking a balloon ride on Wednesday. Little did we know that he would leave us for three hours. After the first 15 minutes, we were all bored and went to the lobby to wait. Iris and Hank fell asleep sitting in chairs. I was just bored. The cost was exorbitant, so we passed on the balloon ride.

The afternoon game run was great. The highlight was seeing a leopard take his

newly killed baby Thompson's Gazelle up a tree. We took photos and watched him as he climbed up carrying his kill and then wedge it on a tree limb, so it wouldn't fall. He then climbed down. What a sight!! It was like watching National Geographic's only better because the only film involved was ours. By the time we left the area, there were 5-6 vans there and five more rushing to see the leopard. The drivers communicate with each other by two-way radio but luckily we were the first to see the leopard.

Later we rounded a corner and came across a very large herd of zebra running like something was chasing them. Some in our group thought we had scared them off, but I think it was the lioness we saw sleeping in the grass nearby.

On the return, we saw the same herd of elephants, three or four Cheetah in the distance, and a large Eland. The sky was beautiful with dark clouds coming toward us.

During the evening we saw a little bit of lightening. Dinner was excellent. We had soup, spaghetti with meat sauce and caramel custard for desert. In this photo, I think Dick wants to make sure there are no cooked carrots for tonight's dinner.

Wilford, our new guide and driver, sadly advised us that he was running out of money and needed $63 from each of us to continue the tour. We doubted that Destin would be able to reimburse us, but gave the money to Wilford anyway. What choice did we have? Anyway, there are worse things, right? Like not having anything to eat or our driver and cook running away. The negativity is beginning to get to me, so

I go to my tent early. We saw David Otani, Kate and Tina during our afternoon game run and waved to each other.

That night when Harold went to use the outhouse he saw what he thought was a black garden hose lying across the threshold, and thought to himself, "What a strange place to leave a hose." When he came out, the hose was gone. What? At that point, he realized then that it must have been a Black Mamba, the deadliest snake in all of Africa. Good thing he didn't scare it, or it would have bitten him for sure. He warned us to be very careful.

A hyena screamed right next to our tent during the night and scared me half to death. I thought he was inside the tent with us. When I screamed, Hank jumped up and put his arms around me fearing the worst.

Wednesday, October 8,
Serengeti - Ngorongoro Crater Park

We were scheduled to leave at 9 am this morning, but as usual, we were early and left by 8 am, anxious to see some more wild animals. We stopped at the Visitor's Center for a little while. On the way out, we stopped where others were viewing thirteen lions resting under an Acacia tree. Yes, I counted them. Across from them, two lionesses were chewing on a kill. Two hyenas were keeping their respectful distance, waiting to see if there would be any leftovers. We watched as one of them crossed the road while the other checked for some leftover meat. To one side was a round brown spot and in the middle were two skinned large leg bones.

We left there continuing on our way out of the Serengeti. The road again was dusty with large pot holes. My sinuses were bothering me so I took a pill which made me sleepy and crabby. Hank called me to sit with him, so I leaned against him, closed my eyes, and immediately began feeling better.

Our next stop along the road was at the Moldavia Gorge. It is a tourist stop so I stayed in the truck because I was not in the mood. If you are interested in geology and museums, I guess it is interesting, but I didn't think it would be for me. The group that went in saw some Neanderthal foot prints.

We had lunch and went on our way. Some of the Masai by the side of the road were asking for money to have their photos taken with us.

About midway up the escarpment, we stopped at a Masai Village where the inhabitants make a living by having tourists stop and tour their village. For $5 each, it was well worth it. They were all ready, dressed in their native attire. One even put on his war bonnet so we could take his picture. They danced and sang in their native language. The men's form of dancing is jumping up and down. They could really jump high and because all of the men are well over six feet tall, it was quite a sight.

Iris asked the chief if he would let us see inside his home. After he agreed, we went into his three-bedroom hut which is made of dried cow dung. I took about two 36-exposure rolls of film and quite a bit of video. It was awesome. There is no furniture inside the huts, but rooms are divided and their beds are wall-to-wall.

Hank took Polaroid pictures and gave them out. He then showed them the video and they got a big kick out of that, laughing all the time. Every Masai was dressed in their bright red or purple with beaded earrings and necklaces. They willingly posed for photos, smiling broadly. They are so beautiful, especially the children.

I couldn't snap my camera fast enough. The ones I took here at the Masai Village are some of my favorites.

One young man asked if Hank would take a photo of him, his spear, and (as an afterthought added) -- and his wife. It was a great day for all of us and one we will never forget.

On the way to our campsite -- Simba Camp, on the rim of the Ngorongoro Crater -- we saw large herds of cattle being tended to by young Masai boys.

Arriving at camp at about 5 pm, David, Tina and Kate from the Peace Corps were waiting for us. The campsite is beautiful with a good view of the Crater and the sun setting on the opposite side reflecting on the bottom. The evening is clear and cold. At one point on the road, Wilford stopped to gather large logs for firewood. I think we will be having a very large campfire.

The kids from the Peace Corps came over for a visit and we talked until about 10 pm. They are very interesting and not afraid of anything. We had a good time talking to them all evening, hearing of their adventures and telling them of ours. Oh, to be young again!!

Thursday, October 9, 1997
Ngorongoro Crater

The Ngorongoro Crater is an absolutely amazing place. There were hundreds of animals roaming all around. As usual we were awake by 6 am, but it was hard for me to get up because I stayed up late talking to Kate, Tina and David. Ernie reported that he found some fresh elephant dung by the men's room, but the elephants were so quiet during the night that we did not hear them pass by. The morning was again clear and cold. Viewing the Crater and the surrounding jungle is magnificent. Our game drive lasted all day long beginning at 7:30 am. Ernie, Dick and Iris Schutz, Hank and I went in one land rover and Betty, Harold Jan and Dick Sherman in the other. Of course, the road was rough with rocks protruding everywhere.

About half-way down into the crater, I spotted some wildebeest running. I asked Mike, our driver, to stop so we could see what was happening. With field glasses I spotted a female lion stalking them. The wildebeests ran circles around the lioness. She must have been old because she finally gave up and sulked off. Because this is the end of the dry season, there weren't the thousands and thousands of animals that Betty saw here during her trip in the wet season. In Africa there are two seasons -- Wet and Dry.

We were told that in the crater, there are usually one and one-half million

wildebeests and over 300,000 zebra. The wildebeest and zebra have their calves at the same time and will have 10,000 babies a day, every day for the season. The predators eat about 10% or1, 000 per day and then go for one to two days without eating, and then eat another 1,000. AMAZING!!! That would be something to see.

Down on the crater floor, we saw the usual gazelle, wart hogs, wildebeest and zebra. We saw a few Bushbucks, but not many. The first pride of lions we saw was four sleeping females. Three would sometimes lift their heads but only to plop them down again after looking at us.

The dust from the dry lake bed was bothersome and you could see it continuously from anywhere. The next lions we saw sitting together a little farther were one mother with two young males, whose manes were just beginning to grow. You could see their hair blowing in the breeze which was strong all day long. I also saw a male lion with a black mane walk into the bush to sleep. I was told that lions with black mane are the oldest and higher in the hierarchy.

We stopped for lunch on a grassy spot around the lake with a bunch of other land rovers. I couldn't believe there were so many because we didn't see them driving around. We had to eat in the car because the Black Kites will fly down and steal your food right out of your hands; I saw one take a sandwich out of a woman's hand.

After lunch we drove back to where we had seen the sleeping White Rhinos from a distance in the hope that they would be up and feeding. We did see one walking around but as we drove up he plopped down and we got no photos. They were so far away, that unless you used field glasses you couldn't even tell what kind of animals they were.

During the day, we saw hippos in three or four ponds. One of the ponds was deep and there so many hippos in the water that we couldn't count them. In an adjoining pond, we saw four half submerged. If you didn't know any better, you'd think they were large boulders.

We drove over a lush green area which was beautiful with black and white zebras in the foreground. What a photo opportunity! At the restroom area, we saw Vervet monkeys all over the buildings. We were told that elephants usually hang out here too but there were none that day.

We left at 2:30 in order to get through the gate by 4:00 or we would be charged for another day. At Kudu Camp we met the boys and the trucks. The ride from there was extremely dusty and bumpy -- but what else is new? And, of course, we were tired, hungry and dirty -- we had worn the same clothes for the past three days. However, the scenery was extraordinary with the red earth and bright green foliage, so it didn't matter. We arrived at camp at about 6 pm and dinner again was excellent -- beef stew, boiled potatoes and eggplant. We are eating very well. I went to write in my journal and the rest went to the bar to see some African dancing. I think I just needed some "alone" time after such a long day.

Friday, October 10,
Ngorongoro Crater, Tanzania

Tonight is the last night of sleeping in a tent. Even though I had become used to sleeping in it, I was looking forward to sleeping in a bed again.

Of course as usual we were up way before the scheduled 9 am departure time. It rained lightly for a little while. Hank took the tent down while I sat in the truck to update my journal. He is such a jewel; I am lucky to have him in my life.

The drive again was dusty, rough, windy and cold. Hank & I cuddle under my Masai blanket to keep warm. The drive though the hills is beautiful with the ever-changing colors of red, light copper, tawny and then black. What a marvelous view.

We saw many Masai men along the road and Hank threw them empty film canisters as we drove by. Some Masai were herding cattle. They make their fences, called "Boas "by piling up dry thorny brush to keep the wild animals out. We see several villages along the route. Young boys begin tending the cattle and goats at about the age of 10.

 At noon, when I thought I could bear the cold no longer, we arrived at the African Cultural Center, a very touristy complex with rooms full of expensive African art for sale. We bought a few small items as we were already overloaded with gifts.

At the open market in Arusha we stopped for vegetables I took about a half roll of film of the activity. I love the hustle and bustle of the people all around.

We saw a shoe factory on the porch of one of the buildings. One man was outlining the patterns, another cutting them out, another sewing pieces together with an old treadle sewing machine and another gluing the remaining pieces together. What an assembly line! In front of them on the ground sat women selling tomatoes, oranges, potatoes and other vegetables. There were so many people on the street that it was mind-boggling.

We arrived at Masai and found Destin walking along the road. It was good to see him again. We had lunch and then Destin took us into town to buy more touristy things. We had Cappuccinos and sweets in the pastry shop and then returned to camp.

Destin told us that he still had to go to the bank again tomorrow, so we should do our laundry because tomorrow we wouldn't get to Nairobi until late that night. Hank & I washed only a few things to get by. For dinner we had an exceptional chicken cooked in a sauce, rice, carrots and peas with fresh fruit salad for desert.

After dinner Hank explained that he spoke with Destin about the money owed to us by Tracks being divided amongst him and the crew as their tips.

Everyone agreed. I asked a question about the accounting, which I thought was reasonable, but immediately it started an argument. I got my feelings hurt, got mad and left in a huff. Hank came into the tent. He gave me a hug and kisses, and immediately I felt better. What a great guy he is, and I'm fortunate that he is my husband.

Saturday, October 11, 1997
Last day of Safari

It was rainy, cold and damp so we took our time packing and getting out of our tent. Destin came to the campsite early and then walked to Arusha to be at the bank when it opened. He still had not been able to get the money from Tracks. Since we had agreed to use the money we advanced Tracks for the boys' tips, we really had nothing to worry about. It was Destin's problem.

We breakfasted under the canopy of the truck, took our showers and then got organized for our trip to Egypt, the last leg of our trip. I can't believe our Safari is over.

Hank packed our big bags with the items we had purchased and I packed his smaller film bag with the clothes we would need for Egypt. He is so organized that it helps me to be organized too. We just waited in the truck for Destin to get back from the bank. It was still rainy, cold and damp with most of us reading or "doing whatever" to pass the time Hank cut my hair sometime during the week and it is the shortest I have ever worn it.

At noon, some of the group made sandwiches for lunch, and Willie, Juma and Wilford hung around waiting for Destin to return too. I think they wanted to get paid.

Finally, Hank, Betty and I went into a local restaurant and had chili and fresh-baked rolls. Jan and Dick joined later. Destin finally showed up at about 1:30 and we were ready to go in 15 minutes.

The sides went up and down about four times on our drive to Nairobi depending on the weather conditions. It would get sunny and then hot, then it would start to rain again. During one dry spell, we got a flat tire and while Destin was changing it, took a "hunk" out of his finger. The guys finished up for him.

The remainder of the ride was boring and cold. Hank sat up in the cab with Destin. I tried to sleep but was too cold.

We arrived at the 680 Hotel in Nairobi at about 9pm. What a pleasant surprise! The hotel is about 10 stories high and across the road are beautiful Jacaranda trees in bloom. We had great rooms with private baths. The first thing I did was fill the bathtub with hot water and gets in just to soak. My feet and hands were so black with dirt that it took about four scrubbings to finally get them clean and back to a normal sunburned color. The bath was wonderful; it was luxury at its best."

During dinner Hank told us that during the drive they came across two road blocks; the first one was legitimate, but because the second one was in the dark, Destin ran through it. He said that you never know why they want to stop you. Thank Goodness for Destin; he kept us safe throughout the trip.

After a light dinner, we went to bed about 10 pm. The bed was so comfortable that I fell asleep immediately.

Sunday, October 12, 1997
Nairobi, Kenya

Woke up early, but stayed in bed enjoying the luxury of the smooth sheets. Hank and I went down for breakfast about 9 am, joining the rest of the group.

We talked to a man by the name of Patrick and made arrangements to be picked up at 5 am the following morning in two mini-vans to take us to the airport. The cost would be $55 for all of us.

We walked down to the City Market after being told it was the only place open on Sundays. We were warned to look out for pick-pockets both there and along the way. The haggling with the sellers is one of my greatest enjoyments on this trip. We bought two t-shirts and miscellaneous stuff -- a purse (which I'm still enjoying after 13 years) and a hand carved shoe horn for Hank's dad. Jan bought a t-shirt for Dick but when he took it out of the bag at the hotel found that they had switched it and given him one that looked like it had been run over by a truck several times through mud. Walked around the town for a while and were back at the hotel by noon. David, Kate and Tina came by to say "Hi" and "Goodbye." For some reason, I got tears in my eyes when I saw them leave.

We had sandwiches for lunch and since there was nothing else to do, spent the afternoon in our rooms. Hank tried to confirm air and hotel reservations for our trip to Egypt, but no one would pick up the telephone. We then repacked the luggage. I tried to take a nap again but couldn't because I was getting excited about going to Egypt.

At 6:30 we met downstairs for dinner. Iris and Dick went to an Italian Restaurant. Iris got all dressed up and looked absolutely beautiful. We waited in the bar for the restaurant to open at 7 pm only to sit and wait another hour before being served. How frustrating! Oh, I forgot we're still on African time.

After checking out of the hotel and leaving wake-up calls for 4:30 am the next morning, we retired for the night.

Monday, October 11, 1997
Nairobi, Kenya to Cairo, Egypt

Hank and I both woke up before the call. The porters were in the hall by 4:32 am, ready for our luggage. We rushed to get ready and were downstairs by 4:50 am to meet Patrick with the mini-van. All nine of us rode in the mini-van and he rode in the taxi with the luggage. Next time I go anywhere, I'll travel light and not buy heavy items. Yeah, right!

Dick Sherman and Iris Schutz got sick during the night and were sick all day long. Ernie is still feeling poorly from the rash he has on his chest.

Patrick took charge at the airport. He took all of our luggage (except our carry-on bags), tickets and passports to the counter. When he came back, he explained that they wanted to charge an additional $300 for not confirming our flight. We argued that Egypt Air did not answer the phone when we tried to confirm the previous day. They waived the charge.

When Patrick put our entire luggage together to be weighed, we were way overweight. He returned to our group with figures and told us that they wanted to charge an additional $600 for the overweight luggage. Hank & I felt bad because we knew it was my fault. After a lot of negotiations, Dick Schutz (thankfully) calculated with the officials and we only had to pay $50. Since Dick Schutz paid the extra charges, we reimbursed him when we got home.

Thank goodness for Patrick. He got our exit tax paid, stickers, boarding passes and stayed with us through Customs. The waiting was hard on Iris, Ernie and Dick Sherman because they were all sick. While the rest of us were waiting, we talked to other tourists we had met at the Masai Camp in Arusha who were from Australia and New Zealand. We also talked to another group from Pennsylvania who had been on a "luxury" safari with cots, bathrooms and tents. One day, maybe we can do it that way, but I wouldn't have changed one day of this trip for anything.

Monday, October 13, 1997
Cairo, Egypt

The plane was an hour late boarding and it took us four and a half hours to arrive in Cairo. I had a window seat and enjoyed watching the Nile River as it wound through the desert. Looking down at Cairo was like a picture postcard. Unbelievably beautiful with their buildings the color of the sand. Cairo is bigger than I anticipated -- we heard it was home to from 16 to18 million people. Of course like most big cities it is also very smoggy.

We were met by a guide from Imaginary Traveler, our tour service. He helped us through the hassle of getting through the airport. He showed us where to get our visa and change money. His name is Diia. He took care of the luggage and had a bus waiting to take us to the hotel.

The bus driver spoke no English. He drove through the streets mostly in the middle of the road regardless of marked lanes. Another picture postcard view was the avenue lined on both sides with soldiers (or police) in uniform, one every 25 yards or so. They wore white uniforms with black berets, boots and belts and stood facing away from the traffic. We were told it was in honor of the President who was expected to pass through. Watching the bus driver maneuver through traffic was quite an experience. He weaved through the crowded streets as if he were driving a sports car. No one, I mean no one at all pays attention to the marked lanes. When we arrived at the narrow street the hotel was on, he drove between cars parked on both side of the street. I would not even try this in my Camry at home. He finally got through but not before he got a kid to guide him and two others to push one car forward about two feet. It is a miracle that he didn't even damage a side mirror. Upon arriving unscathed, we simultaneously burst out in applause.

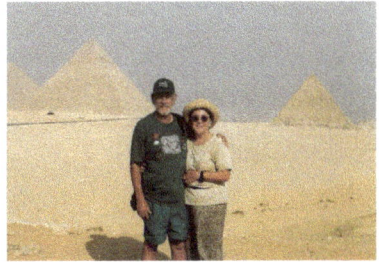

After checking into the hotel and washing up, we met in the lobby to find some lunch. Daniella, our tour guide for the Nile Tour was ready for us. She recommended that for lunch we try the TAZA -- an Egyptian Take-Away. Those of us, who were not sick, went there to see what was available. Betty, Hank and I had chicken Taouk, which is chicken shish-kebob wrapped in bread similar to pita bread. It was, very good.

After lunch, Hank & I decided to take a walk to familiarize ourselves with the area. We were soon approached by a young man who saw us with dollar signs in his eyes.

The local custom with tourists is quite devious. First, a young man befriends you on the street, tells you he has a relative in the US, and then invites you to come to his home for tea. What you don't know is that their "home" is really their shop, and you will not be able to leave until you buy something.

After you are relaxed, they start their sales pitch to sell their wares. Believe me, they are worse than used car or time-share salesmen. We couldn't get out of there until we bought something (because we were his friends, right?) We ended up spending $40 US for two papyrus drawings, two cartouche and chains, and a bookmark. What suckers! It turned out to be an expensive lesson.

We learned later that Harold had walked across the street to the Green Star Shop. A man and his nephew work there and keep an eye on new tourists. When they see a tourist walk out of the hotel, they make a phone call and the "game is on." Harold said he spent two and a half hours in the shop across the street before buying a papyrus.

For dinner, the nephew from across the street guided us to another fast-food restaurant a few blocks where the locals eat. The food was not as good as TAZA.

Tuesday, October 14, 1997
Cairo, Egypt

What an exciting city, swarming with people doing their thing everywhere. We woke early wanting to go for a walk to experience the sights, sounds and smells of Cairo. We feel safe walking in Cairo carrying our cameras. The children like to practice their limited English on us, constantly repeating, "Welcome to Egypt," "Welcome," and "Hello."

We were back at the hotel by 7 am for breakfast with the group. We learned that Ernie, Iris and Dick Sherman were going to see the doctor at the local hospital, so we took another walk. Our second walk was way more interesting because the whole street is an open market with people selling whatever it is they have to sell. We saw donkey-drawn wooden carts, and horse-drawn wooden carts loaded with all kinds of produce, and women sitting on the sidewalk behind their produce hoping to sell something. There was bright color around this otherwise drab city.

When we regrouped with everyone except Ernie who had some carbuncles excised from his lower chest and needed to rest, we decided to walk to see Cairo Tower. It turned out to be a long walk through busy, hot, and smoggy traffic-congested streets. Betty (the trooper that she is), Hank, Harold and Dick Sherman climbed to the top of the tower. The rest of us decided to wait and perspire in the shade. The only restaurant open was too expensive, so we decided to walk back to the TAZA where we knew we could get a good reasonably priced lunch.

Late in the afternoon, we arranged for two taxis to take us to the Old Cairo Market. This was by far my favorite place in all of Cairo. The drive in the taxi through the traffic was much like the bus ride from the airport -- crazy and reckless.

If a pedestrian is crossing the street, the driver just goes right up to him, stopping within inches. Pedestrians will not give way to the vehicles; they just proceed across, not making eye contact with the drivers, walking at

their own pace. When the pedestrians pass, the vehicle will then proceed. It is amazing that we never saw an accident.

We got a kick out of watching a young couple cross two streets at a roundabout (traffic circle). They were arm-in-arm, looking into each other's eyes and talking. Never looking at the cars, they just proceeded. The drivers of the cars slowed down to let them go by. Unbelievable!!!

The Old Cairo Market -- or Khan-al-Khalidi Bazaar -- is absolutely amazing and right out of "The Arabian Nights." We are told that one side of the main road is the bazaar for locals and on the other the bazaar for tourists. Of course, we would choose the one for locals first. The buildings were built in the 13th Century. People are everywhere selling everything you can imagine. It is dirty, noisy, hot, humid, confusing and absolutely wonderful. First, we located the papyrus store and watched them making both paper and mosaic boxes. Again, a local young man approached us, but we were ready for him. The children are pesky little things, repeating the one or two English words they know, but I still enjoyed taking their photo.

We crossed the main street to the tourist bazaar. Here men are barking constantly everywhere trying to get you into their shop to show you something, anything, in the hopes that you will be tempted to buy. They are very aggressive. We didn't stay long and bought nothing that afternoon.

During one of our walks, Hank and I were thrilled to see a tall handsome Sheik. He was dressed all in black with a white head cover and black rolled band. He looked like he was from the movie set of "Lawrence of Arabia." Not only was he tall and dressed beautifully, he was absolutely gorgeous. I couldn't take my eyes off him. I wanted to take a picture but was too embarrassed to ask. On our way back down the street, we saw him again. How handsome he was!

Wednesday, October 15, 1997
Cairo, Egypt

Malaria Pill Day! We all take our Malaria pills on the same day so no one forgets.

We were in no rush for breakfast at the hotel. At 8:30 we met in the lobby to talk about what we wanted to do for the day. Our tour would not start until Thursday, so we were on our own for another day. Ernie had to return to see the doctor, so he would stay back at the hotel to rest but first he needed to get some cash. Iris and Dick Sherman had recovered. We decided to walk up to the Sheraton Hotel where we could get cash on our credit cards.

Ernie returned to the hotel and the rest of us walked to the Sadaat Metro Station where we would ride to see the Old Cairo Coptic Church. The metro is easy to ride, much like the metros in Paris or the States, but a funny thing did happen on our first metro ride in Cairo.

When the metro arrived, we all boarded in one car not noticing that all of the other passengers were women. At the next stop, two young men saw that there were men onboard and boarded our car. Immediately the women started to yell at them. They looked around and got off at the next stop. We learned later that there are specific car assignments – one for women, one for men and one for married couples. What did we know?

The museum is very interesting. It's hard to believe we are there looking at all of these old buildings and artifacts. As I was wearing shorts, I was not allowed into the church.

While waiting for the others, Hank and I decided to buy seven cartouches for the girls in our family. After showing the clerks how we wanted them, they was agreed to deliver them to the hotel by 10 pm that night.

We were getting hungry, tired, hot and very sweaty. Iris and Dick stayed to do more shopping but the rest of us left to go back to the hotel. Betty was so dehydrated that by the time we got to the Sheraton, Dick and Jan decided to take her inside to rest a bit and get some water for her. Harold, Hank and I were ahead and went to the TAZA for lunch. We didn't know about Betty until they arrived for lunch and told us what had happened. We felt bad that we hadn't waited. Back at the hotel, I took a nap and slept for a while. The heat can really take it out of me.

At 6:30, we met downstairs to go for a dinner cruise on the Nile. Betty was still not feeling well so stayed at the hotel. We took taxis to the ship which was named, what else -- The Pharaoh. The décor was Egyptian and tastefully decorated. There was live music and entertainment. The buffet dinner and deserts were not only tasty but beautifully arranged. Hank and I danced and I admired him with his white beard. We had a wonderful time.

Back at the hotel, the jeweler was waiting with the cartouche. The next day would begin the Nile Cruise.

Thursday, October 16, 1997

Luxor, Egypt

We put most of our luggage in storage and after breakfast had our briefing on what to expect for the day. There are two groups running together. Our group would be 16 plus Daniella and James, our tour directors. In our group besides our usual group is an older couple (not that we're so young), and a young couple from Australia, plus Ralph from Ontario and Monica and Rachael from Australia.

First stop was the Cairo Museum by air-conditioned bus. The Museum itself was hot and extremely crowded with people from all over the world. Little did we know that a few weeks before, a bus in the parking lot had been bombed by terrorists and the tourists killed.

The exhibits were like nothing I had ever seen before, quite beautiful with lots gold everywhere. After the museum, we were taken to an Egyptian restaurant for typical Egyptian food which was delicious.

We then were driven to the Pyramids of Giza. What an experience that was! Everyone should see the pyramids once during their lifetime, but not go inside. Hank talked me into going inside one. I'll never do that again. It was dirty, smelled like urine, and once inside we had to walk up a lot of stairs bent over at the waist.

Egyptian men with camels were trying to get tourists to go for a ride. Having ridden one of those nasty beasts as a child at the Zoo in San Antonio, I passed on that. No thank you -- not again.

After seeing the Sphinx and taking hundreds of photos, we were back at the hotel by 5 pm. We were then rushed to change and shower and be ready to go to the train depot for our train ride to Luxor by 6:30

At the depot while waiting for our train to arrive, we saw an old train arrive with the poor locals. It reminded us of the movies we saw as children of trains full of Jewish prisoners during World War II riding to the gas chambers. These people were dirty and carried their clothing in cloth bundles. One poor man wanted to get off with his parcels, but the train wouldn't stop.

He threw his parcels off the train onto the adjoining train tracks, and then jumped from what looked like a box car. He was really mad, shaking his fist and yelling.

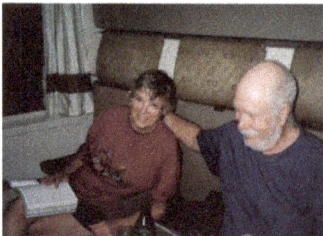

Our train was much cleaner and nicer than that one. I watched Egypt go by in all of his history, as if I was watching it hundreds of years ago. There were men and boys fishing with nets from small boats, men and boys driving donkeys loaded with hay, or just walking at a brisk pace. We saw small mud homes and women here and there. They all stopped what they were doing to stare at the train as it went by; a few waved.

We had dinner of roast beef and rice in the dining car, which wasn't too bad. Our berths were made up by 10 pm, so we retired.

The accommodations in the berth were not the greatest. I tried to sleep but couldn't because it was uncomfortable in the small berths and we didn't have enough blankets.

Friday, October 17, 1997
Luxor, Egypt

A purser woke us up about 4 am and brought us breakfast of hot coffee and cold rolls.

Upon arriving at the hotel at about 5:30 am, of course, our rooms were not ready at that hour of the morning. Hank and I went for a walk to look around and took some photos. Back at the hotel we went up to the roof to wait for the jewelry store across the street to open so we could order wedding bands made in the cartouche fashion like the one Daniella was wearing. Betty and Iris went to see Nephritides tomb and enjoyed it immensely.

It is extremely hot here, but thankfully our rooms are ready by 9:30 am, so we checked in. Hank is not feeling too well, probably because of lack of sleep on the train. We slept for two hours.

At noon, we went to the El Anoun for lunch and ran into some of our friends. Lunch was delicious and reasonably priced. We walked through the bazaar street where locals sell fruit and vegetables.

When we were in Luxor, Daniella took us on a tour of the ruins. She had arranged for an expert to guide us through and explain everything. Well, this guy, Salleyah, lectures like a college professor. He constantly looks at everyone to make sure they were paying attention. Harold kept walking off to take photos. Salleyah didn't like that one bit and kept telling him to come back. Harold was there for the photography not to hear this man talk.

For some reason Salleyah took a liking to me and kept telling me to stand next to him. It was kind of embarrassing. Hank just laughed. As a gift at the end of the tour he gave me a good luck charm, which is a green *scarab*. I love it and wear it to this day

While walking around looking for something to wear for the Gallebeya Party on the cruise ship, we ran into a very handsome young man who looked like an Arabian Hugh Grant who knew his craft of selling well. We also know his technique but went along with him anyway.

In his shop, Hank selected a white Gallebeya and I a red one with gold trim. They are both beautiful. Hank also selected a black t-shirt. "Hugh Grant" put them aside and then pushed us to buy more, never giving us a price for any one item.

He began by wanting 185 EP. We laughed and offered 60 EP and then he laughed. We haggled for quite a while. I would stand up to leave, and he would sit me down. We did that about three times. We finally left after paying 70EP. Not bad for tourists! Hank & I enjoyed that shopping experience immensely.

We continued on our walk along the streets and watched people selling their produce, food and wares. I enjoyed it a lot even though we were hot and sweaty.

Back at the hotel, we relaxed while waiting to join the others downstairs for dinner and a briefing. Hank was not feeling well but was able to hide it from everyone.

The typical Egyptian food of soup, condiments and salad at the hotel dining room was very good. We were told we would be awakened at 4 am for our trip to the Valley of the Kings by donkey. Say What? Donkey? We were told that Imaginative Travel wanted to give us the true Egyptian experience. They lived up to their word

After dinner we walked to the jewelry store to pick up our rings and the 12 cartouches and 20 chains we had ordered. We have a very large family.

Saturday, October 18, 1997
Luxor, Egypt

Promptly at 4 am we were awakened by a knock on the door by the Australians who roomed next door. We rushed to be ready and downstairs by 4:20 pm. In the hotel restaurant they had coffee and tea ready for us as well as a bag with our breakfast.

A small ferry took us across to the West Bank. We then walked up a short distance where our donkeys and their handlers were waiting for us. This was going to be a new experience indeed! I had ridden donkeys as a child but never as an adult in a foreign country. Having short legs, one of the handlers helped me get on – what a laugh. Abdul, the donkey handler who accompanied tried his best to keep all of us together. Betty's saddle was loose and she fell off immediately. They gave her another donkey, but she wasn't too happy about that. It took us about an hour riding along a rough trail to get to the Valley of the Kings. The surrounding sights of the locals living their normal lives were something I will never forget.

The valley, where the burial tombs are, was a sight to behold. I chose not to take my camera on this trip because of the difficulty of managing it while riding a donkey. Of course, I was sorry afterwards. I missed some fantastic photo opportunities.

We saw several tombs. I paid an extra fee to see King Tut's tomb, which was absolutely amazing. It's hard to imagine that the Kings were buried in this fashion.

It was really hot, so we drank lots and lots of water. Salleyah was again our guide. He is extremely knowledgeable, but is annoying because if someone is not paying attention, he calls out their name. Harold ignored him again.

After visiting the last tomb, Betty, Iris, Dick, and Hank chose to ride the taxi back to Luxor with Salleyah.

Those of us returning by donkey had to climb a very large hill overlooking the valley where our donkeys were waiting. The climb was very difficult because of the steepness and the heat. I kept saying "You can do it. You can do it. Just put one foot in front of the other. You can do this." And I did reach the top. The view was spectacular and made the difficult climb worthwhile.

Riding our donkeys back, we came down on the east side of the hills overlooking the green valley, the desert and a narrow river canal. About halfway down the hill, we got off our donkeys and walked them the rest of the way to the village where the workers live. There we saw two more small tombs.

Back on the donkeys, we rode for 45-50 minutes through the streets of a village and then through the fields. Abdul showed us the village where he lives. It was amazing and one of the biggest highlights for me. To be able to look into a window of their lives is indescribable.

We rode the ferry back to the East Bank and then had to rush to be ready with our luggage to board our ship in one hour. Hank went to the hotel for our luggage and I went to the jewelry store to pick up the scarab Salleyah had given to me that I had it mounted in silver. Also, my ring was too tight and it had to be made larger. I went to the pharmacy to get medication for Hank. The enlarging of the ring took longer than expected and I was in a panic for fear of missing the cruise ship. They delivered the ring just as the group was leaving the hotel. Poor Hank, he is so sick and all this rushing around made him worse. But, bless his heart, he insisted on carrying my carry-on luggage as well as his own. The larger bags were delivered by taxi, but we still had to get them into our cabin.

We congregated in the lounge for a briefing and Hank and I were assigned to Cabin No. 4, which is in a perfect location, and even had a private bath. I loved it. It was just below the roof deck and at the end of the stairs. I took a much-needed shower and we were the last ones to arrive for lunch. The tables were all set with white tablecloths and napkins with good white dishes and silverware. What luxury after living in the bush for so long or eating at the Take-Away in Cairo.

The lunch was more like dinner – spaghetti with rolls, beef in a brown sauce and cauliflower. We took another nap until 5 pm after our big lunch.

Topside on the viewing deck, we watched Egypt pass by along the Nile. What a view! We were relaxed and enjoying ourselves immensely.

Dinner was at 8 pm. Another big meal! We had fresh baked rolls, soup, chicken, vermicelli, green beans with carrots (much to Dick Sherman's distaste) and a very sweet cake for desert.

Men and boys rowed alongside the ships selling Egyptian dresses and tablecloths. They would throw them up to the passengers, hoping they would be caught before falling into the water, and the passengers would buy them by throwing them money. What a crack-up! They all spoke English, French, Spanish, German and no telling what other language. Of course, I couldn't resist and bought one of the dresses I caught. We also enjoyed watching the young boys in their small make-shift boats with hand paddles singing "Row, Row, Row Your Boat," in all languages over and over again. They had nothing to sell, just wanted you to throw them money for the entertainment, which we did.

Topside again to view the stars, the rocking of the ship began to make my eyes close, so I went downstairs to bed.

At about midnight we were awakened by the ship's movement – or lack of. The crew was preparing to enter the Locks. We came upstairs to the viewing deck to see what was going on. We watched until we were through the first one. It was surprising to see how quickly the water rises in each lock. There were armed guards all around. It was a little frightening, but it didn't keep me from sleeping like a rock that night.

Sunday, October 19, 1997
Nile River Cruise, Egypt

We awoke leisurely and came topside to the viewing deck to join the others. Breakfast of fresh baked bread, cheese and coffee was delicious. What a treat!!

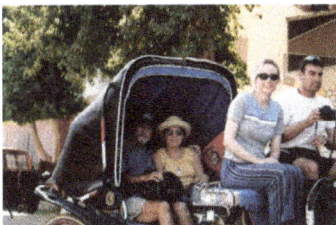

At 9:30 am, we disembarked to ride in horse-drawn carriages to the Temple of Horus and Effu Temple. It is by far the best preserved, very big and by far one of the most impressive ruins. We had fun haggling with the vendors who were selling

t-shirts, decorated dresses, gallabiyahs, scarf's and whatever they thought that a tourist would buy. On our return to our ship, we relaxed topside to take roll after roll of photos while Egypt and the Nile passed by. After lunch, there was not much to do, so I took another nap. It's amazing out traveling makes me sleepy.

Hank and some of the guys dove or jumped into the Nile for a swim. I wouldn't because I knew that the Egyptians used the Nile for "everything."

We stopped by another Temple at Kom Ombo. It was very pretty and all lit up with lights all around. Some of the group disembarked to get a closer look, but we did not.

We sat topside to watch the beautiful sunset and then the amazingly bright stars. What a sight!!

Monday, October 20, 1997
Nile Cruise, Egypt

We were well-rested and ready for breakfast by 8 am. After breakfast, we disembarked to see the impressive temple ruins. Of course, in front of the temple people were selling souvenirs. I bought Hank and I t-shirts at 10 EP and a Nubian crocheted hat. While Betty and I were walking to the ruins, we stopped to watch a man playing a flute in front of a basket with a Cobra -- just like you see in the movies. Only the tourists were paying attention to him. After giving him a few Egyptians coins, we walked on. The ruins were again magnificent.

We left there, had lunch on the boat, and arrived at Aswan during the early afternoon, and then took a brief walk on the Cornish. A little later, we took a ride around Elephantine Island aboard a Felucca. Upon disembarking via a 12" plank board between the Felucca and land, Iris lost her balance and fell into the

water which was only about to her waist. Thankfully, she kept her wits about her and remembering her camera, held it high above her head so it wouldn't get wet. Good going, Iris! Of course, this was another event to tease about for days on end.

On a nearby island we went to see a botanical garden. It was beautiful and very, very green. We returned on the Felucca to the Old Cataract Hotel to watch the sunset and have drinks, however, we missed the sunset by 10 minutes. The hotel was very crowded with tourists so we chose not to stay for drinks. The view, however, was beautiful and the cameras never stopped clicking.

Iris, Dick Schutz and Hank and I went to the local market to look around and had fun joking and talking with the young boys who hang around the tourists. That is until the tourist police "busted" them. It is apparently illegal for locals to interact with tourists without a license. We really felt bad and tried to defend the boys because we had encouraged them. The police were manhandling them as if they had murdered someone.

Back on the cruise ship, we had dinner and packed our "stuff." We would be leaving in the morning.

That evening was our Gallebeya Party. Everyone dressed up in their newly purchased dresses to have their photos taken. Hank looked so handsome in his white outfit with his white mustache and beard. After dinner the youngsters partied well into the night.

Tuesday, October 21, 1997

Egypt

We were awakened at 3 am and ready to go in 15 minutes despite a power failure. Grabbing a quick cup of coffee and box breakfast, we boarded an air-conditioned motor coach for our three hour ride to see Ramses II and Nephritis's Temple. Because we are not far from the Sudanese border, we had to travel in a convoy at that hour of the morning. There were several men with machine guns riding jeeps to guard us.

We slept most of the way as there was nothing to see along the route. The trip, however, was well worth the inconvenience. This is the most impressive Temple of all. The fact that it was moved from the bottom of a valley in order to build the dam and Lake Nasser is remarkable. Each stone was marked and moved one block at a time. This was another of the highlights of the trip. Just to see how large and impressive it

is one thing, but the colors are still fresh after so many thousands of years. Hank and I loved this tomb the most.

We had two day rooms at the Cleopatra Hotel to wash up and leave some of our belongings. We went for a long leisurely lunch on a floating restaurant called the Aswan Room. It was really nice.

Back at the bus by 4:30, to take the train back to Cairo. The train left promptly at 5:20 pm. The train ride was rough and bumpy and it was hard to get comfortable enough to sleep

Wednesday, October 22, 1997
Cairo, Egypt

The train steward awoke us at 5:30 am for breakfast, which was again hot coffee and cold, hard rolls. We arrived in Cairo at 6:30 am and were taken immediately to our hotel by bus. Not all our rooms were ready at the King Hotel, so Dick and Iris waited in our room and Daniella came by for a visit. Daniella is such an interesting person. The young girl is from New Zealand, has traveled extensively and does an exceptional job as a guide. After getting settled, we decided to go to the Citadel and then Khan Al-Khalili. We took a taxi to the Citadel and spent a couple of hours there. Betty was tired so took a taxi back to the hotel to get some rest. Dick Schutz talked to a couple of boys who said they could walk us to the musical instrument bazaar. After walking a good distance, we found a taxi. Dick Schutz bought a lute and I bought a small drum for my granddaughter.

From there, we walked toward Khan Al-Khalili, and on the way ran into a guy who said "Hello" and told us he was going to his father's bakery. If we wanted, he would take us there to show us how their bread is made. We walked through a most amazing and interesting area. First we went through a covered market of meat with blood dripping on the ground around us. People kept saying, "Welcome," Hello," "Good Morning," or "Welcome to Egypt." This is indeed a most friendly Country.

We continued through an industrial area where woodcarvers were making chairs, men

cutting rubber from tires, iron workers making gates, and the like. Finally, we found the bakery. Inside they demonstrated how the Egyptian flat bread is made, baking it in fire ovens and gave us each a taste. Delivery boys carry large loads of bread on their head while riding bicycles. Amazing they don't tip over as the loads of bread are much larger than they are. We found the tent makers' Sauk and saw several stalls with men sewing appliqués to make patterns. What beautiful handwork! Hank I couldn't resist and bought a wall hanging about five feet long with a Pharaohs design for $17.50 US -- $60 EP.

For lunch our guide took us to an open lunch room, which was like someone's back yard. He ordered us a "Very Special Egyptian" meat dish. After about two hours of waiting, we were finally served. They charged us an exorbitant fee each, including the guide's lunch. We felt like we were "taken," but walking through areas we would never have seen without him, was well worth the extra charge.

Back through the tent Sauk, we noted a building built in the 12th Century. Amazing! Walking further, we came to the main street, crossed the bridge and took a taxi back to the hotel, arriving at about 4 pm. On the bridge, we saw a family of Sudanese refugees. Bless their hearts they were dirty, tired and begging for food. It is always sad to see refugees when we have so much.

We had dinner at the hotel with the rest of the group and discussed plans for the following day. Dick and Iris and Hank and I decided to hire a taxi to take us to an Oasis, 63 miles to the south by the name of El Fayoum. Daniella arranged for the taxi to pick us up at the hotel at 8 am the next morning.

Thursday, October 23, 1997
Cairo – Cairo to Madina El Fayoum, Egypt

What an experience!! I was so excited to be going to the outskirts of Cairo where few tourists venture. Since there were only four of us plus the driver, we were comfortable in his station wagon for the 100 km drive. The drive through Cairo was comical as usual with people and cars, donkeys and carts going in every direction carrying all sorts of loads, plus the constant honking of horns.

After passing the barren desert and going through two or three police stops, we began to see the Oasis – lush, green farmland with date palms and canals throughout. People walking or riding on donkeys along the roads, donkey

carts and an occasional motorcycle were the norm. The people work hard in the fields and then go to markets in towns to sell their produce. Donkeys, donkey-drawn carts, cars, and people either walking or riding on a donkey are all competing for road space.

El Fayoum was a total surprise. I expected a small village, but it turned out to be a large city with multi-storied buildings made of cement. In the center of town we found an ancient water wheel that has not stopped for thousands of years. Our driver spoke very little English, so was not much of a guide.

As we walked around the canal that runs down the center of town, we were approached by a Tourist Police (who also spoke no English). He pointed to the badge on his sleeve which shows that he is in fact a "Tourist Police." He began escorting us around and then guided us to the Sauk, which was a short distance away. He kept watching us to make sure we stayed together. There were no other tourists around so we drew a lot of attention and were constantly greeted with "Welcome to Egypt," "Hello," and "Welcome.

The walkways through the open souks are narrow and crowded with women selling their produce. At one point, it was so crowded that I had to put my hand with my camera up over my head. The locals kept looking at us as if we were aliens from outer space, but that was okay; we were looking at them too. I'm sure this Sauk hadn't changed in several thousand years.

We were finally able to make our way out and back to the waiting taxi. The Tourist Policeman wanted "Baksheesh," which is a fee for his services. Dick gave him 5 EP, but he was upset with us because he wanted a fee from each of us. Then another man came to talk to the taxi driver and the taxi driver gave him some money. Then, another man came up and there was a long discussion after which the taxi driver told Hank to get in the back seat so the man could ride in front. What is going on here?

After more discussion, we were told that we had to go to the police station. What? Why? At the police station, the driver and man went inside. Then, the driver came out to get Dick Schutz and they stayed inside for a few minutes. Dick Schutz came out and explained to us that the Police Chief told him that the man was a surgeon and had to accompany us for security reason. What? Why? Amazing?

So, the man got in and accompanied us during the rest of our trip in El Fayoum. (We dropped him off at the security stop on the way out of town. I think he just wanted a free ride).

We wanted to have lunch at a local restaurant before going to the lake. The restaurant offered a beautiful view of the almost barren area, which was totally empty of customers. It was a large restaurant with play areas for children. There was no menu, only offering two fish dishes – one fried and one grilled. The cost was high plus we had to pay for the driver and the hitchhiker. The lunch was not bad, but not that good either. We took photos of the lake and then returned to Cairo. We made it back to Cairo without further incident. What an adventure!

Back at the Hotel, Hank told me that "he was just sick;" he had lost his new wedding ring. Poor Hank, I could see the pain in his face. So, I suggested that we go to the gift shop in Cairo Tower and have another one made. The salesman there said he could make us what we wanted and we selected some blank rings. He said it would only take a short while, so we sat down and waited for two hours. The rings were so poorly made that we would not accept them. Luckily, he refunded our money.

While there, we saw a beautiful Egyptian woman, clad in all back up to her eyes. I can only imagine that she was beautiful because she had beautiful black eyes.

On our way back to the hotel, we passed a silver shop, went inside and told the jeweler what we wanted. He said he was an artists and could make better rings but with the same design. The price was 220 EP for both – about $33 US each. So, we ordered them

We didn't get back to the hotel until almost 8 pm, so missed saying good-by to Daniella. Everyone else had gone to dinner, so Hank and I want to the TAZA one last time. We would be on our own now for the rest of the trip in Cairo.

Back at the hotel, we gathered with the others who told us that they wanted to go to the Camel Market on Friday morning.

We crossed the street and talked to the brothers about ordering the cartouche for the men in our family. We bought them only after he had reduced his price from 240EP to 130 EP –about $10 each.

Friday, October24, 1997
Cairo, Egypt

The front desk clerk awakened us at 5:45 am. We expected there would be at least coffee and rolls for breakfast but were disappointed. The two taxis arrived promptly at 6:30 am and we were off. Iris and Dick Schutz and Hank and I were in one cab and Harold, Betty, the Sherman's and Ernie were in the other. It was the same cab and driver we took yesterday...

Traffic was light as it is the Muslim day of rest. We drove through some of the poor slum areas before getting to the countryside and the farmlands. There were canals with pumps pumping water into the fields. We saw many people working, donkeys, donkeys pulling carts and people just walking. It was all very exciting and we took lots and lots of photos.

As we got closer to the Camel Market, we came behind a truck carrying two camels in a truck bed with just their heads sticking up over the cab. What a comical sight that was with the camels looking down at everyone they passed.

The Camel Market was amazing with too much going on to do justice in the telling or in photos. The handlers hobble the camels by tying the front leg back, so they can only walk on three legs, thereby not escaping. Then they control them by striking them on the rump with a long stick. The market itself is dusty and dirty and horribly noisy with the camels and handlers yelling constantly. Had we been able to understand Arabic we would have been able to understand the sales practice.

At one point, a big black Mercedes arrived with three Sheiks riding in the back seat. They got out and began to pick out their camels. The selected camels are marked with paint on their head, neck or rump. It was all so confusing but fun to watch. There were many children running around.

Iris Schutz didn't want to leave the market after only one hour because we had paid for two, but was quickly out-voted. We had seen enough.

Back at the hotel by 9:30 am, we had breakfast. Hank and I decided to take a walk to give housekeeping a chance to clean our room. On the way, we spotted a McDonalds and had milk shakes. The day before was their opening so they had given away t-shirts with McDonalds on them. I talked the manager into selling Hank and I each one for our grandsons. Who was I kidding? He knew perfectly well they were for us. Oh well.

Back at the hotel, I read a little and then took another nap. When I woke up we sorted our luggage to pack for our trip home. Our trip was coming to an end.

For dinner some of the group wanted to go to TAZA one last time, but Hank and I and Dick and Iris chose to go to Pizza Hut, just for kicks. It wasn't bad. Their menus showed what they served in pictures, so all we had to do was point at our selection. No language barrier here. Outside the door was a delivery bicycle.

Our rings were delivered to us by a young boy at about 9:30 that night.

Saturday, October 25, 1997
Last Day

As Hank and I were all "tombed out," so we chose not to go with the rest of the group to Memphis, Sakarrah and the step pyramids. We woke leisurely, had breakfast at the hotel and then took a long walk to Central Cairo.

Central Cairo is a modern city with old buildings mixed in. Few men wear turbans and gallabiyahs. What struck us was the number of stores selling shawls – nine in a half block area, five on one side and four on the other. We went into a couple of bookstores, bought some sweets and ended up at McDonald's for lunch. Amazing Huh? In Cairo, having a McDonald's hamburger! But what can I say?

We stopped by the jewelers to thank him for the rings and went back to the hotel until 5 pm. We packed a few items and then went to KFC for a light dinner – what? KFC? On the way back, we had an ice cream cone. I guess we're homesick for foods back home.

We were downstairs by 1 am to take taxis to the airport. We had to be there by 2 am. While waiting at the airport, Hank still isn't feeling well and is running a slight temperature. And then, while waiting in line, Ernie slides down into a sitting position. Being the former firefighter and caregiver that he is, Harold immediately got a wheelchair for Ernie. We are worried about him, but we all needed to get on the plane. We made it just fine, Harold took care of Ernie all the way home.

Going through Customs Hank and I were a little concerned because we had bought so much stuff. But thanks to Harold, he went through first and told the officer that we were all with him. The officer just waived us through.

Although it was a wonderful trip, it is always good to be HOME....

The Trip of a Lifetime

Sylvia is published author. She has written an historical book about her ancestor Pasquier Leo Buquor who was an Indian Fighter, Texas Ranger and Mayor of San Antonio and an accomplished person in Texas history. She is currently writing her life's story and a novel about another ancestor Joseph De La Baume who was born in 1731. He was a French Nobleman, American Patriot, Spanish Soldier, and a Texas Pioneer. She is a member of the Bullhead City Writers Club and volunteers as writing coach at the local middle school.

Sylvia Villarreal Bisnar
genealogy is my passion

6192 Kodiak East,
Fort Mohave, AZ 86426   email: slybiz@aol.com
928.768.1474. 562.400.1320 web:slybizgenealogy.com

The life of:
P. L. Buquor

Indian Fighter
Texas Ranger
Mayor of San Antonio

Sylvia Villarreal Bisnar

Not long after our return home, we purchase a RV. This was the start of our traveling around the US and Canada. In 2003, we sold our home in Long Beach and purchased a 36' 5th Wheel and a new 2003 Ford Crew Cab truck. We traveled for the next three years, visiting all the US states and all the Canadian proveniences.

In July of 2005, we stopped in Fort Mohave AZ. to visit our son Andy and his family. With all the places we had been we didn't really find a place we both agreed where to settle down. Andy said we should build a house and stay in Arizona. "The worst thing that could happen is you'll make some money on the house if you don't like it here". Sylvia convinced me that it was a good idea and so we built a very nice three bedroom home in Fort Mohave. It is

now 2014 and we are still here and have adjusted to desert life. We are happy with our choices.

Brent Anthony Bisnar

March 24, 1958

Brent was born in Long Beach CA. at St. Mary's Hospital. He is our first born and like all first born he had to deal with inexperienced parents. He was a very good baby once he got over his colicky stage. Being the first grandchild on Val's side of the family, he got a lot of attention from his grandparents and aunts and uncle. He learned to walk at about one year and had trouble with words that had an 'S' in them until he was around five years old.

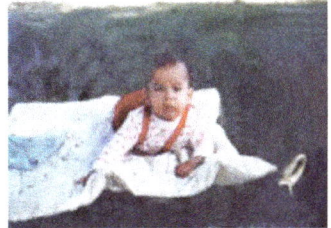

Brent was a finicky eater until he became an adult. Now he eats all kinds of food and thinks he's a wine connoisseur and food critic. He does know more about wine than anyone else in the family.

All of my kids were really good about going to bed, but Brent had this habit of coming to our bed during the night. He put his blanket over his head and held his arms out like a ghost and stand next to our bed until I pulled him up into bed. I learned if I made him lay in the middle, he wouldn't stay more

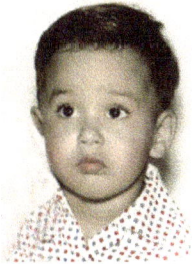

than a few minutes before he went back to his own bed. I wish I had a picture of him standing there with that blanket over his head.

Brent went to St. Pancratius Catholic School from Kindergarten to 2nd grade, and then we sent him to public school. There were so many children in his classes at St. Pancratius that when he finished his work in class he disturbed the other children. The teachers couldn't keep him busy enough for him to stay out of trouble. He did well at Riley Elementary and Hoover Jr. High, Lakewood High, Long Beach City College and The University of Cal State Long beach.

Brent loves all sports and athletics are an important part of his life into adulthood.

Lakewood Park League football, baseball and basketball

Little League Baseball

Pony and Colt League Baseball

American Legion and Connie Mack Baseball

High School Baseball   Surfing

Wakeboarding

Coaching

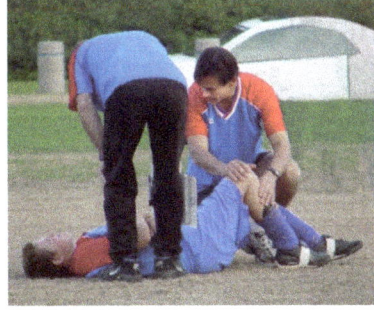

Fishing

Triathlon

Take your pick

Most high school coaches would be content with one pitcher. John Herbold of Lakewood has five — kneeling, Brent Bisnar (left) and Joe Zalesis; standing, Stan Williams (left), Rick Arnold and Sam Giethan. Collectively they are 31-0 or a team that has been seeded No. 1 in CIF 4-A playoffs.

Brent was very fortunate to be on several championship teams. The Pony League World Series in Washington, Pennsylvania, the Connie Mack World Series in Farmington New Mexico. His Lakewood High School team won the 4A CIF Championship.

Brent got his driver's license at age sixteen but had two bad experiences early on. One night, as Val and I were on our way home, I saw my truck going in the other direction with Brent at the wheel. Brent and two friends, Stan and Don, were out for a joy ride. I immediately made a U-turn and pulled them over. Of course, I made Stan and Don walk home and Brent lost his driving privilege for a month.

"Dad can I take the truck up to the batting cages with Stan?" "OK but don't go anywhere else and be home by 10:30." One hour later, I received a phone call. "Dad, somebody just ran me off the road." "Are you OK and where are you." When I got to his location in the Lakewood Country Club, I found Brent, Stan, and two Lakewood Sheriffs standing behind my truck. Brent had jumped the curb and ran over a tree and knocked down a concrete light standard. Brent's story was that some guys forced him up on the sidewalk and he couldn't stop before hitting the tree and the light standard. Thank God it was a small tree and he was in the truck and not our car. Of course, the story was all "a bunch of BS." He was driving way to fast, turned a corner and lost control. When I bought the truck it had a Long Beach Police Motorcycle decal on the front windshield. I'm sure the Sheriffs saw that decal and decided to give Brent a break. They did not site him or even reprimand him. They did point out to me the tire marks were acceleration marks and not breaking marks. They never asked if I was a police officer. By the way, the Lakewood Country Club is nowhere near the batting cages.

The insurance company paid the repairs on the truck and the city never billed for the street light, but for Brent, two months without driving privileges was a lesson learned.

Why do teenagers do what they do? Reflecting back on my own teenage years, I know I did some "off the wall stuff" but never broke to law.

Don't get the wrong impression. Brent was a good kid who respected his parents and adults. He was polite and friendly and had good grades all though school. He was 100 % boy and I'm sure there's many of his adventures I don't know about and I don't want to know.

After high school Brent went to Long Beach City College and Long Beach State University. He lived at home and paid his own way through college. Falling just short of his degree, he felt he needed adventure and decided to take an extended trip to Mexico with three of his buddies. They bought a 1964 International 4 wheel truck and worked on it for months before taking off for Mexico. They carried their surfboards on top and a motorcycle on the back. About two or three nights out, Brent called home and said that someone had stolen one of the surfboards while they were sleeping in the truck. "We ran after him but couldn't catch him. He knew the neighborhood." I don't remember exactly how long he was gone; more than a month and less than three months. The day he returned I was working in the front yard and Brent and one friend came walking down the street carrying only my cooler and his guitar. A trip he will always remember.

After his Mexico trip he chose not to continue college. He tried his hand at landscaping for a while. His friend Jerry had a communications company and wanted Brent to work for him. Brent wasn't interested in that job, but after Jerry's constant encouragement he relented and said he'd give it a try. He not only flourished in his new job, but became part owner of the company. The company grew from three employees to nearly six hundred with offices in thirty eight states and Australia. As of this writing those numbers are somewhat lower due to the nationwide economic downturn.

Brent's career has been highly successful and very profitable

Note: In 2016 Brent and Jerry sold the company for a large profit. They agreed to stay on for another three years at their salary and 7% ownership.

In 1997 he married Dawn Radison. Dawn had two children, Chasen five, and Savannah three. Brent adopted Chasen, and after a few years they had a boy of their own who they named Colten. I'm sure he would have adopted Savannah, but her Dad was active in her life. The marriage lasted about eight years. I know Brent did his best to make the marriage work but Dawn no longer wanted to be married.

In April of 2011, he married Lori Johnson. Lori has three children: Tayte, thirteen, Tyler, ten, and Tessa, eight. She is a wonderful wife and mother. They travel quite a bit building memories for their family. Brent is as happy as I've ever seen him. Left to right. Savannah, Colten, Chasen, Tessa, Brent Tyler, Lori and Tayte.

Brent

Lori

Chasen

Savannah

Tayte

Colten

Tyler

Tessa

Hopefully Brent will write his own Ramblings some day and share more of his adventures.

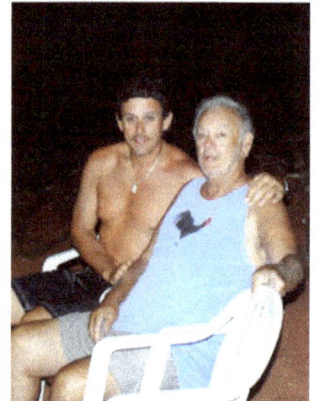

Andrew Richard Bisnar

May 19, 1959

Andy was born in Long Beach CA. at St. Mary's Hospital. He is the second son only fourteen months after his brother Brent. He was the best sleeper of our three children. He would get on his hands and knees and rock his crib back and forth while sound asleep.

His brother Brent was ever so nice with him until he got old enough to become competitive.

Even though they are both in their fifties now the competitive spirit is still alive.

All young boys have their stories to tell. Here are a few of Andy's.

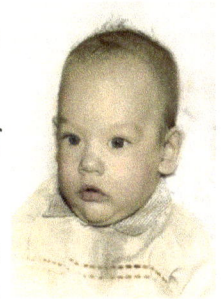

Andy got a pair of roller skates before he learned how to tie his shoes. He kept taking his skates off and, of course, that meant I had to tie his skates every time he wanted to put them back on. One day, I got smart and told him if he wanted to skate he had to learn how to tie his shoes himself. It took about three times showing him how and he never asked me again to tie his skates or shoes again.

We had a pet turtle name "Theodore" who would eat out of your hand. One day Theodore took a bite out of Andy's finger and all the blood sent his Mother in to "panic" mode. She rushed him to the doctor only to find out that the doctor didn't know what to do with a turtle bite. They gave him a tetanus shot and sent him home.

I had built storage shelves in our garage which were maybe five or six feet off the floor. Guess who fell off the shelf and broke his arm?

Our dog, Tien, was a runner. Any time the gate was left open he would run like a rabbit, and the only way to get him back was to drive the car and open the door. One day after chasing the dog several times, Val said to the kids,

"If the dog gets out again I'm not going after him." Later that afternoon she couldn't find Andy. After checking all the usual places and asking all the neighbors, she called the Sheriff's Department. When they showed up, their attitude was that she was this terrible mother who couldn't keep an eye on her children. She felt awful. They found Andy about five blocks away over at the junior high school with the dog. When he got out of the Sheriff's car he was carrying the dog, and they were both soaking wet. "Got him Mom, but I had to chase him though the sprinklers".

Andy went to St. Pancratius Catholic School for the first and second grades. He came home one day all excited about being in the school play. He was one of the background kids without a speaking part. Three days before the play, the lead kid got sick and couldn't perform. Andy's teacher asked him to take the part. So "WE" studied for two nights learning the narrator's part. There was no doubt he knew the script but I wanted to make sure he could be heard "in the back to the hall." "Andy, I'll be in the very back of the hall and I want to hear you loud and clear". That may have been a mistake on my part because to this day you can hear Andy from blocks away. He played his part perfectly and made his Mother and I veryproud.

Andy started playing sports at age six and is still active as a volunteer baseball coach at the local high school.

Park League baseball, football and basketball.

Little League baseball.   **Junior High football and baseball**

High School baseball   **Pony and Colt League baseball**

American Legion and Connie Mack baseball

LBCC baseball   **Irvine University baseball**

Minor League baseball

' Montreal Expos' Golf

Hole-in-one

Snowboarding

Wakeboarding

Hunting

Coaching

Hunting

Andy went to St. Pancratius, Riley, and Madison grammar schools, Hoover Junior High, Lakewood High School, Long Beach City College and the University of Irvine.

Leaving college without his degree he spent one year playing minor league baseball for the Calgary Expos in Calgary Canada.

When his baseball days were over he found he needed to find a job. For a short time, he worked at a door and window company owned by myself and a partner. From there, he spent the next ten years or so working for a company doing design and set-work.

Andy's first marriage was to Judy McCloud in 1984 or 1985. They have two sons, Michael and Taylor. Their marriage lasted about ten years.

In 2001 Andy and Gina Harris married in Hawaii. They live in Fort Mohave AZ. and are owners of a real estate company in Bullhead City Az. Together they have five boys, Andy's Michael and Taylor, and Gina's; Shawn, Lance and Tyler. They have six grandchildren. Frankie, Leila, Emma, Tristan, Gabriel and Anthony.

Andy

Gina

Shawn

Aja

Frankie

Lance

Mandy

Leila

Jessica

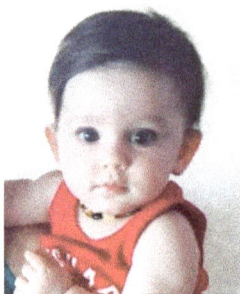
Emma

Tyler

Tiffany

Tristan

Taylor

Michael

Nicole

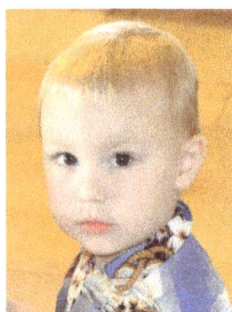
Gabriel

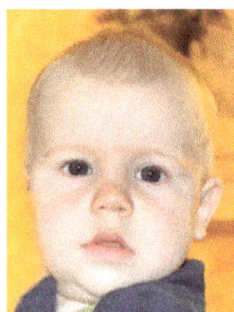
Anthony

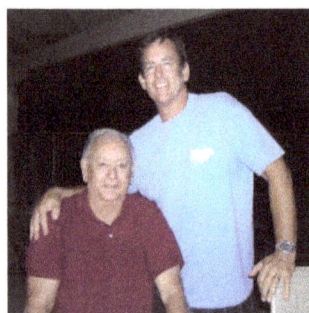

Of course there is much more to Andy than these few highlights. I'll leave them for to him tell when he writes his own Ramblings.

Jacqueline Marie Bisnar

July 9, 1967

Jacki was born in Long Beach CA. at St. Mary's Hospital eight years after her brothers. Of course, being a girl she was special.

She was the perfect baby, slept good, ate everything, playful, happy and spoiled. About the time she was born is when I really got interested in photography, and I couldn't stop taking her picture.

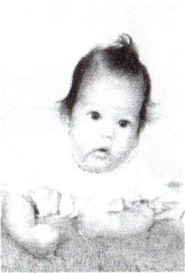

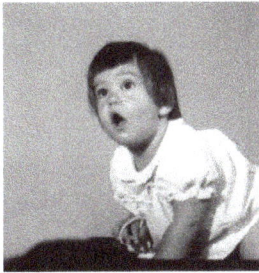

When she was little she loved to wear hats. She even wore them to bed. She didn't spend much time playing with dolls. She likes games and sports.

A few stories about Jack.

Jacki learned to swim at age four. She would jump off the diving board into my arms at age three.

When she was in third or fourth grade she was in the school yard at recess time. The school was doing some work on the playground and there were pieces of asphalt on the ground. For whatever reason Jacki picked up a chunk of asphalt and tossed it in the air, only to have come down on the top of her head. Big bump on the head, but no real damage.

I took Jacki and her friends horseback riding when they were ten or eleven. As we started up the trail she was about thirty yards ahead of me when her horse turned and ran for the barn. Jacki lost the rains and the horse was

309

running free and fast. It scared me to death thinking she was going to all off, but she managed to hold on to saddle and ride it back to the barn. She wanted off and no part of horses. I made her get back on. She cried at first but after a long easy ride she enjoyed herself.

I took Jacki and her friend Kathy to Knott's Berry Farm for her birthday. We were there all day and they rode all the rides several times. I timed the actual ride time and for the entire day it amounted to eighteen minutes.

Jacki's Pets

Schooner

Tabby

Jacki's Playhouse

Jacki was a real "diamond rat" having to go to all of her brothers games for twelve or thirteen years. At age eight she was one of the bat girls for the local Connie Mack team. One night she was sitting in the dugout and a foul ball hit her in the side of her head. She spent the night in the hospital and lost most of her hearing on the left side. The loss of hearing has never held her back in any way.

She learned to drive in my 1958 Volkswagon (stick shift), and although she had a few accidents, she is a really an excellent driver and able to handle ambulances and fire trucks.

She was a good student all though Riley Elementary, Stanford Junior High, Lakewood High School and Long Beach City College.

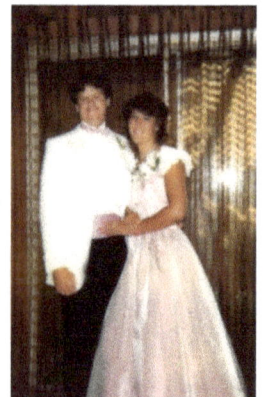

Jacki was a consular at St. Anne's Home for Unwed Mothers in Los Angles California for a couple years and decided to move Arizona. She lived in Bullhead City and worked across the river in Laughlin Nevada at the Flamingo Casino. She was a maid, cashier, and an EMT. She received her EMT certificated from Mohave Juror College.

From Bullhead she moved to Benson AZ. working as an EMT and became a licensed Paramedic. From Benson she moved a few miles west to Mescal AZ. She worked as a volunteer Firefighter and before long she was elected Fire Chief. Her career as a Firefighter has been on the fast track since she moved to Vail AZ. where she became a full time Firefighter. In just a few short years she progressed from EMT, Paramedic, Rookie Firefighter, Lieutenant, Captain and now a Battalion Chief. Jacki has achieved her Bachelor's Degree in Fire Science from Columbia Southern University and is now working on her Master's Degree.

She likes sports and adventure

Softball   **Pool**   **Rafting**

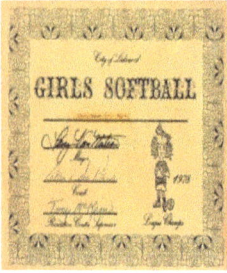   

Snowboarding Repelling Snorkelling   Fishing   Running

Although Jacki has no children of her own she taken on the responsibility of raising two beautiful girls.

 **Lindsay Lopez** is Jacki's Goddaughter. She has lived with Jacki off and on for many years as she were Jacki's daughter. Lindsay is part of our family and she's called me "grandpa" all her life. Now at twenty two she has her own son Joaquin.

Sadie Palma is the daughter of Paula Palma Jacki's roommate. From the time she was born, Jacki has been like a second mother to Sadie. She shares all the parenting with Paula and as she did with Lindsay she treats her as if she was her own daughter.

I'm very proud of all Jacki has accomplished and know she'll continue to reach for her goal's in life.

THE HOUSES I LIVED IN

1935 120 Golden Ave.

I was born at this address. It was a duplex.

Long Beach CA. The Long Beach World Tread Center now sits on the property

1935 Loma Vista DR.

I don't know how long we lived here.

Long Beach CA.

1936-1957 820 Dawson Ave. Long Beach CA.

I lived here from age two to twenty two.

Fort Ord, Monterey, CA

Basic Training Sept. 1954 to Jan. 1955

1955 - 1956 US Army Kelly Barracks Stuttgart Germany

1957 - 1958 801 Alamitos Ave. Long Beach CA.

1958-1959 1329 Market St. No. Long Beach CA.

1959-1978 2829 Centralia St. Lakewood CA.

1978-2003 4144 Stanbridge Ave. Long Beach CA.

2003-2006 RV Traveling All US States and Canadian Provinces.

2006- ???? 6192 Kodiak East Ft. Mohave AZ.

The Schools I went to

1940-1948 St. Matthew Grammar School
Long Beach CA.

1948-1949 Southern California Military Academy
Signal Hill CA.

1949-1953 St. Anthony High School
Long Beach Ca.

1953-1954 Long Beach City College
Long Beach CA.

The F-Stops 1983 to 2016 and counting

In 1983 I met two women when on photography class field trip to Yosemite National Park.

It was the last field for that class and Sylvia and Betty wanted to start a camera club with the class members. They took names and phone numbers of those interested.

About one year later I enrolled in another photo class at a different collage and as luck would have it both Sylvia and Betty were in the same class. I ask them what ever happen to the club they wanted to start. They answer we lost our motivation. I said if they would make all the phone calls we could have the first meeting at my house.

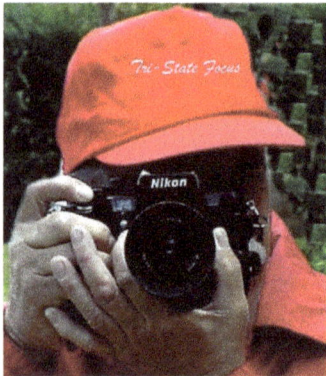

About twenty people showed up and we formed a club and named it The F-Stops. We only had two by-laws. 1. I would never hold any office (I had plenty of that stuff at my work). 2. The club would be limited to no more than twenty five members.

All though there were some really good photographers the club evolve in to a traveling club that took pictures. We traveled all over the US and a few other countries.

Don't ask me to show you my photos because it could take a few days to see them all.

Original Members

Sylvia

Betty

Hank

Harold

Carol

Ottis

Don

Don

Ernie

Gary

Iris

Lynn

Mary

Peggy

Tom

Toni

Sequoia Nat. Park

Big Sky Country Wyoming

45th Parallel

Glacier Nat. Park

Nile Cruise

Hank and Sylvia Wedding

Arctic Circle

Lake Watson Canada

Yellowstone Nat. Park

After 33 years the club is still going strong with five of original members. There are many newer members I am not acquainted .

1983 to 2016

Things I Remember

Toys

Bow and Arrows
Cork Pop Guns
Electric Trains
Erector Sets
Huffy Radio Bicycles
Lincoln Logs
Model airplanes
Movie Projector
Orange Create Scooters
Steam Engine
Tinker toys
Toy Submarine

Football board Game
16mm Movies / Cartoons
Baseballs
Footballs
Rubber Guns
Tennis Balls
Peashooters

Volleyballs
Foot Scooter
Baseball Glove
Toy Battleship

Baseball Bats
Sling Shots
B-B Guns
Marbles
Wagon
Jump Rope
Pogo Sticks

Boxing Gloves
Tin Soldiers
Yo Yo's
Toy Cruiser

People

Benny and Cecil
Car Hops
Charlie Chan
David and Chet (news)
Ernie Banks
Eve Arden- Our Miss Brooks
Howdy Doody
Marlin Perkins
Red Buttons
Sky King
The Fuller Brush Man
Timmy and Lassie

The Ice Man
The Ink Spots
The Milkman
Gracie Allen
Cassius Clay
Gene Autry
Lois Lane
Rudolph Valentine
Fabian
Sugar Ray Robinson
Mickey Mantle
Mighty Mouse

Randolph Scott
Steve Reeves
Lassie

Clark Gable
Mary Martin
Chef Boyar Dee
Doris Day
Errol Flynn
Popeye
The Lone Ranger

Places

Airplane Hill	Joe Joist	Terminal Island Navy Station
Alamitos Bay Sand Dunes	L. B. Naval Shipyard	Terminal Island Pontoon Bridge
Marine Stadium	Drive-in movies	Art Theater
Frosty Freeze	F. W. Woolworths	Belmont Pool
Hoff's Hut	Rexall Drug Stores	American Bandstand
Bixby Park	Municipal Auditorium	Naples Bridge
Cabart Theater	Naples Canal	Casting Pool Rec. Pk Pier Pier Point Landing
Carnation Ice-cream Plant	Pine Av. Tunnel	Cherry Beach Tunnel Softball Complex Rec. Pk Coast
Theater	Strand Theater	Crawdad Creek
Terminal Island Draw Bridge	Crest Theater	San Pedro Ferry
The Hamilton Bowl	Douglas Aircraft	Sand Dunes
Alamitos Bay	The Lagoon	Douglas Aircraft
Rainbow Pier	The Villa Riviera	Ritz Theater
Town Theater	Drive-In-Restaurants	Shell Hill
UA Theater	E-Bell Theater	Signal Hill
Will Rogers Park	Fish Cannery	Terminal Island

Games

Boxing	Over the Line	Hot Potato
Caroms	Red Rover / Red Rover	Jump Rope
Dirt Claw Fights	Step Baseball	You're It
Ditchem	Touch Football	Hide and Seek
Dodge Ball	Marbles	Red Light / Green Light
Fly's Up	The Marble Game	May I?
Hop Scotch	Red Light / Green Light	Jump Rope
Kickball	Kick the Can	

Things

102 Beer	Clamp on Roller Skates	Salty Fish
5¢ Dill Pickles	5¢ Cokes	Duck and Cover Drills
Gasoline 23c per gal.	Model Airplanes	Speedy Alka-Seltzer
$ .75 Hair Cuts	Falstaff Beer	Smallpox
Studebaker Cars	Cracker Jacks	Popsicles
15¢ McDonalds Burgers	Metal Ice Trays	Blue flash Bulbs
TV Test Patterns	Tom & Jerry Cartoons	Captain Midnight
16¢ Pack of Cigarettes	S & H Green Stamps	The Helms Bakery Truck
5¢ Popcorn at the Movies	Gum Wrapper Chains	The Red Car (Streetcar)
3¢ Stamps	Jiffy Pop	The Cisco Kid
The Lone Ranger	Boston Blackie	Lighting Bugs
45 RPM Vinyl Records	Mimeograph Machines	Kool-Aid
Wax Coke bottles w/ Sugar Water	Playing cards in bike spokes	
Ding Dong Avon Calling	Nash Metro Cars	WWII Blackouts
5¢ Baseball Cards	Blackjack Chewing Gum	Penny Candy
WWII Rationing	eeny-meeny-miney-mo	do over
Brownie Box Cameras	Polio	Cracker Jacks
3-D glasses	Fallout Shelters	Zippo lighters
Brylcream	Reel to Reel Tape Recorders	Tom & Jerry's
Burma Shave Signs	Double- Dog-Dare	Orange create scooters
Butch Wax	Roller Shake Keys	Dick Tracy
Candid Camera	Royal Crown Cola	Dashboard ignition switches
Topo Gigio	Hi-Fi Systems	Head light Dimmer Switches
Washtub Ringers	Telephone party lines	The Green Hornet
Red Rider and Tonto	Superman	Plastic Man

Batman	Car heaters on the fire wall	Ice Boxes
Pant leg clips	Candy cigarettes	Juke boxes in coffee shops
Home milk deliveries	Newsreels	P. F. Flyers
Packard's	Keystone 8mm Movie Camera	D.Crockett Coonskin Caps
Vitalis V7	Zenith Cobra-Matic Record Changers	Schlitz Soft-top Cans
Brownie Cameras	Saddle Shoes	Bendix G-15
Computers Transistor Radios	Bell & Howell Projectors	Flashbulbs
Mobil Flying Horse	View Masters	Flat Top Hair Cuts
Hula Hoops	Pizza at age 23	TV Dinners
Cardboard Milk Bottles Stoppers	Newsreels	Solarex Sunglasses
Shaving Mugs	Home delivery Milk & Ice	Hand Signals for cars

<u>Vehicles I've Owned</u>

1932 Ford five window roadster

1953 Ford Hard Top Convertible

1956 Oldsmobile Coup

1957 Ford Station Wagon

1965 Chevrolet Sedan

1958 Volts Wagon

1974 Toyota Hatchback

1981 Toyota Hatchback

1987 Camry

1972 GMC 3/4 Ton Pickup

1972 Ford 1 ton Crew Cab

1983 El Camino

1974 Chevrolet ½ Ton Pickup

1973 Dodge Van

1991 Dodge Van

1997 Toyota Four Runner

1991 Ford Capri

1987 Toyota Camry

1994 Fleetwood 24' class C RV

2000 Coachman 32' class C RV

2003 Ford 1 ton Crew Cab

2003 Nu Way Hitchhiker 35' 5th Wheel

2005 Nissan sedan

2009 Ford Flex

Life's Events 1935 -2010

1935

Jan. 01	1st. Sugar Bowl and 1st. Orange Bowl
Jan. 02	Hank Bisnar's Birthday
Jan. 11	Amelia Earhart flies from Honolulu to Oakland California
Jan. 24	1st. canned beer, "Krueger Cream Ale," by Kruger Brewing Co.
Feb. 08	1st. NFL draft, Jay Berwanger first pick by Eagles. He never plays in NFL
Feb. 22	Airplanes are no longer permitted to fly over the White House
Mar. 16	Hitler orders German rearmament, violating Versailles Treaty
Mar. 20	"Your Hit Parade" debut on radio
May 01	F. D. R. commemorates Boulder Dam
May 05	Jessie Owens sets long jump record at 26' 8"
May 24	1st. Major League night baseball game, in Cincinnati (Red s, Phil 1)
Jun. 02	Babe Ruth, 40, announces his retirement
Jun. 13	James Braddock beats Max Baer for heavyweight title
Jun. 25	Joe Louis defeats Primo Carnera at Yankee Stadium
Jul. 05	F. D. R. signs National Labor Relations Act
Jul. 16	1st. automatic parking meter installed in Oklahoma City, OK.
Aug. 14	Social Security Act becomes law

Sep. 12	Howard Hughes flies his designed plane at 352.46 mph
Sep. 15	Nuremberg Laws deprives German Jews of citizenship and the swastika becomes official symbol of Nazi Germany
Nov. 05	Parker Bro. launches game of Monopoly. Invented by Charles Darrow
Nov. 09	Japan invades Shanghai China
Nov. 14	F. D. R. Proclaims Philippine Islands a free commonwealth
Nov. 22	China Clipper left Alameda Ca. carrying 100,000 pieces of mail. 1st. trans-Pacific airmail flight
Dec. 28	W P A Federal Art Project Gallery opens in New York City

1936

Jan. 04	Billboard magazine publishes 1st. music hit parade
Jan. 16	1st. photo finish camera installed at Hialeah Race Track in Hialeah Fla.
Jan. 24	Benny Goodman and orchestra record "Stompin' at the Savoy"
Jan. 29	1st. Baseball Hall of Famers - Ty cob, Babe Ruth, Honus Wagner, Christy Mathewson and Walter Johnson
Jan. 31	1st. "Green Hornet" audio show head on WXYZ Radio in Detroit
Feb. 05	National Wildife Federation formed
Feb. 06	4th Winter Olympic games in Garmisch-Partenkirchen, Germany
Feb. 06	Felix the Cat, Cartoon Character
Feb. 11	Building of Treasure Island in San Francisco Bay begins
Feb. 14	Maribel Vinson wins U.S. Female Figure Skating Championship
Feb. 14	Robin Lee wins U.S. Mali Figure Skating Championship
Feb. 15	Hitler announces building of Volkswagen
Feb, 15	Sonja Henie of Norway wins 3rd. consecutive Olympic Figure Skating Gold

Feb. 16	Valerie Pegg's Birthday
Feb. 17	"Phantom" cartoon strip by Lee Falk debuts
Feb. 29	F. D. R. signs 2nd Neutrality Act
Mar. 01	Rene Villarreal's Birthday
Mar. 04	1st. flight of airship Hindenburg, Germany
Mar. 05	Spitfire 1st. flight
Mar. 07	Hitler sends troops to Rhineland. Breaks Treaty of Versailles
Mar. 26	Mary Joyce ends a 1,000 mile trip by dog slid in Alaska
Mar. 29	Nazi propaganda claims 99% of Germans voted for Nazi candidates
Apr. 03	shortest boxing bout with gloves lasts only 10 seconds
Apr. 29	1st. pro baseball game in Japan. Nagoya defeats Daitokyo, 8-5
May 30	Joe DiMaggio 1st major league game
May 05	Edward Ravenscroft patents screw-on bottle cap with a pour lip
Jun. 01	Queen Mary completes its maiden voyage, arriving in New York
Jun. 19	Max Schmeling KOs Joe Louis for World championship
Jun. 20	Jesse Owens sets 100 meter record at 10.2
Jun. 26	1st. flight of Fw61 Helicopter
Jun. 30	40 hour work week law approved
Jul. 18	Spanish Civil War begins, Gen. Francisco Franco led uprising
Jul. 29	RCA show 1st. real TV program
Aug. 01	Adolph Hitler opens 11th Olympic Games in Berlin
Aug. 05	Jesse Owens wins his 3rd. Olympic medal
Aug. 09	Jesse Owens wins his 4th. Olympic medal
Aug. 11	Chaing Kai-shek's troops conquers Kanton

Aug. 14	1st. Olympic basketball game (Berlin)
Aug. 23	Bob Feller's 1st. game. At 17 he strikes our 15 St. Louis Browns
Sep. 02	1st. transatlantic round-trip air flight
Sep. 07	Hoover Dam begins operations
Sep. 11	F. D. R. Dedicates Hoover Dam
Sep. 13	Bob Feller strikes out record 17 A's
Sep. 27	Walter Alston plays his only major league game
Oct. 09	Hoover Dam begins transmitting electricity to Los Angeles
Oct. 11	"Professor Quiz," 1st. radio quiz show premieres
Oct. 22	1st. commercial flight from mainland to Hawaii
Oct. 28	F. D. R. rededicates Stature of Liberty on its 50th anniversary
Nov. 02	1st. high-definition TV broadcast by BBC in London
Nov. 12	Oakland Bay Bridge opens
Nov. 16	German air force begins bombing of Madrid
Nov. 17	Edgar Bergen and Charlie McCarthy become a success on radio
Nov. 23	1st. issue of life magazine, created by Henry R. Luce
Dec. 01	Bell labs tests coaxial cable for TV use
Dec. 12	Chinese leader Chiang Kai-shek declares war on Japan
Dec. 13	Green Bay Packers win NFL Championship
Dec. 24	1st. radioactive isotope medicine administered, Berkeley Ca.
Dec. 30	United Auto workers stage 1st. sit-down strike, at Fisher Body Plant

1937

Jan. 11	First issue of LOOK Magazine
Jan. 09	Howard Hughes set record flying from Los Angeles to New York in 7 hours, 28 minutes and 25 seconds.

Jan. 20	Franklin D. Roosevelt sworn in for second term.
Feb. 11	General Motors recognizes the United Automobile Workers Union.
Feb. 16	Wallace H. Carothers receives a patent for nylon.
Feb. 21	First successful flying car, Waldo Waterman's *Arrowbile*, makes its initial flight.
Mar. 01	First issue of comic book *Detective Comics*. Twenty-seven issues later in introduces *Batman*. Longest continually published comic magazine in history.
Mar. 26	Crystal City TX. Erect a statue of the cartoon character Popeye.
Mar. 26	William Henry Hastie first African-American appointed a federal judgeship.
Apr. 09	First Japanese Kamikaze aircraft arrives at Croydon Airport in London.
Apr. 17	Debut of *Daffy Duck* by Looney Tunes series.
May 01	17 million unemployed in the USA.
May 06	The German Airship *Hindenburg* bursts into flame in Lakehurst, New Jersey.
May 12	The coronation of King George VI and Queen Elizabeth at Westminster Abbey, London.
May 27	The *Golden Gate Bridge* opens to pedestrian traffic. The next day President Franklin D. Roosevelt pushes a button in Washington D.C. starting vehicle traffic.
May 30	*Memorial Day Massacre*. Chicago shoot and kill ten unarmed demonstrators.
Jun. 08	First total solar eclipse to exceed 7 minutes in over 800 years.
Jun 14	Pennsylvania first State to celebrate *Flag Day*.
Jun 28	*Civilian Conservation Corps* (CCC).
Jul. 01	First sighting of the *White River Monster*.

July 02	Amelia Earhart and navigator Fred Noonan disappear after takeoff from New Guinea.
Jul. 02	First guard takes his place at the Tomb of the Unknown Soldier in Washington D. C.
Jul. 07	Japanese forces invade China.
Jul. 13	Krispy Kreme opens, MB.
Aug. 05	The Soviet Union commences on the *Great Purge*, to "eliminate anti-Soviet elements". At least 724,000 people were killed, many chosen for shooting by their ethnicity.
Sep. 02	The *Great Hong Kong Typhoon* of 1937 kills 11,000 persons.
Sep. 17	*Abraham Lincoln's* head is dedicated at Mount Rushmore.
Sep. 26	First radio program of the, *The Shadow*, with Orson Welles in the title role.
Sep. 27	The last *Bali Tiger* dies.
Oct. 05	Roosevelt famous *Quarantine Speech* in Chicago.
Oct. 15	Ernest Hemingway's novel *To Have and Have Not* is published.
Dec. 04	*The Dandy*, the world's longest running comic book in published.
Dec. 12	Japanese bombers sink the American gunboat USS Panay.
Dec. 12	*Mae West* makes risqué appearance on NBC *Chase and Sanborn Hour* that eventually results in her being banned from radio.
Dec. 13	The *Battle of Nanjing* ends and the *Nanjing Massacre* begins. Japanese slaughter over 300,000 civilians and prisoners.
Dec. 21	Walt Disney's *Snow White and the Seven Dwarfs* opens. First animated cartoon with sound becomes a smash hit.
Undated	*Of Mice and Men* by John Steinbeck is published.

1938

Jun. 03	*The March of dimes* is established by Franklin D. Roosevelt.
Jan. 16	*Benny Goodman* and his orchestra become the first jazz musicians to headline a concert at Carnegie Hall.
Jan. 27	*The Niagara Bridge* at Niagara Falls, New York collapses due to an ice jam.
Jan. 28	First *ski tow* in America begins operation in Vermont.
Feb. 04	A nylon bristle toothbrush becomes the first product to be made of nylon yarn.
Mar. 03	The *Santa Ana River* in California spills over killing 58 people.
Mar. 03	Oil is discovered in *Saudi Arabia.*
Mar. 12	*Anschluss:* German troops occupy Austria; annexation is declared the next day.
May 17	*Information Please* debuts on NBC Radio.
May 28	Hitler declares his decision to destroy *Czechoslovakia* by military force and orders mobilization of 96 *Wehrmacht* divisions.
Jun. 12	The *Roma* and *Sinti* peoples in Germany and Austria are rounded up and jailed.
Jun. 15	*Laszlo Biro* patents the *Ballpoint Pen* in Britain.
Jun. 19	*Italy* beats *Hungary* 4-2 to win the 1938 World Cup.
Jun. 22	*Joe Louis* knocks our *Max Schmeling* for the heavyweight championship
Jun. 23	The Civil Aeronautics Act signed into law.
Jun. 23	*Marine land* opens near St. Augustine, Florida.
Jun. 24	A 450-metric-ton meteorite explodes about 12 miles above the earth near Chicora, Pennsylvania.
Jun. 30	*Action Comics #1* is published. First comic book featuring *Superman.*

| Jul. 03 | The *Steam Locomotive Mallard* set world speed record of 126 mph. |

Jul. 14   *Howard Hughes* sets a new record completing a 91 hour airplane flight around the world.

Jul. 18   *Wrong Way Corrigan* takes off from New York, ostensibly heading for California.
He lands in Ireland instead.

Jul. 24   First ascent to the *Eiger* north face.

Aug. 18   The *Thousand Islands Bridge*, connecting the United States with Canada is dedicated by President Franklin D. Roosevelt.

Sep. 10   Hermann Goring in Nuremberg calls the Czechs a "miserable pygmy race".

Sep. 21   *Winston Churchill* warns of grave consequences to European security if *Czechoslovakia* is partitioned. Soviet Maxim Litvinov makes similar statement.

Sep. 21   The New England Hurricane of 1938 strikes Long Island and Rhode Island killing over 600.

Sep. 22   Olsen and Johnson's musical comedy *Hellzapoppin'* opens.

Oct. 16   *Winston Churchill* address the United States, condemns the *Munich Agreement* and calls upon America and Western Europe to prepare for armed resistance against Hitler.

Oct. 18   The German government expels 12,000 Polish Jews living in Germany. 4,000 go to Poland and 8,000 are forced to no-man's land on the German-Polish frontier.

Oct. 24   The minimum wage is established in the United States.

Oct. 30   Orson Welles's *The War of the Worlds* is broadcast, causing panic in parts of the United States.

Oct. 31   *Great Depression: The New York Stock Exchange* unveils a 15-point program aimed to upgrade protection for the investing public.

Nov. 01   *Sea biscuit* defeats *War Admiral* by four lengths at Pimlico Race Course in Baltimore, Maryland.

Nov. 10   *Armistice Day:* Kate Smith sings God Bless America for the first on her weekly radio show.

Nov. 16   *John L. Lewis* is elected by the Trade Union as the first president of the *Congress of Industrial Organization.*

Nov. 30   *President Roosevelt* agrees to loan *Chiang Kai-shek* $25 million cementing the Sino-American relationship and angering the Japanese government.

Dec. 13   The *Neuengamme* concentration camp opens near Hamburg.

Undated   *Adolf Hitler* is 'Time magazine's "Man of the Year", an award that usually goes to the most influential person of the year.

Undated   The first *Bugs Bunny, Porky's Hare Hunt* is released.

www.ingramcontent.com/pod-product-compliance
Lightning Source LLC
Chambersburg PA
CBHW040255100426
42811CB00011B/1268